Teaching and Learning with Microsoft® Office 2010 and Office 2011 for Mac

Teaching and Learning with Microsoft® Office 2010 and Office 2011 for Mac

Timothy J. Newby
Purdue University

Judith Oates Lewandowski
Indiana University, South Bend

Boston Columbus Indianapolis New York San Francisco Upper Saddle River
Amsterdam Cape Town Dubai London Madrid Milan Munich Paris Montréal Toronto
Delhi Mexico City São Paulo Sydney Hong Kong Seoul Singapore Taipei Tokyo

Acquisitions Editor: Kelly Villella Canton
Associate Editor: Anne Whittaker
Editorial Assistant: Annalea Manalili
Executive Marketing Manager: Krista Clark
Production Project Manager: Liz Napolitano
Manager Central Design: Jayne Conte
Cover Designer: Susanne Behnke

Cover Image: © Shutterstock
Editorial Production Service: Element LLC
Electronic Composition: Element LLC
Text Printer/Binder: Bind-Rite Graphics/Robbinsville
Cover Printer: Lehigh-Phoenix Color/Hagerstown
Text Font: Minion

Credits and acknowledgments borrowed from other sources and reproduced, with permission, in this textbook appear on appropriate page within text.

Every effort has been made to provide accurate and current Internet information in this book. However, the Internet and information posted on it are constantly changing, so it is inevitable that some of the Internet addresses listed in this textbook will change.

Library of Congress Cataloging-in-Publication Data

Newby, Timothy J.
   Teaching and learning with Microsoft Office 2010 and Office 2011 for Mac / Timothy J. Newby, Purdue University, Judith Oates Lewandowski, Indiana University, South Bend.
      pages cm
   Includes index.
   ISBN-13: 978-0-13-269809-2
   ISBN-10: 0-13-269809-9
      1. Microsoft Office.   2. Application software.   3. Microsoft software—Study and teaching.   4. Computer-assisted instruction.
   I. Lewandowski, Judith Oates.   II. Title.
      QA76.76.A65N455 2013
      005.5—dc23
                                                                                                                2011046779

10 9 8 7 6 5 4 3 2 1

ISBN-13: 978-0-13-269809-2
ISBN-10:   0-13-269809-9

BRIEF CONTENTS

CONTENTS

PREFACE

VISION OF THE TEXT

Teaching and Learning with Microsoft® Office 2010 and Office 2011 for Mac has been designed to give busy (and often overwhelmed) preservice and practicing teachers a quick way to understand the basics of key software applications. Our goal is to provide a foundation of the basics of common application software and to offer a vision and a path of how to integrate and use the software within classroom settings to create a learning environment that is engaging, interesting, and effective. We employ a basic approach for the following reasons:

1. Teachers have more demands put on them now than ever before.
2. Application software (e.g., a word processor) is more powerful (i.e., has more features) and can offer more help to the teacher than ever before.
3. More than 90 percent of the time that teachers spend working on the computer, they are using basic features of the most common software programs.

An understanding of the basic features will help you use the computer in the classroom. With that foundation, you will know what information to request and how to find additional, more advanced features as needed.

WHAT IS NEW AND IMPROVED?

Although we have previously published *Teaching and Learning with Microsoft® Office* books, this version has been designed to support the use of new Microsoft® Office 2010 and Office 2011 for Mac software. Additionally, we have worked on enhancements to improve format and content of previous versions of the book.

1. **Office 2010 software.** With the recent upgrade to Microsoft® Office 2010, all chapters have been completely updated to include explanations and screen captures of all tool ribbons and other features of Microsoft Word, Excel, PowerPoint, and Publisher.
2. **Revised Chapter 1 System Software.** This chapter addresses the upgraded Windows 7. Although it is still relevant for other operating systems, all screen captures and discussions are based on Microsoft's newest system software. Please note that we also have added a full MS Office 2011 for Mac interchapter on the Mac OS X system with similar screen captures, text, and mentoring videos.
3. **MS Office 2011 for Mac.** At the conclusion of the Word, Excel, Excel database, and PowerPoint chapters, an interchapter is included that focuses entirely on the respective chapter's Orientation, Level 1, and Level 2 from the perspective of Office 2011 for Mac. Those using a Mac computer are able to get all information and complete all assignments specifically written (with accompanying screen captures) for the Mac.
4. **MS Publisher.** Our new version of this text reflects that MS Publisher in Office 2010 has been upgraded to the ribbon format similar to the other MS Office applications (this was not true of Publisher 07). This chapter follows the same format as all other chapters (three levels) and has desktop publishing projects that are integrated with other chapters within the text.
5. **New PDToolkit site offers mentoring videos.** Mentoring videos have been created that focus specifically on MS Office 2010 and Windows 7 for the PC as well as MS Office 2011 and Mac OS X for the Mac. Videos are now available for all Orientation, Level 1, and Level 2 features discussed within the text. Moreover, there are a similar set of mentoring videos for all Orientation, Level 1, and Level 2 features of the corresponding Office 2011 for Mac. Mac users have the same resources as those users of PC-based computers.
6. **Updated examples, Workouts, and projects.** Within each chapter, the examples, Workouts, and projects have been updated based on the updated MS Office software. In most cases, the new version has allowed for expanded use of various tools and those

changes are reflected within the examples and Workouts that are described. Explanations, step-by-step procedures, and the accompanying videos now reflect the changes that have been implemented.

7. **Updated National Educational Technology Standards (NETS) for teachers and students.** With the new NETS for teachers and students, it was necessary to upgrade each chapter's section (found within the respective Level 3) that directly focused on the integration of the technology within the context of the standards. A special emphasis has been placed on helping the reader understand and use the MS Office applications to accomplish the NETS for teachers and students.

8. **Collaboration and MS Office tools.** Twenty-first-century skills focus on how to develop the ability to work in groups to solve problems and accomplish various learning tasks. One of the new additions within several of the applications explored within this version of the text encourages learners to use Windows Live to incorporate and use a number of different individuals to work on the same document and project. New exercises and Workouts have been incorporated within the text to give the reader experiences using these new software capabilities in the context of teaching and learning.

WHY EMPHASIZE MICROSOFT OFFICE?

First, this software is prevalent in the majority of homes and schools. Second, because the applications are from the same family of software, they work in an integrated manner with many common toolbars, tool ribbons, menus, and so on. For the novice, a feeling of familiarity when going from one program to the next is important in building confidence as well as in increasing the speed of acquisition.

WHY USE A THREE-LEVEL APPROACH?

A three-level approach is used within this text to help preservice or practicing teachers who enter a college or PD course at various levels of expertise.

Level 1 is for the true beginner or novice. It is designed to give step-by-step "hand-holding" help on accomplishing basic tasks with the software. It also offers a good review of key features for the more experienced user.

Level 2 requires the use of additional and often more advanced features of the software—with guided assistance and help in finding the help that is needed. In this level, the student uses the software's Help feature, as well as the extended help offered at www.office.com and www.apple.com on the Internet, to find solutions to questions and problems encountered. Keywords and content locations are given as support to help the student grasp how to effectively access and use the Help features. In addition, guidance is given in the form of added procedures, images, and insights on how to implement the features. The goal is for students to gain independence and confidence by answering their own questions with the assistance of Help—but also not to become frustrated by the search process.

Level 3 addresses integration of the software. Examples are given and students practice designing and developing technology-integrated learning experiences. Moreover, the relationship of the use of the software with the NETS is emphasized.

HOW ARE THE CHAPTERS OUTLINED?

All chapters are structured in a similar fashion. However, each is independent and thus the chapter sequence can be modified to fit the schedules and desires of the course instructor or the personal needs of the reader.

1. **Introduction**

    This section explains the goals of the chapters, the purpose of the software, reasons for learning, and some basic ideas of how it can be used by teachers and students.

2. **Orientation**

   This section allows one to view and work with the main workspace of the target software. Key ribbons and menus of tools are examined and keywords, organizational concepts, and specific features are highlighted and explained.

3. **Level 1**

   One or more short scenarios or cases are given that incorporate projects previously completed using the targeted software. Key steps in the process of constructing each project are highlighted and students are guided through a step-by-step procedure to create a similar project.

4. **Level 2**

   The scenario from Level 1 generally continues within this lesson and an additional, more complex project is outlined and completed. Users are then directed to alter the program and construct their own version. In this case, users are encouraged to use the program's Help, as well as go to www.office.com or www.apple.com for the tutorials, information, and insight needed to determine how to complete specific processes. Keywords and phrases relevant to completing the task are listed for the individual to use with Help if it is needed. Insights and guidance are also given on how to use needed features. The focus is on using Help to acquire the desired results.

5. **Level 3**

   Integration is the focus of this level. Beginning with a presented lesson plan, users are shown how integration of the software can occur. Moreover, they are given opportunities to attempt to develop technology-enhanced lesson plans given specific situations. They are taught to use the integration assessment questionnaire, and they explore and reflect on the relevant NETS and how their work pertains to those standards.

MS Office 2011 for Mac

Although Microsoft has developed Office versions for the PC (Office 2010) and the Mac (Office 2011) and the two programs have many similarities, there are some definite differences in how one uses the software. This interchapter focuses specifically on the Mac version of Office and how to complete the key Level 1 and 2 activities within the respective System Software, Word, Excel, and PowerPoint chapters.

WHAT ARE THE TEXT'S KEY FEATURES?

Lists: The text attempts to present most information in a concise fashion using frequent bulleted and numbered lists.

Workouts: Workouts are regular exercises and projects that the student is directed to work through. These are designed to get the student actively involved early and often with the software. Many of these exercises are augmented by practice items that can be accessed through PDToolkit.

Modeling: Example products and exercises are used to help students understand what is desired and how it can be achieved.

Reflective or guiding questions: These are used to encourage students to go beyond the immediate application of the software to envision how it could be integrated and transferred to other situations and settings.

Examples: Hundreds of examples of the use of the software are given across all age groups and content areas.

Help emphasis to gain independence: The use of the software's Help programs are highlighted, practiced, and implemented within this training in order to encourage independence and confidence in solving problems encountered when using the software.

National Educational Technology Standards: Both teacher (NETS*T) and student (NETS*S) standards from the National Educational Technology Standards are provided on the inside cover. Within Level 3 of each chapter the use of the standards is discussed, and students demonstrate how they are used and assessed as the software is integrated within self-generated lesson plans.

HOW CAN THE AUTHORS BE CONTACTED?

The easiest and fastest way is generally through e-mail, but here is all of the needed information.

Tim Newby
Purdue University
Room 3138, BRNG
100 N. University St.
W. Lafayette, IN 47907-2098
Phone: 765-494-5672 Fax: 765-496-l622
E-mail: newby@purdue.edu

Judy Lewandowski
Indiana University—South Bend
Greenlawn Hall
1700 Mishawaka Ave.
South Bend, IN 46634
E-mail: jllewand@iusb.edu

If you contact us directly, we will be happy to share our ideas on how we use this text. We also enjoy visiting classes via phone or video conference to discuss issues with students and faculty members. Just let us know what we can do to help.

WHAT SUPPLEMENTS AND ALTERNATIVE DELIVERY OPTIONS ARE AVAILABLE FOR THIS TEXT?

New PDToolkit

Accompanying *Teaching and Learning with Microsoft® Office 2010 and Office 2011 for Mac*, there is a new website with mentoring videos that, together with the text, provide you with the tools to learn how to effectively use and integrate the Office suite to motivate and engage your students and help them succeed in learning.

The PDToolkit site is available free for six months after you register with the password that comes with this book. After that, it is available by subscription for a yearly fee. Be sure to explore and download the resources available at the website. Currently, the following resources are available:

- Concise mentoring videos can be accessed via this website. These videos show the exact steps needed to complete all outlined features within the text—for all chapters and all levels in each chapter.
- Downloadable items that allow for further practice.

COURSESMART AND OTHER E-BOOKS

CourseSmart is an exciting new choice for students looking to save money. As an alternative to purchasing the printed book, teachers and preservice teachers can purchase an electronic version of the same content at a reduced price. With a CourseSmart eTextbook, teachers and preservice teachers can search the text, make notes online, print out reading that incorporate notes, and bookmark important passages for later review. For more information, or to purchase access to the CourseSmart eTextbook, visit www.coursesmart.com.

ACKNOWLEDGMENTS

No book can be completed without the help of numerous individuals. In particular we wish to acknowledge both our in-service and preservice teachers who have presented hundreds of questions to ponder, consider, and respond to within this text. Through the years, their questions have heavily influenced the vision, design, and development of this work.

We would like to thank the following individuals for reviewing and offering their constructive suggestions on *Teaching and Learning with Microsoft Office 2007 and Expression Web: A Multilevel Approach to Computer Integration, Second Edition*: Peggy A. Lumpkin, Georgia State University; Timothy Cushman, Greenville County Schools; Monique Whorton, Georgia State University/Cross Keys High School; and Margaret Kostal, Amherst County Public Schools.

ABOUT THE AUTHORS

Timothy J. Newby, Ph.D.

Tim is a Professor in the Learning Design and Technology program area of the Department of Curriculum and Instruction at Purdue University. He received a Ph.D. degree in Instructional Psychology from Brigham Young University. At Purdue he conducts research on issues pertaining to technology integration within the classroom, as well as motivation, human learning, and the impact of instructional strategies on the learning process.

Judith Oates Lewandowski, Ph.D.

Judy is an Associate Professor of Instructional Technology at Indiana University South Bend. She received a Ph.D. degree in Curriculum and Instruction from Purdue University. At Indiana University South Bend, she focuses upon the integration of technology into learning, instructional strategy selection, and best practices for professional development.

Teaching and Learning with Microsoft® Office 2010 and Office 2011 for Mac

INTRODUCTION

What's This All About?

Read Me First!

In many cases, when you open a new purchase that requires a little assembly (e.g., computer, bicycle, shelf unit for your office), there's a set of directions that indicates you should *read me first*. You may not have to assemble this book, but it's wise to take a look at this introductory section. It sets the tone, provides insights, and helps you get set for the learning that's about to begin. It helps you to know what is expected and what you can expect from exploring and working on these pages. Things just go smoother when you begin here.

WHAT ARE WE TRYING TO DO?

We want you to be able to use computer software such as word processors, databases, and spreadsheets. More important, we want you to use the software in ways that enhance your teaching, your curriculum, and your impact on your students (or future students). That is our goal, plain and simple.

IS THIS ONLY "CLASSROOM SOFTWARE"?

We wrote this book as if we had on the eyeglasses of a teacher and a student. That means, our examples and projects are focused on how teachers and students can use this software to enhance learning. These basic applications, however, can be used by individuals in all walks of life and in all times of their lives.

Don't shy away just because you are going to cooking school, are in the military, or want to become a fireman, dancer, or magician. We have all been in the classroom before—these examples and projects should make sense from all different perspectives.

HOW DOES THIS RELATE?

This is the big question that we want you to ask over and over again as you go through this material. Think to yourself, "How does this relate to my teaching?" "How does this relate to the work that I have to do?" "How does this relate to a positive impact on my curriculum and ultimately on my students?" "How can the implementation of this software affect my learning?"

We provide you some examples and some ideas of how these concerns tie together and how they work. Always be mindful of ways to find relevance for your personal classroom or learning situation. Constantly look for ways to make these tools work for you. It is then that you will come to view them as something worthwhile and not just another thing to learn this week and never use again.

We want you to reflect back on these tools and think, "How did I ever get along without them?"

WHY SHOULD I LEARN THIS?

- Saves time
- Saves energy
- Improves quality

There isn't a job in this world that doesn't require these three objectives—and this is especially true for those of us in the teaching profession.

It would be great if we could just hand you those benefits. However (here's the catch), for you to reap them, you have to invest a bit of time and energy.

Our goal is to make your investment as efficient and painless as possible. We figure that if we can have fun along the way and help you get some of your work done as you learn this stuff, you'll stick with us.

WHY USE MICROSOFT OFFICE?

Two reasons:

1. This software is very prevalent on home, business, and school computers.
2. Many of the same tools, menus, and so on are used from one application program to the next (this will help speed the learning process and the feelings of familiarity).

Note: We realize there are *different versions of this software* and that there are other publishers of software that you may be more familiar with. We focus on important skills that can be learned with whatever software you have available—it may not be done in exactly the same way as the Microsoft products—but it will be close, and you'll soon learn how to figure out the small differences.

WHERE ARE WE GOING?

The key tools we explore include the following:

- Navigating the system (Windows 7 and Mac OS)
- Word Processing (MS Word)
- Spreadsheet (MS Excel)
- Data management (MS Excel)
- Presentation software (MS PowerPoint)
- Desk top publishing (MS Publisher)

Each of these topics receives attention. We suggest that you go through the section on navigating the system first (just to lay the needed foundation); however, after that, go with what you need. If you are in a class, your freedom might be limited, but if you're working on this independently, look over what you need to get done and where the emphasis in your life is—then go in that direction.

Note: Start thinking now about current or future projects that you might be able to work into the projects for each of these applications. Remember, we want you to use your own. From the very beginning we want you to see the importance of this software for helping you and your students achieve.

HOW ARE WE GOING TO GET THERE?

Basically, the format of each of the applications is similar.

You will explore some basic background (short and sweet) about the software and complete some quick exercises. This will familiarize you with the software (what it looks like and how it works) and orient you about the basics of what, when, and why it is important.

Level 1 application: This is directed at the novice. We provide you examples of something produced with the software. We supply step-by-step guidance so you can produce something similar that can be altered for use in your own classroom.

Level 2 application: To achieve increased independence, a second set of examples are given at this level. Key features of the products are highlighted and you will learn how to find critical "how-to" information as you create your own set of products using the software. That is, we will provide less step-by-step guidance but more general suggestions. Remember, our goal here is *not* to hold your hand, but to help you become more self-sufficient. We want to show you how to find the answers to your questions. Then when you're on your own, you should be better prepared to find your own solutions to the unique problems you confront.

Level 3 application: With the basics learned, this level provides opportunities to explain, teach, and integrate the software within classroom settings. It's a time to solidify your own understanding of the basics, but most important, to consider the possibilities of its use and application for yourself as well as your learners. Here we want you to envision how this could be used and give you additional ideas on how to integrate and apply your new skills.

Mentoring videos: All along the way there are references to *mentoring videos*. These are short (most are about 60 seconds in length) video demonstrations of each of the steps within the various levels. For example, in Level 1 of the chapter on word processing we may explain the steps needed to cut and paste information. If you feel you need to see how that works, you can simply go to the website that accompanies this book and select the video that will demonstrate it on your computer. You can watch these videos over and over until you understand exactly how the feature works and why it works the way that it does.

Go to PDToolkit for **Teaching and Learning with Microsoft® Office 2010 and Office 2011 for Mac** to locate the appropriate mentoring videos.

DO I REALLY NEED TO LEARN ABOUT THESE SOFTWARE PROGRAMS?

Maybe . . . maybe not. There are several ways of finding out, but because most of you are associated with teaching and/or learning, we felt that a short assessment (nice word for *test*) would be in order. So take a crack at this, then ponder over your answers.

Circle the number on the scale about how closely the statement resembles something you could or should have said about yourself.

	That's Me				Not Me
1. I have been told that the computer will reduce my workload, but every time I try to use it, it costs more time, energy, and effort than it is worth.	5	4	3	2	1
2. I feel comfortable using the computer for some things, but I'm frustrated because I know I should be using it to do a lot more.	5	4	3	2	1
3. When asked to *cut and paste*, my thoughts wander to grade school, blunt-nosed scissors, and Elmer's glue.	5	4	3	2	1
4. I think I have lost things in my computer and I have a feeling I'm not going to get them back.	5	4	3	2	1
5. When I hear the word *spreadsheet*, I think back to the last time I attempted to make my bed.	5	4	3	2	1
6. Everyone else seems to know a lot more about how to use the computer than I do.	5	4	3	2	1
7. In the past, I have usually found someone else to use the computer when I needed something done.	5	4	3	2	1
8. Computers and feelings of inadequacy, for me, seem closely related.	5	4	3	2	1

Now add up your total score and divide by 8 to calculate your average response. Check the scale below for our suggestions on using this book and learning the software.

3.0+	You've got the right book and there are lots of good things in store.
2.0–3.0	Buzz through the Level 1 exercises and quickly get to the Level 2 assignments.
1.0–2.0	Review the Level 1 and Level 2 materials, see if there are some examples that you haven't experienced or thought about, then look closely at the integration and examples found in Level 3.

IS THERE A CONNECTION BETWEEN INFORMATION IN THIS TEXT AND THE NATIONAL EDUCATIONAL TECHNOLOGY STANDARDS (NETS)?

Standards are being developed, examined, and used throughout all aspects of education, and they are also being generated for and applied to computers and other technologies within the realm of education. The Appendix lists the NETS for teachers and students. Within each chapter devoted to word processing, spreadsheets, databases, presentations, or publications, we highlight and emphasize those standards that are being addressed by the various learning activities and workouts. Look for these as a part of the Level 3 workouts. Within those workouts we highlight sections that apply to specific standards and insert reflective questions that should help you contemplate and visualize the relationship of a standard to the learning activity you are completing and/or designing.

WHAT ARE SOME PHILOSOPHIES GUIDING THIS BOOK?

1. **We aren't going to teach you everything.** There's no need for that. The programs we work with can be wonderful for the right job—they can also be overwhelming if you get into things you don't really need. Our goal is to focus on what you need and to show you how to find solutions to specific problems you come across.
2. **We believe in application.** If you use it, you won't as easily lose it. We quickly have you working with this book right alongside of your computer. Actual participation (you working the keyboard) is much better than watching someone else do it—we want and need you to be an "active participant."
3. **Kill two birds with one stone.** We want you to develop skills with the computer programs that will help you in *your* work. Make this information as relevant as possible. Look around and find some projects that need to get done at work, home, or school. As we show you different programs, think of ways that you could get an assignment done by finishing something that you have to do anyway.
4. **Let's keep it short and sweet.** You have limited time and we know that. We use all kinds of job aids, such as numbered and bulleted lists and other means to help shorten the amount of reading you need to do, to help you find what needs to be found.
5. **Having fun is *not* a crime.** We think that we can have some fun going through this assignment. We try to add some smiles along the way—which you can either enjoy or ignore. We have had a lot of classroom experience, and some of them are hilarious and can be used to illustrate different points in this text—so we have chosen to include them to some degree.
6. **We are not the final word.** You are going to find out (if you don't already know) that there are several ways to get the job done. That is the way that most things work, and it is definitely the way most well-designed software works. We show you how we do it, but in some cases you may know of other ways. If it works for you, use it.
7. **Keep frustration under control.** Listen, you're working with computers—computers are one facet of technology—and technology means that funny things will happen—and usually happen when you least expect it and least need it to happen. So be prepared and the problems will be only molehills, not huge mountains, to overcome.

HOW SHOULD I USE THIS BOOK?

A few points to note here:

- We don't think most of you should read this text like a novel. Use the margin headings to get to the information you need in as efficient manner as possible.
- After reading this introduction, jump to the chapter that will service your current needs. That is, if you have a need for upgrading your skills with spreadsheets, go to that chapter and work there. You don't have to work through the other chapters first. An efficient way to figure out what you should do next is to look at the "hot" projects that you need to get done as soon as possible. If there is a project that could be enhanced with the development of a mail-merged letter, then perhaps you should look to the chapter on that

application, but if you have a pressing project on an upcoming presentation, then by all means go to the chapter on PowerPoint. You'll learn this much quicker and in greater detail *if* you are working on a project that has relevance to you.

- We have included **mentoring videos** to help you reference and quickly recall some of the basics. The videos are on the website that accompanies this book and can be quickly accessed and viewed. There will be times when it helps to see a short demo of a specific feature within your selected program. These videos can also be used to help you remember some "forgotten" skill that you once had. Once you get through the chapters, use these features to help you retain and continue to use the key features of the software.

A SPECIAL NOTE TO MAC USERS

As you can probably guess, a PC was used during the initial development of this text. However, in this edition, we have developed a special Mac interchapter for each of the relevant chapters. Each of those chapters now has a special section that highlights how the chapter orientation, as well as the Level 1 and Level 2 information, works from the perspective of the Mac user. In addition, Mac-oriented mentoring videos have also been created and placed on the website that accompanies this book.

SOME "RULES TO LIVE BY"

1. *Save, save, save and then *save* your work again.* Get in the habit of frequently saving your work. It isn't as hard as taking out the garbage and you can do it in a matter of 1 to 2 seconds. If you don't, you *will* get burned—it's only a matter of time. Don't depend on the software to do this for you—sometimes that may rescue you, but in many cases it won't.

2. **Think *content* first, *pretty* later.** In most cases it is better to enter and edit the content of your work first and worry about the formatting (making it look good) later. If you get sidetracked on working on the "pretty" (which is frequently done in today's world), your message may never be developed.

3. **Simple is better.** With so many bells and whistles found in these programs, it's very easy to get into the throw-in-the-kitchen-sink syndrome. Just because you have hundreds of type fonts, pictures, hyperlinks, audio, or video clips available, it doesn't mean that you should try to include them all.

4. **Keep your eyes open.** Look for examples of different ways to design and present your information. Sometimes other teachers, texts or magazines, web-based documents, or even your students may offer some answers to problems and predicaments that you find yourself in. Pay attention and the solution may present itself.

5. **Store and use *examples* and *templates*.** Once you have either developed or located a good example, store it so that you can use it later. For instance, if you develop a spreadsheet grade book, a newsletter, a seating chart, a brochure, save copies so the next time you need to do something similar you can begin with that original as a template. The second time around you can speed up the process and actually make higher-quality products. Templates launch you forward into your next project—use them.

1

SYSTEM SOFTWARE
MS Windows 7: The Basics of Navigating the System

INTRODUCTION

What should you know about system software?

If you don't know the rules of the game, it's very difficult to succeed. With the computer there are some general things you need to know and do (in most cases, these will turn into automatic skills) so that your interaction with the computer is simplified. If you don't understand how these work, you're going to be fighting an uphill battle—forever. When it comes to understanding the ground rules of the computer, you need to know some basics about the operating system software. Here are some of the things you should be familiar with:

- How to communicate and interact with the computer
- How things are reliably created, organized, stored, and then retrieved
- What tools are available and how they are accessed
- How to get help

Terms to know

click	Help	mouse	toolbar
desktop	hold	point	window
drag	icon	preview	
file	jump list	Start menu	
folder	menus	taskbar	

What is the system software and what does it do?

System software tells the computer how to perform its fundamental, basic operating functions (e.g., turn on, save things, run application programs). In other words, it is the master control program. When the system software is functioning properly, life is good—when it isn't, life can be miserable.

What are some commonly known system software?

Two types of system software (sometimes called *platforms*) dominate the school and home market at the present:

Microsoft's Windows Operating System   Apple's Mac Operating System

What gets a little confusing is that new and improved versions of these systems are continually being introduced. For example, you might be working on Windows XP, Vista, or 7; however, you might also have experience working with the Mac OS 8, 9, or X. As these versions are upgraded, new releases of the same operating system take on new version numbers or even names. For example, one version of Apple's Mac OS X is 10.7, which is also referred to as Lion.

Although there are some basic differences between the main systems (and even within the different versions of a system), their purpose is very similar—to control how the computer functions.

Why bother learning how to use and navigate the system software?

From the time the computer is turned on until it is shut down, the system software is involved and actively participating. Its role is similar to that of the director of a play. The audience may not see the director, but the director controls what transpires on the stage.

Understanding the system software will allow you to control the following:

- Starting up and shutting down the computer
- Storing, moving, and retrieving your work
- Installing and uninstalling other software on your computer
- Finding **folders, files**, and so forth in your computer storage areas
- Controlling how peripherals (e.g., keyboard, **mouse**, monitors, scanners) interact with the computer
- Using application software (e.g., word processors, spreadsheets)

ORIENTATION

What's the workspace look like?

When you walk into a new school building for the first time, it's often easy to get lost. It generally helps if you can find out where you are (perhaps by visiting the main office) and then see a picture of the building and how it is laid out. Key landmarks (e.g., the main hallway, the faculty lounge, the numbering system of the rooms) then can be noted and the logic of the building begins to be clarified.

Similarly, this is how we need to handle the computer and its various applications. We will begin each explanation section with an overview map of what the workspace looks like so that you can get a feel for how it's laid out and what the major landmarks, or tools, are.

Review Figure 1.1. This is a view of a Windows-type computer **desktop**. After starting the computer and allowing it to go through its getting-ready stage, the desktop appears. This is a key landmark and a place where you will frequently find yourself visiting and working from.

Mac Users: Refer to the Mac addendum at the conclusion of this chapter. There you will be able to see how that operating system compares to the Windows version.

What's the desktop?

In a usual working office, the top of the desk is where most of the work is completed. There are tools (e.g., pencils, paper clips, writing paper) that are sitting on the desktop so that when needed they are readily available. This is very similar to the computer's desktop. It is here that one has ready access to the needed tools and files so that real work can be accomplished.

Note: Don't be concerned if your desktop looks a bit different than the one in Figure 1.1. The top of the desk in your home or office probably looks different from that of any other person's desk. We can customize the desktop to fit your needs—just like you have done on your personal desk. Generally, there are some basics that you will find (e.g., Recycle Bin, taskbar and toolbars, some folders) in and around the desktop. Look for those key landmarks.

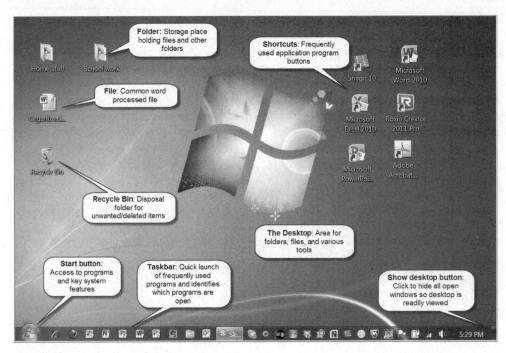

FIGURE 1.1 View of a Windows 7 desktop

Getting it to do what you want

The centerpiece of a good relationship is the ability to communicate. Teachers have to be good at this—you have to handle a variety of students, parents, administrators, and so forth—all of whom may require different communication skills.

Guess what? When working with the computer, communication is also essential. Yes, it can be even more frustrating than telling little Billy not to bring his pet lizard to school for the eighth time. Early on, your biggest problem will be finding the way to effectively communicate to the computer what you want done. Sounds a lot like the give-and-take within any relationship, doesn't it?

For most computer systems today, *the mouse and keyboard are the critical means of communication*. So look them over, tap on them, play with the keys, and note what the different buttons do. You'll be using them before long.

The "power of the mouse": *pointing, clicking, selecting,* and *dragging*

The power of the mouse (or any mouse substitute—such as the trackball, touchpad, pencil eraser, your finger) is that it allows you to tell the computer what to pay attention to and, in many cases, exactly what to do.

Here are the key skills:

POINT:

Move the mouse and watch how the pointer or cursor on the screen moves with it. You need to be able to tell the computer which things to work with—the power of the mouse is that it allows you to **point** to exactly what you want the computer to attend to.

CLICK:

Note that the mouse has a button or two (maybe more) on it. When you depress a button once quickly, it is called a *click*. A click gives the computer important information about what to do with the item you are pointing at. Generally, for a PC the majority of clicks are on the left button. At times you will need to expand your clicking repertoire into a

- Double (or even a triple) click
- Right click
- Click and hold

If you do not have access to a mouse (perhaps you are working on a laptop), note that there is still some kind of point-and-click mechanism provided. Don't worry. They all are designed to accomplish basically the same task.

SELECT OR HIGHLIGHT:

Often you need to identify a specific item (e.g., a picture, word, number) that you want the computer to work on. To do this, you typically put the mouse pointer on top of the item and click. In some cases, you'll need to click and **hold** in front of the item, then **drag** over the item until it is fully selected. When it is selected, it will change colors (typically becoming darker). If you want it to be deselected, you just click anywhere else on the screen. Here is an example of a selected word:

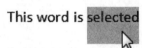

Here are examples of selected and nonselected folders:

Nonselected   Selected

DRAG:

This is when you point at some object, click and hold (don't release the button), and then move the mouse. The item you have clicked on will then move (drag) or be highlighted in some way. For example, this is one way that you can move a file from one place on the screen to another. Point at the file, click and hold, and drag it to the new location.

For more information about the use of the mouse (e.g., clicking, dragging), view the mentoring video on the website that accompanies this book.

The "power of the keys"

For the computer to be really helpful, there are times when you need to spell out what needs to be done. That's when the keyboard comes in handy. Yes, there will be times ahead in which the keyboard may become obsolete—however, for the near future you will continue to type in the words and commands that are needed via the keyboard.

Start menu

The **Start menu** (see Figure 1.2) is important for you to become familiar with. This is where you go to gain access to most of the key functions of the computer. Review Figure 1.2. The inserted callouts highlight a few of the important activities that can be accomplished through the use of the Start menu. This is the place where you go to launch specific programs, complete a search

PDToolkit
for
*Teaching and Learning with
Microsoft® Office 2010 and
Office 2011 for Mac*

Go to PDToolkit for **Teaching and Learning with Microsoft® Office 2010 and Office 2011 for Mac** to locate the mentoring videos for Chapter One.

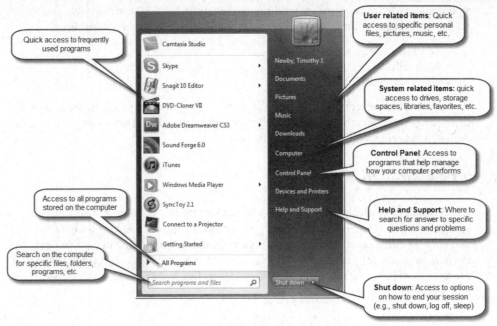

FIGURE 1.2 Start menu from Windows 7

for specific documents and/or folders, gain access to your flash drive, and change settings on the computer (i.e., through the control panel).

Help and Support

With our use of the computer, right after getting a good orientation of the computer layout, it is important for you to know where you can get some help if it is needed.

The main operating systems today have **Help** sections built into their programs. We will constantly suggest that you turn to Help to get many of the answers to your questions.

To find the Help section, look in the Start menu (see Figure 1.2) and note the Help and Support button that has been highlighted. We will discuss Help and Support in greater detail in the Level 2 section of this chapter.

The three *big* metaphors

The following three metaphors will help you learn the basics about the computer:

1. *Office filing systems metaphor.*   Any well-run office (whether at home or at a business) has a means of storing important information. Today, most offices still have file cabinets with drawers full of folders. Each folder holds valuable documents containing all kinds of information. Similarly, for the computer to be used efficiently, a filing system devoted to storing and retrieving key documents and files within folders is used.
2. *Restaurant metaphor.*   Each time you go to a restaurant to eat, you have a selection of food and drink from which to choose. This is most readily accomplished by looking over the menu. Likewise, the computer has menus from which to make a selection of what you want to achieve.
3. *Construction worker metaphor.*   Just as a builder has a toolbox and a number of tools to access and use when building a new home or business, the computer user has access to many tools available within the computer software. Some tools are used more frequently by the builder, but knowledge of many of the others allows the builder to accomplish great things. The same philosophy applies with using the computer.

Often, throughout this text, we refer to these metaphors to help you quickly grasp the new information. Get used to them—you'll be using them yourself before long.

Why do I need to organize and clean my room?

With the large storage capacity of a computer (one of its greatest assets), you need to have an organizational plan. This will allow you to store and retrieve your stuff easily.

Organization plays a key role. If you don't attend to how your files and folders are organized, you'll quickly find that working on the computer can be more frustrating than it needs to be.

In the next few sections, we make some suggestions on what you can do to help organize your computer so it is efficient and effective to use.

Using the Search function

Once you become accustomed to using the computer for many of your daily tasks, you'll soon be amazed at how many things you can store within it. Soon you will have thousands of pieces of information. Those bits and pieces may include photos, letters, files of data, book reports, math exercises, and so on. It's almost scary how fast the bits of information accumulate. We quickly become very dependent on the computer to hold all of this stuff. But it can be a problem when you need to find that information and you can't remember exactly where you put it. With only a small amount of stored information, looking through it by using your own pair of eyes may be more than sufficient; however, if you have thousands of folders, each of which may contain multiple files and documents, it may take a tremendous amount of time to find certain things. That is where the Search function comes in.

Within Windows 7, you can use the computer to quickly search its own contents by merely giving it a clue as to what to look for. Review Figure 1.2 and note that at the bottom of the Start menu is the place where you can enter the key words and have the computer search for your needed document, file, and so on.

Important Organizers

FILES AND FOLDERS.   To organize what's on the desktop and what's stored within the computer, a simple visual metaphor is used. Just like a filing cabinet in the office contains labeled folders and documents placed inside the folders, so too are objects organized in your computer's system platform. The filing system is critical to organizing your workplace (the computer) so you can get the most from it.

An example of files and folders:

1. Whenever you create something using one of the software applications (e.g., word processing), we will call it a *file*. That file can then be stored by putting it on top of your desktop *or* by filing it away within a folder. On the picture of the desktop (Figure 1.1) look for a file that is called *Organize.docx*. This is a word-processed document that has been created, named, and stored on the desktop.
2. Look at the desktop in Figure 1.1 again. Note that there is a picture, or **icon**, of a folder that is called *School work*. This folder is a place where files and other folders related to school can be put and organized.

Note 1: Both files and folders have names associated with them. This is a great convenience! You can name these so that you can remember what they contain.

Note 2: You have an endless supply of folders and the size of each can be expanded to hold a huge amount of files, other folders, programs, and so on. You never have to go to the store and buy another package of folders.

Note 3: If you want to name them a specific way, you can easily do so. Likewise, if tomorrow you figure out a new way to name your folders and files, you can rename them with relative ease.

RECYCLE BIN.   An important part of organizing is *getting rid of the stuff you no longer need*. This is easily done by dragging the item to the Recycle Bin (trash) that's located on the desktop. Once there, it's possible to take out the recycles or trash and empty it from your system.

Note: Discarding trash or recycles on the computer is generally a lot easier (and less smell) than taking out the kitchen garbage. A comforting thought is that the Recycle Bin or Trash is a temporary holding spot. If you delete something you later decide you need, you can open the Recycle Bin and retrieve your disposed material. However, once you decide to empty the Recycle Bin, the contents are gone for good.

Menus and taskbars

WHY MENUS?   Why not? Restaurants have found them effective. Menus allow you to see lots of choices of food to eat or (as in the case of the computer) activities to perform.

   Menus on the computer are often pulled down (or up) and are there until you have made your selection. Once used, they (similar to the restaurant variety) disappear until called on for other selections.

   In all programs we discuss, there will be menus and toolbars that you can access and select from. It's really a very efficient way to access different tools and other important things. The Start menu (Figure 1.2) is a good example of a menu of items from which to choose computer activities. Generally, by selecting a menu button, file name, and so on, the menu of alternatives is revealed in some way (e.g., a drop-down menu appears, a new window is revealed, a pop-up window comes into view). Once a selection is made, the menu then disappears until it is called back into service.

TASKBARS.   The computer is capable of many tasks. Subsequently, there are numerous tools and commands that can be used to accomplish these various tasks. To help with this process, many of these tools have been placed on convenient taskbars that can be shown (or hidden) as you determine their need. Figure 1.1 highlights the taskbar that reveals which programs, files, and folders are currently open and can be immediately accessed with a single click. To place or "pin" a tool on the taskbar, merely right click on the icon for the tool and select "Pin to Taskbar" option. If you want to remove a tool from the taskbar, right click on the tool's icon on the taskbar and select "Unpin this program from the taskbar".

   A couple useful features of the desktop taskbar you should find very helpful include the **taskbar preview** and the **jump list**. For example, we often find ourselves involved in more than one task at a time, thus we end up with several word processing documents, a spreadsheet, an Internet browser, and so on, all running at the same time. As shown in Figure 1.3, the taskbar preview feature actually allows you to mouse over the application button (hover your mouse pointer over the button but don't click) on the taskbar and a small preview window of what is running in the program will pop up. Merely click on the preview pane of your desired file and that file is expanded so you can work on it. This is a very quick and easy way to see what it is you are doing.

   As shown in Figure 1.4, a jump list is activated by right clicking on one of the taskbar program icons (e.g., MS Word). A list is then shown of current and recent files that have been accessed within that program. Simply left click on any of those items and they are launched within the program. Basically, the jump list is a quick way to jump to a recently accessed file.

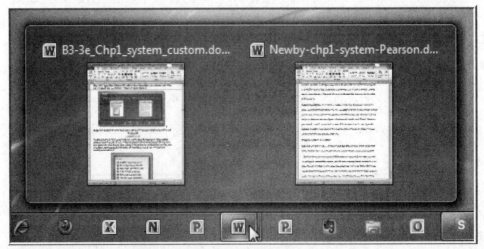

FIGURE 1.3 Taskbar Preview allows you to see and access the currently running files and documents

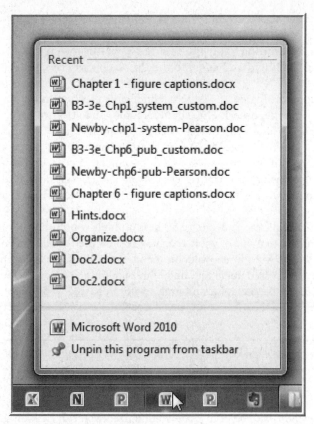

FIGURE 1.4 Example of a jump list of MS Word documents

Windows, windows, everywhere

Take a look at Figure 1.5. This is an example of several **windows** being open on one computer screen. Windows allow you to peer into different programs and different parts of the program.

Note how the windows can be made of different sizes and can be made to overlap each other. As you begin to work with the computer, you'll find that navigating through these windows, and being able to have multiple windows exposed at a single time, can be very

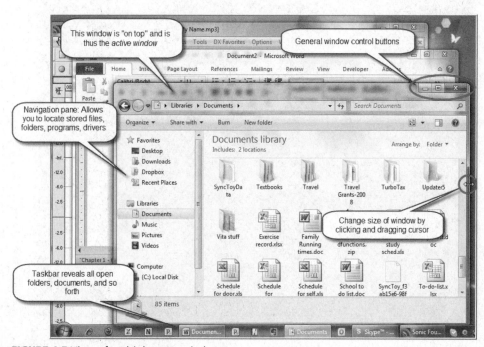

FIGURE 1.5 View of multiple open windows

PDToolkit
for
Teaching and Learning with Microsoft® Office 2010 and Office 2011 for Mac

Go to PDToolkit for **Teaching and Learning with Microsoft® Office 2010 and Office 2011 for Mac** to locate the mentoring videos for Chapter One.

helpful. The window you are currently working on (the one on top) is known as the *active window*. When you have a number of windows on the screen at one time, you can make a specific one active by pointing your mouse directly within the space of that window and clicking once. It will highlight and come to the top (i.e., it will overlay or be on top of the other open windows).

Look more closely at Figure 1.5. Note the highlighted section in the corner of the active window (see the upper right corner). These buttons allow you to control the active window (i.e., hide the window temporarily so you can see what else is on the screen, change the size, or close it altogether). If you want to change the size of the active window, put your cursor directly over a side, bottom, or corner of the active window and the cursor changes into a two-headed arrow. Click, hold, and drag the window to your preferred size and release the mouse button. To see a demonstration of how to work with active windows, review the mentoring video on the the website that accompanies this book.

Think about the application advantage of these multiple windows. For example, you could be grading an assignment that one of your students has submitted and at the same time have the grading rubric in another window showing on the screen at the same time. Or you might find it fun to have a word-processed document up in one window and copy a section of it and paste it into another program (like a graphics program) without having to do much at all other than select, copy, and then go to the other window and paste.

Note: There will be times when you have several windows open and you will find it very time consuming and inconvenient to minimize or close all of them individually in order to review what it on your desktop. By moving your mouse over the top of the Show Desktop button (see Figure 1.6), all open windows will become transparent and you can readily see the desktop. If you want all of the windows to be immediately minimized, you can click on the Show Desktop button. Another click on that same button and all windows are again opened in their original positions.

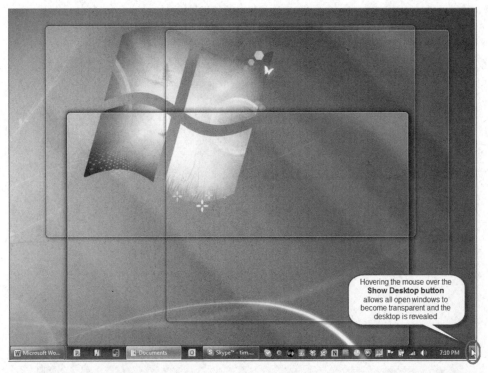

Hovering the mouse over the **Show Desktop button** allows all open windows to become transparent and the desktop is revealed

FIGURE 1.6 Use the Show Desktop button to make open windows transparent in order to peek at the desktop

Orientation Workout: Explore the territory

Turn on your computer and attempt the following on the desktop:

1. Click the Start button and see how it reveals its main menu. Get used to selecting certain parts of the menu and using it to launch various windows or programs.
2. Open several items (e.g., Help and Support). Practice opening, changing size, minimizing, moving, and closing various windows. Check out the menus available within the various windows you open. Also use the taskbar to launch some of the given programs. In addition, use the taskbar to open windows that have been minimized.
3. Try manually changing the size of a window by clicking and holding the side, top, bottom, or corner edge of a window and dragging it slowly (note how the mouse pointer turns into a two-headed arrow as you move it over the edge of the window).
4. Get used to moving the windows from one location on the desktop to another. Point, click, and hold the mouse pointer on the bar along the top of the active window (the title bar). Now drag the mouse and see if the window moves in your desired direction.
5. With several windows open at the same time, use the Show Desktop button to peek at the desktop. Also hide all open windows and then restore them using this same button. **Note:** This feature is not available in the Windows 7 Starter or Home Basic editions.

Note: Each of these key features is demonstrated in a set of mentoring videos on the website that accompanies this book.

LEVEL 1: DESIGNING, BUILDING, AND USING A GOOD FILING SYSTEM

What should you be able to do?

At this level, your focus is on learning how to navigate and access the various tools and features provided within the system software. Moreover, it is important to understand how things are organized and how you can name, rename, and organize files and folders. The emphasis here is on organization—putting things in places where you can find and retrieve them later. If you don't have some grasp of this, it won't be long before you will be frustrated trying to find stuff you seem to have misplaced.

What resources are provided?

Basically, Level 1 is divided into a few common scenarios, selected solutions, and practice exercises (i.e., Workouts). The scenarios have been constructed to allow you to examine common problems and how they can be addressed through the use of the system software. To do this we have provided the following:

a. Quick reference figures that identify (via visual callouts) all of the key features that have been incorporated within the solution presentation. These allow you to rapidly identify the key features and reference exactly how to include such features within your own work.
b. Step-by-step instructions on how to incorporate all highlighted features within your work.
c. Video mentoring support that guides you through the integration of each of the highlighted features.
d. Workout exercises that allow you to practice identifying and selecting which software features to use, when to use those features, how they should be incorporated, and to what degree they are effective.

How should you proceed?

If you have *little or no experience* with Windows 7 or some other similar system software, then we suggest you do the following:

1. Read and review Scenario 1.
2. Examine the reference figure (Figure 1.7).

Go to PDToolkit for **Teaching and Learning with Microsoft® Office 2010 and Office 2011 for Mac** to locate the mentoring videos for Chapter One.

Go to PDToolkit for **Teaching and Learning with Microsoft® Office 2010 and Office 2011 for Mac** to locate the mentoring videos for Chapter One.

3. Using the step-by-step directions, practice creating an organizational structure for storing items on your computer.

4. If you have any confusion or difficulty with how to accomplish these tasks, access the videos and monitor the features as they are demonstrated and discussed within the short mentoring video clips on the website that accompanies this book.

5. Once you feel comfortable, go to Scenario 2 and practice with the features introduced for that scenario. Monitor the quick reference figure (Figure 1.8) closely.

6. After both scenarios have been reviewed, go to the Workout and work through the problems and exercises as it outlines.

If you have *experience* with your operating system, you may want to review the scenarios and the quick reference figures first. If any of the features are unfamiliar, then access and use the step-by-step procedures as well as the mentoring support videos as needed. Once the review has been completed, then move directly to the Workout exercise.

Scenario 1: Organizing your electronic file cabinet

To set the stage, let's imagine that your school has just received a new grant in which all of the teachers at your grade level have been given laptop computers to use. Two weeks before the start of fall classes you receive your computer, but other than how to turn it on, no training will be available until after the first day the students return. You know how hectic the start of school can be and you would really like to be comfortable using the computer before the doors open and the kids show up.

When the computer coordinator drops in to see how things are going with the new computer, you ask for her advice. She suggests that you might try a few things. Here are several of her suggestions:

1. *Turn it on and explore on your own.*
2. *Plan how you think the computer will be used.*
3. *Walk through (with her guidance) some basic implementation activities.*

Your technology coordinator suggests that you plan how you will set up the storage system, that is, how you will know where you will put things you create, where to look for them when you need them at a later date, and so on. This will require the use of folders. Here are some simple steps to follow:

1. *With a paper and pencil, outline the structure of an efficient filing cabinet. For example, if you have an organized filing system at work, look through it and see what works and what could be improved. You may want to replicate this on your computer.*

FIGURE 1.7 Example folder structure

2. *Determine how to label the folders in your filing system and which folders can be "nested" or put within other folders. For example, look at the filing system showing in Figure 1.7. Note how the Classes folder is nested with the School work folder. Similarly, specific class folders (e.g., English, Music) are nested within the Classes folder.*

Note: Don't get too complex or fancy. There's nothing worse than trying to locate a file that's stored in a folder, in a folder, in a folder, that is in a folder. Keep it simple. Also, you can always change folders, rename them, put new things in, and take other things out. Over time, you'll find that you need to change and alter your structure.

No.	Feature	Steps to Get It Done
1.	**Create a new folder**	1. Point your cursor at a blank spot on the desktop. 2. *Right* click and a menu will appear; go to New and then left click on Folder from the options given.
2.	**Name a new folder**	1. Once a new folder has been created (and before you do anything else), type in the name that you have selected for your folder. It will appear below the folder icon. 2. Once you have it typed in, press Enter.
3.	**Rename a folder**	1. Point the mouse pointer on the current name of the folder and click twice (slowly). The name should become selected (highlighted). **Note:** If it's easier, you can also point the mouse on the current folder and right click once. A menu will appear and you can select to Rename the folder from the alternatives given. 2. Once the old name is selected (highlighted), type in the new name and it will replace the old one. 3. When you are finished entering the new name, press Enter. **Note:** Naming and renaming files and documents can be accomplished using these same procedures.
4.	**Open a folder to see what is inside**	Put the pointer on top of the folder and double click. A window will open and you will now be able to see the contents of the folder.
5.	**Create (or place) one folder inside another folder**	1. Open the existing folder (double click on the folder). 2. With that open, follow the instructions for creating a new folder (see Feature 1). The new folder will be created automatically within the open folder. **Note:** You can also create a new folder on the desktop and then click on the new folder and hold and drag it over the top of the folder you want it to go inside of. When the destination folder becomes selected (changes color or shade) then you can release the mouse button. The folder you were dragging will now be dropped into the target folder. To see if it worked, open the target folder and see if the new folder is there.
6.	**Delete a folder**	1. Put the mouse pointer on the folder to be deleted. 2. Click, hold, and drag the folder to the Recycle Bin. 3. Once the Recycle Bin is highlighted, let go of the mouse button. The folder should now be within the bin. This same procedure is used to remove an unwanted file. **Note:** Additionally, you can delete a folder (or file) by putting the cursor on the folder, *right* click, and select the Delete option from the pop-up menu. The folder (or file) will automatically be placed in the Recycle Bin. **Note:** Double click on the Recycle Bin and a window will open. You can look to see if your folder really is in there.
7.	**Take out the recycles**	When you are sure you want to delete something that has been put in the Recycle Bin, you may want to get rid of it for good. 1. Point the mouse pointer at the Recycle Bin and right click. 2. Choose the option for emptying the bin. 3. A warning window will appear to ask you if you are sure you want to permanently delete all of the items in the Recycle Bin. Click on the yes button to complete the task.

Level 1a Workout: Getting organized with folders

Once you have reviewed these different steps and written down your idea of a filing system with various folders, do the following:

1. Create a set of folders as outlined in your plan.
2. Name each of the folders (use names that are relevant to you and your work).
3. Practice nesting some of the folders inside of others.
4. Rename some of the folders.
5. Select and remove some of the folders by putting them in the Recycle Bin.

As additional practice, go to the website that accompanies this book and review its contents.

Do the following:

- Navigate to the Chapter 1 Navigation folder. Copy the folder and paste it on the desktop of your machine. A mentoring video has been created to demonstrate and guide you through this task.
- Once it has been placed on your desktop, open the Navigation folder. You'll see a number of different folders (all of which are empty) nested within that folder. Play with these. Practice naming, renaming, deleting, putting one inside of another, and so forth. The idea is to become accustomed to doing it.
- Develop some type of logical structure for the folders. Create additional folders as needed.

Review what you have just done. It may not look like much, but it is actually quite important. Don't think that folders were the only things you have explored. You have also worked on pointing, left and right clicks, click and holds, dragging, and so on. You have also explored the Start menu and seen the locations of various programs that will be used later.

Note: If you understand how to create, label, and move these types of folders, this basic skill will transfer very easily when you name files, place them within folders, recall them from folders, and so on. This is a major function of the computer and now you know something about how to store and retrieve.

More information about folders, desktops, and creating, storing, and deleting can be found in Windows Help.

Another Note: Pay attention to the necessity of organization. It will amaze you at how fast the number of folders, documents, images, and what-not will pile up in your computer, specifically on your desktop. Soon it will be overwhelming to find what you need. Begin early to organize your data into a set of folders that help identify where your stuff is and how to find it efficiently.

Scenario 2: Make it personal

Recently, I was talking with a group of high school students when suddenly a cell phone began to ring. They all stopped talking immediately and listened to the ring and then one reached into a nearby backpack, pulled out his cell, and began a conversation. Based on the ring, not only did this student know his cell was the one ringing, but he also knew who was making the call. To accomplish this, he had personalized his ring tones. In further examination of his phone, it was also easy to note how he had personalized, for instance, the exterior (e.g., cover with added color), the screen background, list of frequently called numbers, and so on.

That student's personalization of his cell may have been done for a number of reasons (e.g., to make it more efficient, aesthetically appealing, or just to be different). This type of personalization can also be done with your computer through implementing features of the system software. For example, the background on your desktop can be readily altered to include a

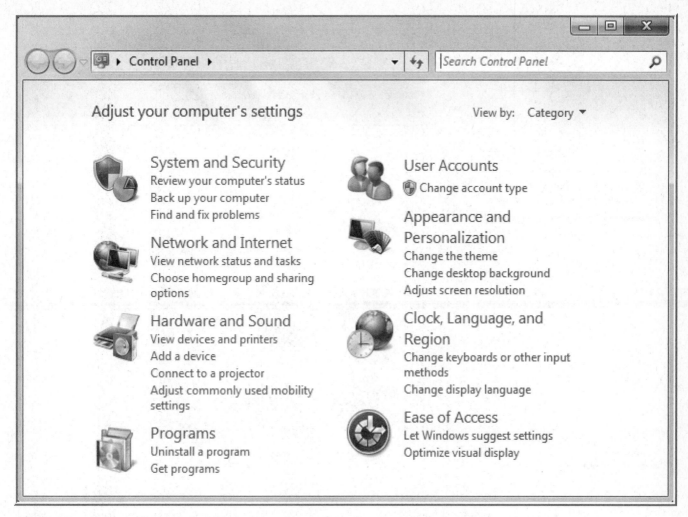

FIGURE 1.8 Control Panel home window that reveals various ways to adjust the computer's settings

picture of your favorite place or person, the size and shape of the cursor or mouse pointer can be changed, or even the look of the windows, taskbars, and Start menu can be altered to fit your personal needs, preference, and desires. In some cases, these changes may be made only to get a new and different appearance; in other cases (e.g., accessibility issues), the changes may be required.

Figure 1.8 is the Control Panel home window (**Start button** >>> right click **Control Panel** button >>> **Open**). From this window you can control and adjust many of your computer's settings (e.g., the clock, language, program install or uninstall, as well as the appearance and personalization of the computer).

The callouts in Figure 1.9 highlight some of the key adjustments that can be made through the Personalization window (**Start button** >>> **Control Panel** >>> **Personalization** or on the desktop right click and in the pop-up window select Personalize). Many of the ways in which you can change the appearance of your computer can be accomplished through this window. In the step-by-step procedures that follow, you can explore the various types of changes that can easily be made to personalize your machine.

Note: In some cases (e.g., school lab computers), customization or personalization of the computer may not be allowed or may require special permission to complete. If multiple users access the computer, specific systematic appearances may be most efficient for that type of environment. Make sure you check with the system administrator before making any changes.

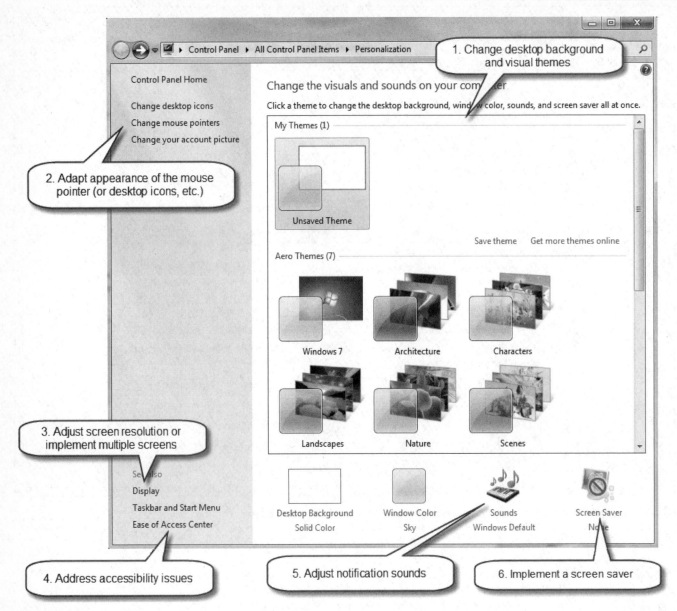

FIGURE 1.9 Personalization window

No.	Feature	Steps to Get It Done
1.	**Change the desktop background and themes**	1. Open the Personalization window (**Start button** >>> **Control Panel** >>> **Personalization** or right click on the desktop and selection Personalize from the pop-up window). 2. In the large area of the Personalize window, use the scroll bar to review all of the possible themes from which to select. 3. Click on a selected theme and preview the result by peeking at the desktop (hover the mouse over the Show Desktop button). Try various themes until you find one that you like. You can also click on the Get more themes online link to review other available desktop themes that can be downloaded.
2.	**Adapt the appearance of the mouse pointer**	1. Click on the Change mouse pointers link within the Personalize window. 2. A Mouse properties window (see Figure 1.10) will appear; click on the Pointers tab. Review the various schemes that can be selected to alter the looks and size of the pointer. 3. Click on the Pointers Options tab to review the various changes to the motion and visibility of the mouse (also review additional options by clicking on the other available tabs). 4. Select your desired options and click on the Apply button.

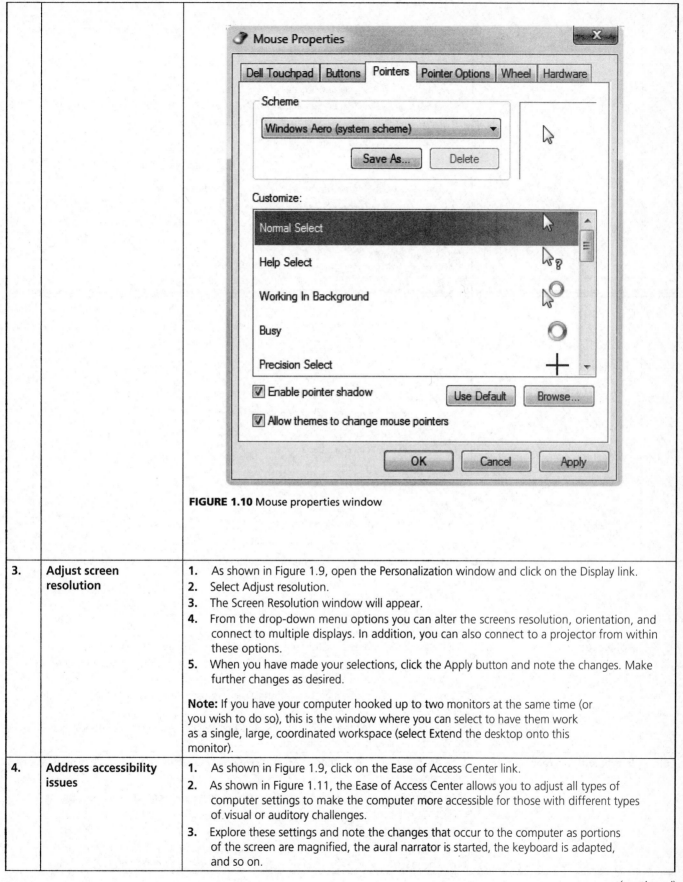

FIGURE 1.10 Mouse properties window

| 3. | Adjust screen resolution | 1. As shown in Figure 1.9, open the Personalization window and click on the Display link.
2. Select Adjust resolution.
3. The Screen Resolution window will appear.
4. From the drop-down menu options you can alter the screens resolution, orientation, and connect to multiple displays. In addition, you can also connect to a projector from within these options.
5. When you have made your selections, click the Apply button and note the changes. Make further changes as desired.

Note: If you have your computer hooked up to two monitors at the same time (or you wish to do so), this is the window where you can select to have them work as a single, large, coordinated workspace (select Extend the desktop onto this monitor). |
| 4. | Address accessibility issues | 1. As shown in Figure 1.9, click on the Ease of Access Center link.
2. As shown in Figure 1.11, the Ease of Access Center allows you to adjust all types of computer settings to make the computer more accessible for those with different types of visual or auditory challenges.
3. Explore these settings and note the changes that occur to the computer as portions of the screen are magnified, the aural narrator is started, the keyboard is adapted, and so on. |

(continued)

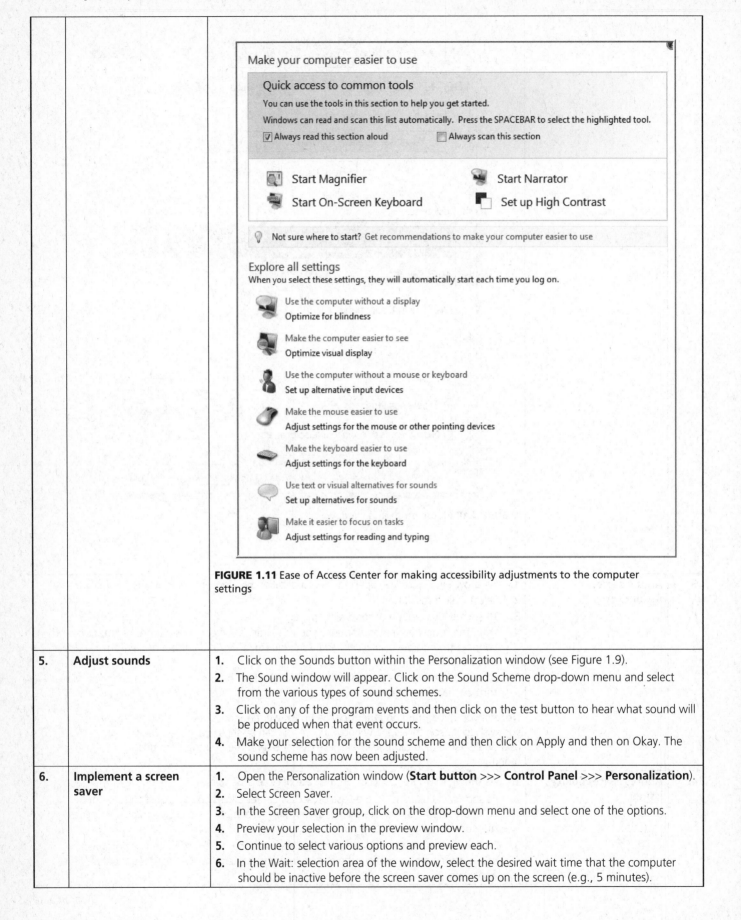

FIGURE 1.11 Ease of Access Center for making accessibility adjustments to the computer settings

5.	**Adjust sounds**	1. Click on the Sounds button within the Personalization window (see Figure 1.9).
		2. The Sound window will appear. Click on the Sound Scheme drop-down menu and select from the various types of sound schemes.
		3. Click on any of the program events and then click on the test button to hear what sound will be produced when that event occurs.
		4. Make your selection for the sound scheme and then click on Apply and then on Okay. The sound scheme has now been adjusted.
6.	**Implement a screen saver**	1. Open the Personalization window (**Start button** >>> **Control Panel** >>> **Personalization**).
		2. Select Screen Saver.
		3. In the Screen Saver group, click on the drop-down menu and select one of the options.
		4. Preview your selection in the preview window.
		5. Continue to select various options and preview each.
		6. In the Wait: selection area of the window, select the desired wait time that the computer should be inactive before the screen saver comes up on the screen (e.g., 5 minutes).

7.	**Adding gadgets**	Another interesting way to personalize your computers through Windows 7 is to add one or more gadgets (see Figure 1.12). Gadgets are small programs that give you useful information (e.g., time, temperature, news updates). These can quickly be added to your desktop (right click on the desktop>>> **Gadgets**). Select and double click (or click, drag, and drop) and the gadget will be placed on the desktop.

		FIGURE 1.12 Gadgets that can be added to the desktop

Level 1b Workout: Your personal touch

After reviewing the various ways that you can change the appearance of your computer system, you should try a few of these things. If you're working on your own personal computer, these changes should be easy to make; however, if you're working in a school computer lab, such changes may not be allowed. Restrictions are frequently imposed within computer labs to keep the computers uniform for the efficient use of the maximum number of individuals.

If you do have the option of changing the various computer settings, here are a few things that you should attempt to do to personalize your computer's settings (each can be accomplished through the Personalization window that can be found through clicking the **Start button** >>> **Control Panel** >>> **Personalization**):

1. Imagine that you want to add a new background to your computer's desktop. Create one that includes your picture or a picture that you have selected beyond the standard pictures offered by the software.
2. Suppose you are currently taking a personal management course that requires the monitoring of the New York Stock Exchange. In fact, you have invested $100,000 in various stocks and you now want to easily monitor their daily performance. Can you add a gadget that will allow you to monitor this easily?
3. Imagine sitting in a computer lab when you notice that the person next to you is having difficulty seeing the screen and following the mouse cursor movement. You offer to help. You need to show that individual how to change some settings to magnify the screen and to enlarge the mouse cursor or pointer to a maximum size. Practice doing this on your computer.
4. You've found that you really aren't very good at opening folders by double clicking them. It is difficult to keep your hand steady and it seems to take forever to get the dumb things open. Find a way to change the double click to a single click to open folders on your computer.
5. You've found a new piece of software that you are using quite frequently. To launch it, however, you have to go into the All Programs section of the Start menu and then through

several other folders before it's finally located. Isn't there a way to just add that program to your Start menu or even pin it to your taskbar? Also, there are a number of programs on the Start menu that you never use. Can you get rid of them or at least just remove them from this convenient location? Resolve these tasks through the same Personalization window.

LEVEL 2: HELP, I NEED SOME INFO

What should you be able to do?

Here, the focus is on getting efficient, effective, and reliable help when it is needed. This is a skill that will be needed and used over and over again as you work with the computer.

Note: There's too much information within the operating system for any sensible person to totally learn and retain. Knowing where and how to access that information is a skill well worth the effort to learn.

Introduction

At this level of performance, we want you to become more independent. That is, we want you to begin to answer questions that you have a need to answer—not something we have conjured up for you. This will allow you to search for and find needed information, get tasks done, solve problems, overcome difficulties, and so on—even when it is just you and the machine.

Don't worry—there will always be questions. You will encounter endless novel situations that will require the use of extra resources. Specifically, the use of the computer's built-in Help should become a natural place for you to turn to.

Note: Help doesn't have all the answers, but it does answer many of the common problems individuals run into. You are much further ahead by using Help as your knowledgeable personal computer assistant.

Another note: There are Help functions within almost all of the major software application programs available today. If you're working in a word processing program, there will be a word processing Help that you can refer to. Likewise, if you're working with a spreadsheet, there's a specific Help for spreadsheets.

Getting some Help

Have you ever bought a new car and then proceeded to *memorize* the owner's manual? Why not? Don't you want to know everything about your new purchase?

For most of us, that type of memorization task would be too time consuming, would take too much energy, and would be too boring with little return. You and I know that when specific information is needed about the car (e.g., Where is the jack located? What is the procedure to change a tire?), we can turn to the owner's manual and find the needed information.

Guess what? This is also true for the computer. The nice thing about the computer, however, is that it has a section where you can electronically look up answers to your questions and solutions for your problems. This is known as the Help program. In Microsoft's Windows 7 operating system, you can access Help and Support by clicking **Start** button >>> **Help and Support**.

Why do you *really* need to know how to use Help?

This question is similar to, "Why do I need to know how to use an encyclopedia?" that some of your students may have asked. Those of us who have worked on this book—and any book out there that has to do with the computer—can't foresee all the situations that you'll find yourself in need of help. In one way or another, you'll find questions that we haven't thought of and definitely haven't attempted to answer.

The goal, then, is to help you find the way to get your own answer. For the long haul, this will be a much better approach than writing a huge text with "all of the answers" that we would want you to memorize. That is a little unrealistic and unwanted.

Help is very efficient and, in most cases, for the novice user it will have more than enough information to get you what you need.

At the present time, Help for Windows 7 comes in two varieties: (1) the help built within Windows 7 and (2) the additional help, information, and ideas that can be found on the Windows website (http://windows.microsoft.com >>> **Help & How-to**).

Scenario 3: Creating the self-sufficient parent

Lexy was having difficulties with her mother. It wasn't a disagreement about Lexy's homework getting done, her friends, or even how many minutes she used on last month's cell phone bill. Lexy's problem had to do with her mother's nonstop questions about the computer. It seemed that each evening Lexy's mom would wait until Lexy was just settling down to a favorite TV show and then the inquisition would begin. In most cases, it began with a simple, "Hey Lexy, can you show me how I can get my computer to . . . ?"

Lexy quickly figured out that the best way to solve her problem was to help her mom learn to help herself. Today, for example, Mom was having difficulty figuring out how to install a new program that she needed to preview for her boss.

"You know, Mom, you can answer many of your own questions by just accessing the computer's Help." Lexy then proceeded to show her mom that she could quickly access Help by clicking on the Start button and then clicking on Help and Support (see Figure 1.13). When she showed her how that was accomplished, she then gave her mom a little assignment: to type in her specific question about installing a program into the search section of Help (see Figure 1.13) and see what topics came up. She was then to select one of the topics that was most relevant and examine if the given procedure was helpful. Mom indicated she would try. Lexy monitored and gave suggestions. Then the computer questioning seemed to abate—which gave Mom more time to ask Lexy about lots of other things—cause moms like to do that.

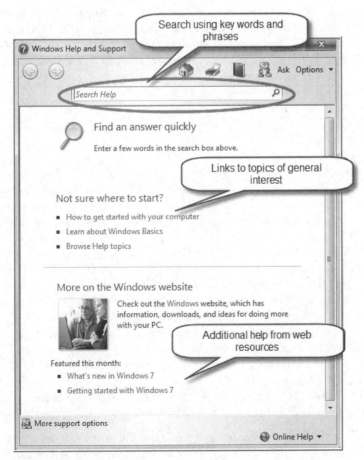

FIGURE 1.13 Windows Help and Support

Using Help

Basically, Help works like an electronic encyclopedia. It is arranged by topics. If you need something, you tell Help the key word or phrase and it will look it up for you and report back the related topics found. You can then select the specific items you feel may have the answer that you seek and the computer will highlight all of the information that it has on the topic.

Sounds simple, doesn't it? There are a couple of things to remember:

- You need to know what the key word or phrase is. If you don't have something at least close to your topic, the computer won't know what to look for. We've given you a bunch of key jargon words for this section of the text as examples of key words that can be looked up in Help.
- Sometimes your selected key word gets you close, but not exactly in the right place (this happens sometimes when you're looking for a book in the library). Don't be afraid to look around and see if some of the topics are related and how they relate to your topic. These may help you find exactly what you are looking for.
- There are times when Help may cause you frustration. Perhaps there isn't the needed information, the information provided is confusing in some way, or you know the information is in there but you can't seem to find it. Skills at using Help are like anything else: they get better as you use them. Throughout this text we emphasize using Help because it's a skill you should develop to gain greater independence with your use of the computer. Your other choice is to memorize everything about this machine and all programs you use with it—and that doesn't seem like a very logical alternative.
- Don't forget about the online help. Just because something doesn't come up from a direct search within Windows Help and Support, don't neglect going to the online version. The online version often has a greater amount of information about the topics and in many cases a greater depth of coverage (e.g., video tutorials, etc.).

Level 2 Workout: Stretching with a little Help

Here are a few exercises to help you get comfortable with using Help.

1. Open Help and Support (**Start** button >>> **Help and Support**). Examine (review Figure 1.13) the various topics in the Help and Support window and the area to insert potential search terms or key words. Within the Help and Support window, click on the Learn with Windows Basics link and investigate several of the following topics:
   - Turning off the computer properly
   - Working with windows
   - Getting started with Paint
   - Desktop gadgets
   - Working with digital pictures
   - Learn about Windows games
2. Open Help and Support, select the Table of Contents (button that looks like a book at the top of the Windows Help and Support window). Examine the various categories of information and how they are organized. If you have a question within a general category (e.g., files, folders, and libraries), you can click on that category and see the various links to all kinds of information. Follow these examples and see what types of information can be obtained from the Help and Support Table of Contents:
   - How do you burn a CD or DVD? (Start at the Pictures, CDs, DVDs, TV, music, and sound category within the Help and Support table of contents.)
   - How do you play music and videos? (Start at the Pictures, CDs, DVDs, TV, music, and sound category of the Help and Support table of contents.)
   - How do I get pictures from my camera to my computer? (Start at the Hardware, devices, and drivers and then look under Cameras.)
   - What is a firewall and how is it used? (Start at Security and Privacy within the Help and Support table of contents.)
   - How do I back up and restore my system? (Start at Maintenance and Performance within the Help and Support table of contents, and then look under Backing up and restoring.)

   Don't spend a huge amount of time playing with this, but do get a feel for what this feature has to offer. There are some really great bits of information readily available to you within Help and Support. Get a feel for what's there and what can be accessed when it's needed.

3. Insert key words and terms in the Search Help area (see Figure 1.13) and practice looking up bits of information that may be useful. For example find out how to
   - Change languages
   - Define HTML
   - Use speech narration
   - Create shortcuts
   - Find a file or folder
   - Install a program
   - Burn DVD
   - Use a calculator

   Try out several of your own terms and see what types of results are produced. Stump your friends by exploring several of the topics in Help. Create some questions about the new things you have found and check with friends, neighbors, colleagues, and so on to see if anyone else knows what you now know.

4. Go To the website that accompanies this book and review the mentoring video that has been created to demonstrate Help and its various functions.

LEVEL 3: INTEGRATION AND APPLICATION

What should you be able to do?

The focus at this point is for you to begin to think of ways that this information can be applied. Using these examples, generate ideas on how to use the features of the system software to facilitate your students' learning and the work that you do.

Introduction

Now it's time to stretch. You need to understand how to use this information on your own and teach it effectively to your students or future students.

Ideas on using the system software as a learning tool

There are a number of ways that the system software can be used to increase the learning of others. Here are some examples to get you thinking about possible ways to use various features of the operating software:

1. Develop a mind-set of finding the answers for oneself by focusing on how to find answers to problems or questions that haven't yet been encountered. An example of this would be setting up a computer scavenger hunt that involves the use of the system software's Help feature. Have students find information that deals with things such as optimizing performance, print queues, or even updating drivers.
2. Develop skills at planning and creating effective organizational filing systems. Have students design a filing system that they can defend as being effective for the storage of their key documents and files. After they have designed it, have them review what others have planned, make revisions, and then create and use the actual folders and nested folders on their computers.
3. Use the system software Search feature to locate specific documents, folders, and so forth on the computer. Have students find specific files on the hard drive and explain the path to the file's location.
4. Learn to adapt the computer settings to best fit the user's preferred style. For example, using the Control Panel, change the settings on the monitor to enhance (or diminish) the size of the screen display, adapt the speed with which the cursor blinks, change the size and shape of the mouse pointer, or even alter the size and looks of the icons displayed on the desktop. Also have the students learn how to change these back to its original setting.
5. Develop the ability to open several folders in separate windows at a single time and transfer documents or subfolders between the different folders. In addition, develop the ability to copy folders and documents and put them on different disks for storage purposes.

PDToolkit
for
Teaching and Learning with Microsoft® Office 2010 and Office 2011 for Mac

Go to PDToolkit for **Teaching and Learning with Microsoft® Office 2010 and Office 2011 for Mac** to locate Workout Level One for Chapter One.

6. Discuss accessibility issues and how the computer can be adjusted to assist those with visual, auditory, or other difficulties. For example, have students use the magnifier or narrator while working on their computer and determine the needed time and effort required to develop skills with those enhancements.

Ideas on using the system software as an assistant

1. Use the computer's system software features to help maintain the computer. Features of the system software such as Disk Defragmenter and Scan Disk can be used to improve the performance of the computer by keeping it in an efficient working order.
2. Use Windows Explorer as a means to view where saved items are located and how they can be rearranged or manipulated.
3. Determine the size of a specific file and/or the amount of disk space.
4. Use the control panels to alter how the computer functions and looks.
5. Create and use shortcuts to facilitate the effectiveness of accessing key programs and files.
6. Add and/or remove programs from the Start menu for easy access.
7. Use the system to enhance the access of physically challenged students.

System Software: Mac OS

Terms to Know
Finder
Spotlight

ORIENTATION

This section assumes you have previewed the full Chapter 1 and have a grasp of system software, its importance, and generally what purpose it serves. This section of the chapter focuses specifically on the operating system of the Apple Macintosh. There are some similarities between the PC's Windows-based system software and that used on Mac computers; however, there are some other significant differences that should be noted.

What's the workspace look like?

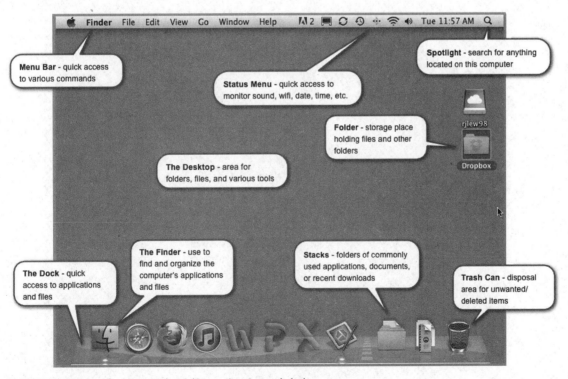

FIGURE 1.14 View of a Macintosh OS (Operating System) desktop

What's the desktop?

In a usual working office, the top of the desk is where most of the work is completed. There are tools (e.g., pencils, paper clips, writing paper) that are sitting on the desktop so that when needed they are readily available. This is very similar to the computer's desktop (see Figure 1.14). It is here that one has ready access to the needed tools and files so that real work can be accomplished.

The dock

When working on various projects or through your usual everyday use, you'll quickly notice that there are several tools you consistently use on the computer. The dock (see Figure 1.14) is the location on the Mac OS desktop where you can locate those tools. Simply locating the icon for the tool you need, pointing the mouse directly on it, and clicking the mouse button will open the application.

The dock can be readily personalized by adding desired tools or removing those tools you don't need. Removing tools from the dock does not eliminate them from the computer, only from the dock itself. If you need them later, you can still get to them in your applications folder.

Note that the dock is divided by a dashed line. Specific applications are on the left side of the dashed line, whereas to the right of the dashed line are stacks (folders that contain applications, recent documents, and downloads) and the trash can.

The menu bar

As shown in Figure 1.14, at the top left of the desktop is a menu bar. The menu bar changes based on the application you are currently using. That is, the menu will be different if you have clicked on the finder icon on the dock than if you had opened a word processing application.

Each of the items listed on the menu bar has a list of drop-down commands. As shown in Figure 1.15, when you click on a selected section of the menu bar, the drop-down list of commands is accessed and can be used.

FIGURE 1.15 The menu bar with access to drop-down commands

The status menu

On the right side of the menu bar shown in Figure 1.14, additional icons reveal the current status of things such as the sound level on the computer, access to wifi, the time and date, and so on.

The trash can

An important part of organizing is *getting rid of the stuff you no longer need*. This is easily done by dragging the item to the trash can that's located on the dock of the desktop. This is a storage place where you can put unwanted documents and so on. If you want to remove items permanently from the trash can, simply click once on the trash can and a window will open exposing all items that are currently in the trash. Click on the Empty button and all items (or those you select) will be permanently removed.

The "power of the mouse": *pointing, clicking, selecting,* **and** *dragging*

The power of the mouse (or any mouse substitute—like the trackball, touchpad, your finger) is that it allows you to tell the computer what to pay attention to and, in many cases, exactly what to do.

Here are the key skills:

POINT:

Move the mouse and watch how the pointer or cursor on the screen moves with it. You need to be able to tell the computer which things to work with—the power of the mouse is that it allows you to point to exactly what you want the computer to attend to.

CLICK:

Note that the mouse for the Macintosh generally has a single button that can be depressed. When you depress once on it quickly, it is called a *click*. That gives the computer important information about what to do with the item you are pointing at. At times you will need to expand your clicking repertoire into a

- Double (or even a triple) click or perhaps a
- Click and hold

If you do not have access to a mouse (perhaps you are working on a laptop), note that there is still some kind of point-and-click mechanism provided. Don't worry; they all are designed to accomplish basically the same thing.

SELECT OR HIGHLIGHT:

Often you need to identify a specific item (e.g., a picture, word, number) that you want the computer to work on. To do this, you typically put the mouse pointer on top of the item and click. In some cases, you will need to click and hold in front of the item and then drag over the item until it is fully selected. When it is selected it will change colors (typically having a darker or lighter background). If you want it to be deselected, just click anywhere else on the screen. Here is an example of a selected word:

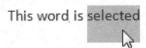

DRAG:

This is when you point at some object, click and hold (don't release the button), and then move the mouse. The item you have clicked on will then move (drag) or be highlighted in some way. For example, this is one way that you can move a file from one place on the screen to another. Point at the file, click and hold, and drag it to the new location.

The Finder

The **Finder** (see Figure 1.16) is an important area for you to become familiar with. It is aptly named because it is where you go to find things on the computer. Opening the Finder on the dock (see Figure 1.14), you will notice a sidebar that appears. Clicking on any of the items listed on the sidebar will reveal all items (e.g., folders, documents, pictures) located on that device or in that location.

Using the view menu, you can see the contents of the Finder location in a number of different ways (e.g., icons, lists, columns). If you would like to be reminded of what the open item looks like, you can use the preview button to see a quick look of what has been saved.

The Finder is also used to help organize your files and folders. You can create new folders, rename files and folders, and change the locations of those items—all within the Finder.

Help

The main operating systems today have help sections built into their programs. We will constantly suggest that you turn to Help to get many of the answers to your questions. Help is one of the options to select on the menu bar (see Figure 1.14). In most applications, Help is located in this same position on the menu bar. Help is specific to which application is currently being used. To get general Mac help, first click on the Finder icon, then the Help menu bar, and then select the Mac Help drop-down command.

Spotlight—Using the Search function

Once you become accustomed to using the computer for many of your daily tasks, you will soon be amazed at how many things you can store within it. Soon you will have thousands of pieces of information. Those bits and pieces may include photos, letters, files of data, book reports, math exercises, and so on. But it can be a problem when you need to find that information and you can't remember exactly where you put it. That is when the search function known as **Spotlight** comes in.

Within the Mac OS, you can use the computer to quickly search its own contents—merely by giving it a clue as to what to look for. Review Figure 1.14 and note the location of the Spotlight (the icon looks like a magnifying glass). Click on the Spotlight icon and enter a

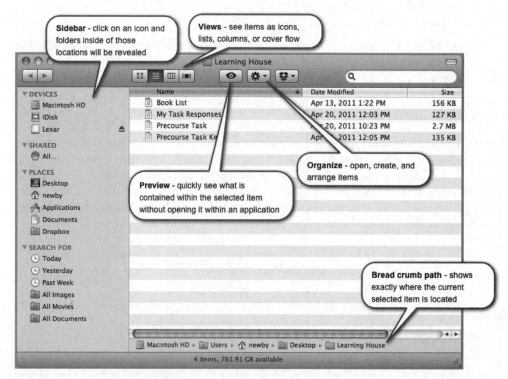

FIGURE 1.16 The Finder in Mac OS

key word that could be found within the document you are searching for. Spotlight will identify the documents, web pages, e-mail messages, media, and so on that include your key word.

Files and Folders

To help organize what is on the desktop and what is stored within the computer, a simple visual metaphor is used. Just like a filing cabinet in the office contains labeled folders and documents that are placed in the folders, so too are things organized in your computer's system platform.

Review Figure 1.14 and note the file titled *Dropbox*. That folder has been given a name and it can hold other files (e.g., documents, figures) as well as additional folders. The use of folders with individual names is a great way to organize related materials for later retrieval.

Windows, windows, everywhere

Take a look at Figure 1.17. This is an example of multiple windows being open on one computer screen. Windows allow you to peer into different programs and different parts of the program.

Note how the windows can be made of different sizes and be made to overlap each other. As you begin to work with the computer, you will find that navigating through these windows, being able to have multiple windows exposed at a single time, can be very helpful. The window you are currently working on (the one on top) is known as the *active window*. When you have a number of windows on the screen at one time, you can make a specific one active by pointing your mouse directly within the space of that window and clicking once. It will highlight and come to the top (i.e., it will overlay or be on top of the other open windows).

Look closely at Figure 1.17. Note the highlighted section in the corner of the active window (see the upper left corner). These buttons allow you to control the active window (i.e., hide the window temporarily so you can see what other things are on the screen, change the size, or close it altogether). If you want to change the size of the active window, put your cursor directly over the bottom right corner and click, hold, and drag to the appropriate size. To see a demonstration of how to work with active windows, review the mentoring video on the website that accompanies this book.

PDToolkit
for
Teaching and Learning with Microsoft® Office 2010 and Office 2011 for Mac

Go to PDToolkit for **Teaching and Learning with Microsoft® Office 2010 and Office 2011 for Mac** to locate the mentoring videos for Chapter One.

FIGURE 1.17 View of multiple open windows

Orientation Workout: Explore the territory

Turn on your computer and attempt the following on the desktop:

1. Click the Finder icon and explore how the computer's storage has been set up. Note the folders and the various names used to name files and folders.
2. Open several items (e.g., Help, a word-processed document, iTunes, a web browser). Practice opening, changing size, minimizing, moving, and closing various windows. Check out the menu bars that are available within the various windows you open.
3. Try manually changing the size of a window by clicking and holding the lower right portion of the window and dragging it slowly.
4. Get used to moving the windows from one location on the desktop to another. Point, click, and hold the mouse pointer on the bar along the top of the active window (the title bar)—now drag the mouse and see if the window moves in your desired direction.

LEVEL 1: DESIGNING, BUILDING, AND USING A GOOD FILING SYSTEM

Scenario 1

To accomplish this Level 1 task, review Scenario 1 (pages 16–17), specifically focusing on Figure 1.7 and how the folder organizational structure was designed. Using Figure 1.7 as a guide, complete the following steps.

No.	Feature	Steps to Get It Done
1.	Create a new folder	1. Point your cursor at a blank spot on the desktop and click and the Finder menu bar will appear. 2. On the Finder menu bar click **File** >>> **New Folder** and a new folder will appear on the desktop.
2.	Name a new folder	1. Once a new folder has been created (and before you do anything else), type in the name you have selected for your folder. It will appear below the folder icon. 2. Once you have it typed in, press Enter.
3.	Rename a folder	1. Point the mouse pointer on the current name of the folder and click twice (slowly). The name should become selected (highlighted). Once the old name is selected (highlighted), type in the new name and it will replace the old one. 2. When you are finished entering the new name, press Enter. **Note**: Naming and renaming files and documents can be accomplished using these same procedures.
4.	Open a folder to see what is inside	Put the mouse pointer on top of the folder and double click. A window will open and you will now be able to see the contents of the folder.
5.	Create (or place) one folder inside another folder	1. Open the existing folder (double click on the folder). 2. With that open, follow the instructions for creating a new folder (see Feature 1). The new folder will be created automatically within the open folder. **Note:** You can also create a new folder on the desktop and then click on the new folder and hold and drag it over the top of the folder you want it to go inside of. When the destination folder becomes selected (changes color or shade) then you can release the mouse button. The folder you were dragging will now be dropped into the target folder. To see if it worked, open the target folder and see if the new folder is there.
6.	Delete a folder	1. Put the mouse pointer on the folder to be deleted. 2. Click, hold, and drag the folder to the trash can. 3. Once the trash can is highlighted, let go of the mouse button. The folder should now be within the trash can. This same procedure is used to remove an unwanted file.
7.	Take out the trash	When you are sure you want to delete something that has been put in the trash can, you may want to get rid of it for good. 1. Click on the trash can and a window will appear that reveals all of the contents of its contents. 2. Click on the small Empty button on the right side of the window. 3. A warning window will appear to ask you if you are sure you want to permanently delete all of the items. Click on the Empty Trash button to complete the task.

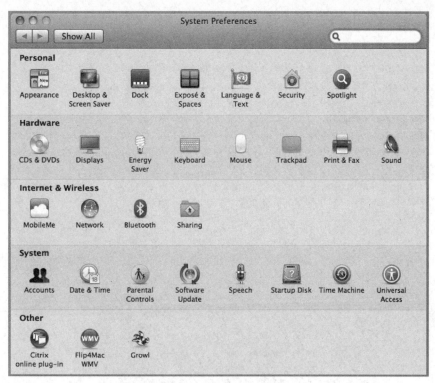

FIGURE 1.18 Use of System Preferences to personalize your Mac

Scenario 2

To accomplish this Level 1 task, review Scenario 2 (page 18). In this case, we want to carry out certain changes to the computer to make it more personalized. This will include changes such as altering the looks of the desktop, adding gadgets, and so on.

Most of the personal preference changes can be made through the Systems Preferences found on the dock (if it isn't located on the dock, look in the applications folder). Figure 1.18 shows the window of icons available once the system preferences has been opened.

No.	Feature	Steps to Get It Done
1.	Change the desktop background	1. Open the Systems Preferences window and click on the Desktop & Screen Saver icon. 2. In the Desktop & Screen Saver window, click on the Desktop tab. 3. Use the scroll bar to review all of the possible pictures or patterns from which to select. 4. Click on a selected picture. 5. Select how you want the screen to be filled (e.g., fill screen, tile) and how often the picture should change. 6. You may also select if you want the menu bar to be translucent.
2.	Adapt the movement and appearance of the mouse pointer or cursor	1. **Systems Preferences** >>> **Systems** group >>> **Universal Access** 2. In the Universal Access window, click on the Mouse tab. 3. Using the slider bars, adjust how the mouse moves as well as the size of the cursor.
3.	Adjust screen resolution	1. **Systems Preferences** >>> **Hardware** group >>> **Displays** 2. Click on the Display tab. 3. Select the desired resolution from the options given. The brightness of the screen may also be adjusted with the slider bar.
4.	Address accessibility issues	1. **Systems Preferences** >>> **Systems** group >>> **Universal Access** 2. The Universal Access window will open. 3. Explore these settings (use the tabs at the top of the Universal Access window) and note the changes that occur to the computer as portions of the screen are magnified, the aural narrator is started, the keyboard is adapted, and so on.

(continued)

5.	Adjust sounds	1. **Systems Preferences** >>> **Hardware** group >>> **Sound** 2. The Sound window will appear. Click on the Sound Effects tab to select the alert sound and volume. 3. The Output or Input tabs allow you to select the speaker or microphone settings.
6.	Implement a screen saver	1. **Systems Preferences** >>> **Personal** group >>> **Desktop & Screen Saver** 2. The Desktop & Screen Saver window will open. 3. Select the Screen Saver tab. 4. Select an option from the various pictures shown in the right selection area of the window. Your selection can be previewed in the right pane of the window. 5. Use the slider bar to set when the screen saver should start.
7.	Adding gadgets **FIGURE 1.19** The Dashboard icon	Another interesting way to personalize your computer through the Mac OS is to add one or more gadgets. Gadgets are small programs that give you useful information (e.g., time, temperature, news updates, stock quotes). To access the gadgets, click on the Dashboard icon (see Figure 1.19) that is generally located on the dock. As shown in Figure 1.20, when the Dashboard is clicked the gadgets are revealed on the desktop. Click anywhere other than on the gadgets and they disappear.  **FIGURE 1.20** Gadgets selected and placed on the dashboard To add other gadgets, simply look for the large plus sign (+) when the gadgets are revealed, click on the + and a list of additional gadgets will be revealed. You can then drag and drop them into the Dashboard area.

Level 1a and 1b Workouts

Return to the Level 1a and 1b Workouts found on page 18 and 23, respectively. Complete the workouts using Figures 1.7 and 1.18 as guides for your work.

LEVEL 2: HELP, I NEED SOME INFO

What should you be able to do?

Here, the focus is on getting efficient, effective, and reliable help when it is needed. This is a skill that will be needed and used over and over again as you work with the computer.

The computer's operating system has a section where you can electronically look up answers to your questions and solutions for your problems. This is known as the Help program. In the Mac's OS you can access Help by clicking **Finder** button >>> **Help** on the menu bar (see Figure 1.21).

Help is efficient and in most cases, for the novice user, it will have more than enough information to get you what you need. Simply type in a keyword and topics related to the key word will be presented.

In addition, as shown in Figure 1.21, general Mac Help can also be accessed through this drop-down menu. The Mac Help presents general topics about the computer and how it can be used. Moreover, additional help can be accessed at www.apple.com (**Support** >>> **Browse Support** >>> **Mac OS** >>> **Tutorials**).

FIGURE 1.21 Accessing the Mac OS Help through the Finder menu bar

Scenario 3

Understanding what can be provided by the Help feature found within the Mac OS will be of great benefit as you begin to use the computer for more and more tasks. Return to page 25 of this chapter and read Scenario 3. That helps to set the stage for why using Help is a needed skill as well as the benefits and limitations of Help.

Please note and remember that Help will not have all of the answers. It is, however, a great resource when you need to get specific information about the operating system. In addition, exploring the various topics within the Help is a very good way to find out about features on the computer that you may not have realized were possible.

As shown in Figure 1.22, Mac OS Help has various topics that can be explored by clicking directly on the links (e.g., Learn the basics about your Mac) or you can enter in specific keywords in the spotlight area of the Help window (upper right corner).

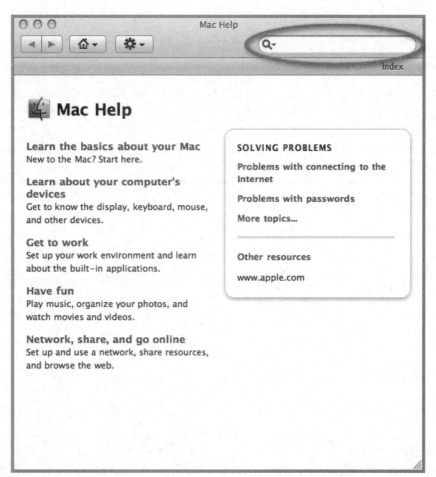

FIGURE 1.22 The Help window in the Mac OS

Level 2 Workout

Here are a couple of things to help you get comfortable with using Help:

1. Open Help (**Finder icon** >>> **Help** tab of main menu). Within the Help window click on the Learn the basics about your Mac link and investigate several of the following topics:
    *   Navigating your computer
    *   Menu basics
    *   Printing a document
    *   Changing your computer's settings
    *   System preferences
    *   Customizing the dock
    *   Working with digital pictures
    *   Exposé

2. Open the Help window and use the search function to get answers on each of the following:
    *   How do you burn a CD or DVD?
    *   How do you play music and videos?
    *   How do I get pictures from my camera to my computer?
    *   What is a firewall and how is it used?
    *   How do I back up and restore my system?

Don't spend a huge amount of time playing with this, but do get a feel for what this has to offer. There are some really great bits of information readily available to you within the Mac OS Help and also at www.apple.com (Support). Get a feel for what is there and what can be accessed when it is needed.

3. Insert key words or terms in the Spotlight area (see Figure 1.22) and practice looking up information that may be useful. For example find out how to
    *   Change languages
    *   Define HTML
    *   Use speech narration
    *   Create shortcuts
    *   Find a file or folder
    *   Install a program
    *   Use a calculator

Try out several of your own terms and see what types of results are produced. Stump your friends by exploring several of the topics in Help. Create some questions about the new things you have found and check with friends, neighbors, colleagues, and so on to see if anyone else knows what you now know.

4. Go the website that accompanies this book and review the mentoring video that has been created to demonstrate Help and its various functions.

PDToolkit
for
Teaching and Learning with Microsoft® Office 2010 and Office 2011 for Mac

Go to PDToolkit for **Teaching and Learning with Microsoft® Office 2010 and Office 2011 for Mac** to locate the mentoring videos for Chapter One.

2 | WORD PROCESSING

MS Word: The Basics of a Writing Assistant

INTRODUCTION

What should you know about word processors?

Word processing is *a* (if not *the*) major software tool used by teachers and students. You need to know a few basics to use it effectively. In this opening section, we want you to know the following:

- What a word processor is, what it can do, and how it can help in teaching and learning
- How to justify the use of the word processor as an effective tool—by knowing when and why it should or shouldn't be used

Terms to know			
alignment	gallery	ISTE	shading
bullet list	grammar check	margin	spell check
clip art	graphic	Microsoft Word	style
columns	gridlines	number list	tables
command groups	handles	page border	text wrapping
command tabs	headers	quick styles	view buttons
contextual commands	hyperlinks	ribbon	view tab
font	integration	ruler	watermark
footers	International Society for Technology in Education	section break	web
format		sections	WordArt

What is a word processor and what does it do?

A word processor is a computer application that allows you to enter, edit, revise, format, store, retrieve, and print text. When you work with text the way that teachers and students do, word processors quickly become a valuable tool.

What are some commonly used word processors?

Standard software varieties include the following:

- **Microsoft Word**
- Corel WordPerfect
- Sun Microsystems StarOffice/OpenOffice Writer
- The word processor within Microsoft Works

Web 2.0 varieties:

- Google Docs
- Zoho Writer

Note: We focus on Microsoft Word in this text. However, *what we present can be done in any of the other word processors listed*, so if you don't have access to Word, don't be alarmed—you can still complete the projects and learn the basic skills.

Why bother learning how to use a word processor?

- We haven't found anything yet to replace reading and writing. As long as those two skills are needed, there will be a need for the processing of words.
- Most of us don't have perfect memories. Word processors are a good way to record ideas, thoughts, research, and instructions and then be able to recall them later.
- We live in a world of repetition. From the written standpoint, word processors help so you don't needlessly start from scratch when confronted with a project that may be the same or similar to one encountered previously. Thus the second time around, you spend your time on improvements instead of reinventing the same thing.
- It just looks better. If this text were handwritten (by me), you would gag. Word processing allows others to be able to quickly decipher what is written. As much as we would like to say that we judge things based on their content, how something looks also matters. Good word processing can help with how information is perceived and processed by the reader.
- It isn't just words anymore. Today's word processors not only handle words, but they also incorporate the use of all kinds of graphics and pictures. These can lead to more proficient and better communication (and possible learning).
- No longer is word processing a lone wolf. That is, what is produced with a good word processor can be coupled with other programs and made even more powerful. Hooking up your words with powerful graphics programs, databases, spreadsheets, and even the Internet can open all kinds of possibilities for classroom projects, fun explorations, and increased efficiency.

How can word processors be used at school? A brief list of ideas

By the teacher:	By the student:
• Newsletters	• Essays
• Classroom handouts	• Book reports
• Student assignments and tests	• Answers to comprehension questions
• Calendars	• Creative writing
• Lesson plans	• Science reports

ORIENTATION

What's the workspace look like?

Figure 2.1 is an example of the workspace of a common word processor (MS Word). Note where you can enter in your information and some of the common commands, **command groups**, and specific tools that can be accessed and used.

What commands can be used?

As in all MS Office applications (e.g., MS PowerPoint, MS Excel), there is a **ribbon** of tools that runs across the top of the work screen. Within each ribbon the actual tools that can be used to input, format, and edit the words to be processed are grouped under the various **command tabs** (e.g., Home, Insert, Page Layout, References). Selecting a specific tab reveals an associated command set or group. Once a command tab has been selected, this specific group remains visible and ready for use. Items within the set may appear as individual items or as a **gallery** of related items. For example, selecting the Insert tab (see Figure 2.2) in Word reveals a group of commands that deals specifically with the insertion of such things as tables, illustrations, links, headers and footers, and of course the text itself.

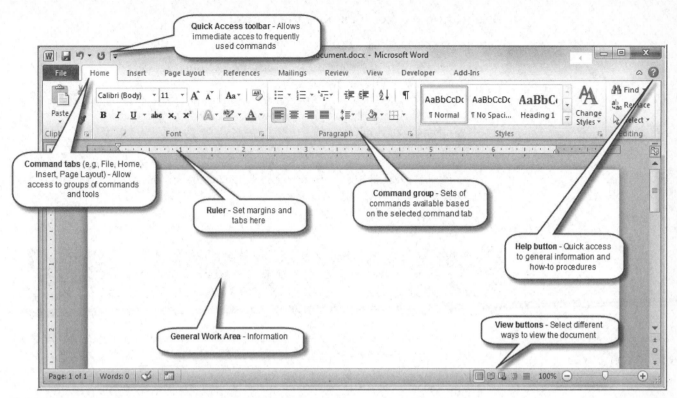

FIGURE 2.1 View of a Microsoft Word word processing work area

The tabs have been developed to make your life easier. No longer do you have to go through hundreds of potential drop-down menu items to find the needed tool; the tabs allow you quick access to related groups of commands.

It should be noted that there are additional commands that are needed on occasion. As shown in Figure 2.3 (Picture Tools), these **contextual commands** appear when a specific object like a picture, graphic, table, or chart is selected.

For more information about the Word ribbon and command tabs, please review the Word Orientation video on the website that accompanies this book.

PDToolkit
for
Teaching and Learning with Microsoft® Office 2010 and Office 2011 for Mac

Go to PDToolkit for **Teaching and Learning with Microsoft® Office 2010 and Office 2011 for Mac** to locate the mentoring videos for Chapter Two.

FIGURE 2.2 The ribbon holds the command tabs, command groups or sets, and individual commands

FIGURE 2.3 Selecting a specific item (e.g., graphic, picture) in the workspace reveals contextual commands that can be accessed and used with the selected item

Orientation Workout: Explore the territory

Turn on your computer and attempt the following:

1. Launch the Microsoft Word software (or a similar word processor).
2. Create a new Word document.
3. Explore the various tabs on the ribbon and examine the different command groups.
4. On the new document attempt the following:
   - Enter a few lines of text.
   - Select some of text and alter its **format** (e.g., size, **style**).
   - Use the different **view buttons** and select different ways to view your document.
   - Alter the paragraph structure by changing the manner in which your text is aligned and whether it is double or single spaced.
   - Practice cutting and pasting portions of your text.

LEVEL 1: DESIGNING, CREATING, AND PRODUCING WRITTEN DOCUMENTS

What should you be able to do?

At Level 1, the emphasis is on using various tools and techniques of an electronic word processor to format a document given specific guidelines and step-by-step procedures.

What resources are provided?

Basically, Level 1 is divided into common teaching scenarios, selected solutions, and practice exercises (i.e., Workouts). The scenarios have been constructed to allow you to examine common problems and how they can be addressed through the use of this software. To do this, we have provided the following:

1. Completed word-processed documents that you can review and compare to see how the features are used to address the problems presented within each scenario.
2. Quick reference figures that identify (via visual callouts) all of the key features that have been incorporated within the solution presentation. These allow you to rapidly identify the key features and reference exactly how to include such features within your own work.
3. Step-by-step instructions on how to incorporate all highlighted features within your work
4. Video mentoring support that guides you through the integration of each of the highlighted features.
5. Workout exercises that allow you to practice identifying and selecting which software features to use, when to use those features, how they should be incorporated, and to what degree they are effective.

How should you proceed?

If you have *little or no experience* with MS Office 2010 and particularly Word, then we suggest you do the following:

1. Read and review Scenario 1.
2. Examine the quick reference figure (Figure 2.5) and all of the highlighted features.
3. Using the step-by-step directions given for each highlighted feature, use the software and practice using each of the features.
4. If you have any confusion or difficulty with these features, access the videos and monitor the features as they are demonstrated and discussed within the short video clips on the website that accompanies this book. Select the short clip that demonstrates the use of the needed feature.
5. Once you feel comfortable with these features, go to Scenario 2 and repeat these same steps with the new features introduced for that scenario. Monitor the quick reference figure (Figure 2.9) closely.
6. After both scenarios have been reviewed, go to the Workout and work through the problems and exercises it outlines.

PDToolkit
for
Teaching and Learning with Microsoft® Office 2010 and Office 2011 for Mac

Go to PDToolkit for **Teaching and Learning with Microsoft® Office 2010 and Office 2011 for Mac** to locate Workout Level One for Chapter Two.

PDToolkit
for
Teaching and Learning with Microsoft® Office 2010 and Office 2011 for Mac

Go to PDToolkit for **Teaching and Learning with Microsoft® Office 2010 and Office 2011 for Mac** to locate the mentoring videos for Chapter Two.

If you have *experience* with Word 2010, you may want to review the scenarios and the quick reference figures first. If any of the features are unfamiliar, then use the step-by-step procedures as well as the mentoring support videos. Once the review has been completed, then move directly to the Workout and create your own Word document by incorporating many of the highlighted features.

Scenario 1: A little story

Sally sat staring at a stubby, chewed pencil on her desk. Her second-graders had just wiggled on home for the day and she was too tired to move. She smiled as she thought about the 2.5 million silly second-grade questions she had answered that day, how much dry-erase marker was on her dress, and how many times she had to tell Jenni Hatcher to quit acting like a bird—although the bird was actually easier to control than the spotted dinosaur that Jenni had been the day before.

From the hallway behind her, Sally heard Brinna Washington's voice. Brinna was laughing as she looked in at Sally and said, "Don't worry, it does get better." During these first two weeks of the school year, Brinna had already shown herself to be a needed friend and mentor. She had great timing for giving support and adding tidbits of advice.

Brinna continued, "During my prep time this afternoon I was thinking about how overwhelmed you must be feeling right now. Two years ago, I was in your exact position and it wasn't that much fun. So I made you a little helper gift. I put it on the flash drive that I borrowed from you this morning." She then handed Sally an envelope that obviously contained the flash drive and a short note. "It's nothing special," continued Brinna, "but it's something I wish I had when I first started teaching."

"Thanks … but you know that I don't do much on the computer," replied Sally.

"Oh, I know that—but you will," Brinna responded as she disappeared into the hallway. Sally unfolded the note and looked over what was written:

Sally—

This flash contains a folder that holds three files. They should be easy to open on your machine in your classroom or on the one you have at home. The first file contains a short newsletter that I sent to my kids last week. You'll see that it's really simple, but it might give you an idea of what could be sent home and what you can build on. The second file is a simple science lesson plan that I was working on for next week. See if you want to use it or adapt it in some way. We might even want to join our classes together to work on it. And the last file is just something that helps me keep things in perspective. I keep a copy inside my day planner and try to read it every once in awhile.

Hope this helps—

Brinna

P.S. Did you do a bird unit today? I kept hearing bird sounds coming from your room—aren't second-graders great!!

A few minutes later, Sally was packed up and heading out to her car for the trip home. In her new "My School Bag" tote bag she carried the flash drive. She'd take a look at the files over the weekend and see what treasures her friend had given her.

Let's take a look at the first item that Brinna offered Sally—"The Happenings …" newsletter. It is a simple word-processed document that can be used as a template for other letters that may use a similar format. Several key word processing formatting features are used within the letter. Figures 2.4 and 2.5, respectively, show before and after pictures of the newsletter. Within Figure 2.5 callout bubbles have been inserted to identify the key features that were incorporated to enhance the formatting of the document.

- Using Figure 2.5 as the guide, follow the numbered features in the step-by-step procedure to learn how each of the features is employed.
- If additional guidance is needed, go to the mentoring videos on the website that accompanies this book and select the short clip that demonstrates the use of the needed feature.

PDToolkit
for
Teaching and Learning with Microsoft® Office 2010 and Office 2011 for Mac

Go to PDToolkit for **Teaching and Learning with Microsoft® Office 2010 and Office 2011 for Mac** to locate the mentoring videos for Chapter Two.

The Happenings...
Mrs. Washington's Second Grade, Room 8

Week of August 26-30

Hello everyone,

This is the second in our weekly series of newsletters. Things have started to settle down into a regular weekly routine. Hopefully you have all had the chance to look over some of the work that is being done in our class.

Highlights of this week:
We've started our group science project on "Whales". The kids were fascinated by the stories we read from our library books. I think some of them were surprised at the size of a blue whale when we attempted to draw one the right size with chalk in the school parking lot! We are now monitoring the "Whale Search" web site. If you have access to the Internet at home, try it out and let the kids show you what they have discovered.

In math, we are working with manipulables. We are trying to count about everything possible in our room. If your child counts things at home, that is why.

We have spent a lot of time in the "reading lounge" this week. After a long summer vacation, it is time to get into the habit of regular reading. Encourage this at home. Pick something fun and have your child read to you out loud.

Things to look forward to:
More whale work is coming. We will soon be creating a world globe that highlights many of the key areas that whales can be found in today's world. We will also create one that represents where the whales were 100 years ago. It should make for an interesting comparison.

We will be doing some classroom reading and math assessments next week. These are to help identify any areas that need special attention and encouragement. I will send home individual reports to each of you about your child's performance and my thoughts.

A little help from parents:
Extra boxes of tissues are needed. Could you send an extra box in the next week or two? Thanks.
The school fund raiser is upon us. We will need help in the organization and distribution departments. I will be sending home a sign up sheet next week. Be looking for it.
Weekly spelling tests will be starting next week on Fridays.

Thanks for all of your support and help. This should be the best year ever!!!!
Mrs. Washington

FIGURE 2.4 Letter from Mrs. Washington *before* formatting

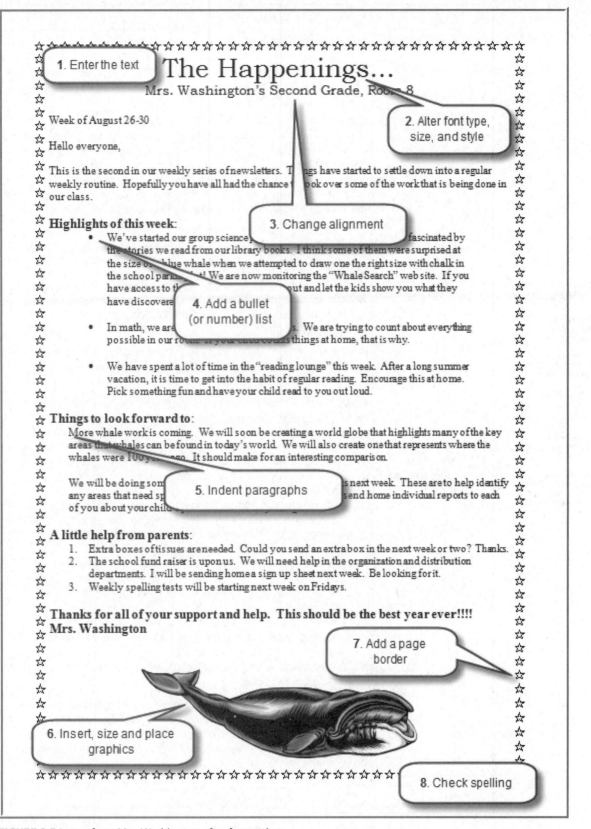

FIGURE 2.5 Letter from Mrs. Washington *after* formatting

No.	To Do	How to Get It Done
1.	**Enter the text**	**1.** Start Word and create a new document (**File** tab >>> **New**). **2.** Select the Blank document (it may already be selected) and click the Create button. A new, blank document should appear and you can begin entering data. **Note**: When you have the New document dialog box open, you can also select from various Word and Office.com templates. Some may be currently available on your machine and others may be acquired by clicking on the preferred template and downloading it from the Office.com site on the Internet. Such templates may help to speed up your work by providing much of the initial design and formatting. These were developed by professionals and they generally look very good and can be great time savers. **3.** Remember one of the key rules—"think content first, then make it pretty." That applies here. First enter the information for the document into the computer. **Note:** If you want to use the content from "The Happenings …" newsletter (see Figure 2.5), it's available on the website that accompanies this book. **4.** Generally, don't worry about how the document looks at this point. You just need the content to be accurate. Making it look fancy will be part of the formatting to follow. **Note:** Check out the Mentor Video, "Copying, Cutting and Pasting," on the website that accompanies this book for guidance and demonstration on different ways to enter infoprmation.
2.	**Alter font type, size, and style**	**1.** Select (highlight) the title of the newsletter, "The Happenings …" **2.** Review the **Font** set of commands (**Home** tab >>> **Font** group) as shown in Figure 2.6. **3.** Click on the down arrow to reveal the gallery of different font types (e.g., Cambria, Times New Roman) and preview the different alternatives by moving your cursor over the different names of types. Click on your preferred type. **4.** Use the down arrow on the font size (e.g., 12) to reveal selected font sizes that can also be previewed in a similar fashion. Follow the same procedure to preview and select the size of the font you desire. **5.** Using this same font group of tools, you can change the font style (e.g., **bold**, *italic*, underline), font color, and background highlighting within the document. **6.** For additional alternatives, select the expansion arrow and a font dialog box will open. **Note:** You can also use the **Quick Styles** feature (**Home** tab >>> **Styles** group) as shown in Figure 2.6. Similar to the previous steps, highlight the text you want to alter, then preview how it will look by moving the cursor over the formatted styles that are on the ribbon. Click on your selection to make the change.

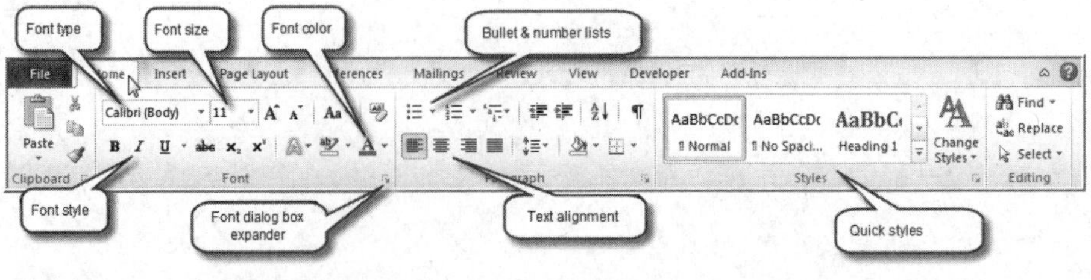

FIGURE 2.6 Home tab with various formatting commands highlighted

PDToolkit for *Teaching and Learning with Microsoft® Office 2010 and Office 2011 for Mac*

Go to PDToolkit for **Teaching and Learning with Microsoft® Office 2010 and Office 2011 for Mac** to locate the Happenings Newsletter within Workout Level One for Chapter Two.

PDToolkit for *Teaching and Learning with Microsoft® Office 2010 and Office 2011 for Mac*

Go to PDToolkit for **Teaching and Learning with Microsoft® Office 2010 and Office 2011 for Mac** to locate the mentoring videos for Chapter Two.

3.	Change alignment	1. Select the first two lines of the newsletter. 2. As shown in Figure 2.6, click on the center **alignment** tool (**Home** tab >>> **Paragraph** group). **Remember:** Alignment allows you to quickly line up text on the left, the right, equally between right and left, or in the center of your page.
4.	**Add a bullet or number list**	1. Highlight all items in the list to be bulleted or numbered. For your newsletter, select all three paragraphs under the "Highlights of This Week …" heading. 2. Click on the **bullet list** icon (Figure 2.6) within the Paragraph group of commands within the Home tab. 3. Review what has been done to your document. Bullets should now appear in front of the items or paragraphs that were selected. The items are indented and there's an extra bit of white space between each bulleted item. 4. Next, on the newsletter highlight the three paragraphs under the subheading "A little help from parents …" 5. Click on the **number list** icon (Figure 2.6). **Note:** If the default bullets or numbers are not appealing, you can change them. After selecting your list of items, click on the down arrow icon next to the bullet or number icon. A gallery of alternative versions of the bullets and numbers will appear. Preview the items by moving your cursor over the alternatives and then click on your selection.
5.	**Indent paragraphs**	1. Locate the **ruler** at the top of the document (if it's not showing, go to **View** tab >>> **Show** group >>> **Ruler** (click the check box)). Note the sliders or paragraph markers sit on both sides of the ruler. The left one pertains to the left text margin and the right one to the right text margin. 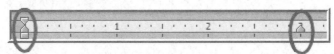 Ruler with paragraph indention markers 2. Select the text where you want to alter the paragraph indents (e.g., select the text under the heading Things to look forward to). 3. On the bottom square (left marker) icon, left mouse click, hold, and drag the mouse slowly to the right. A vertical dashed line will appear and it will move the margin of the selected text to the right. Adjust it in and out to get a sense for how this works. This adjusted margin only pertains to the highlighted paragraphs of text. If nothing is highlighted, it pertains to the paragraph where the cursor is currently located. 4. See what happens if you point only at the top triangle marker and move it to the right or left. The first line will change on your selected text. If you wish to indent the first line of the selected paragraphs, then you would use this tool. Note what happens when you move only the bottom triangle. This is known as the *hanging indent*. This leaves the first line where it is and moves the rest of the paragraph. Try each of these to see how they can be used to set and reset any text that is selected. 5. Use the right margin marker set (triangle on the right of the document on the ruler) to set the right **margin** of the selected text. **Note:** If you begin your document by setting the first line marker, the left marker, and the right marker, all the paragraphs that follow will use this same margin setting. Later you can come back and change any and all of the settings as is needed. If you have already entered the text, then highlight those sections that need to have similar margins and set it one time.

(continued)

6.	**Add, size, and place a graphic**

		1. *Get the **graphic*** (e.g., picture, **clip art**).
		   a. On the main ribbon, click **Insert** tab >>> **Illustrations** group >>> **ClipArt** … The Clip Art task pane will appear.
		   b. In the Clip Art task pane, enter a key word that describes the type of clip art you are searching for (e.g., *sports*) and then click on the Go button. Various small versions of the clip art should appear in the task pane.
		   c. Scroll through the different alternatives presented in the task pane. Use Find more at Office.com to expand your search if needed (e.g., where to search, types of media to search for).
		   d. Click on your selected clip art and the picture will automatically be inserted within your document.
		
		2. *Size the graphic.* If your inserted clip art is the perfect size for your document—great, leave it as it is. However, in many cases, the size will not be perfect. So point your mouse at the picture and left click once. You'll note that a box is drawn around the picture and **handles** are placed at each of the corners and in the middle of each of the sides. The handles are small circles and squares. You can grab a handle by putting your mouse pointer on the handle (note that your pointer will change into a double-headed arrow), left click, and hold it. Dragging a handle causes the picture to be altered. Try different handles and see what happens to the shape and size of the picture.
		
		3. *Place the graphic.* Once your picture is inserted and sized appropriately, you can move it to a different location on the slide by putting the mouse on top of the graphic and then clicking, holding, and dragging it to the new location.
		
		4. *Adapt or adjust the quality of the graphic.* You should also note that once you have selected your picture (the picture has the box around it with the handles), a special set of Picture Tools (see Figure 2.7) becomes available (look for the Picture Tools tab immediately above the Format tab on the main ribbon). You can use these tools for the following:
		
		• Adjust the picture (brightness, contrast, color)
		• Change the picture style (border, shape, special effects)
		• Arrange the picture in relation to other items (bring to the front, send to the back)
		• Size (crop, alter height and width)
		
		Note: Working with clip art and other graphic files may take a bit of practice. Some won't look as nice when their size is changed to a drastic degree—others work great. You'll also find that access to the Internet gives you an endless supply of various clip art photos, pictures, and so on that you may want to insert within your documents. When you choose to add such items to your documents, be sure to consider protection provided by the current copyright laws.

		FIGURE 2.7 Picture tools

7.	**Page border**	1. Click **Page Layout** >>> **Page Background** group >>> **Page Border**. 2. The Borders and Shading dialog box will appear (see Figure 2.8). Click the **Page Border** tab if it isn't already selected. 3. Under the section titled Settings click on the Box option. Notice what happens in the Preview section on the right-hand side of this window. 4. Under the section titled Art, click on the down arrow and scroll through all of the different borders that could be selected. Select one that you think would be appropriate. Look at the Preview box to see what has occurred. 5. Explore this window and try several different settings. See what appeals to you by watching how the changes affect the Preview box. When you have made your final set of selections, click OK. **Note:** This Borders and Shading dialog box will become very handy. Make sure you take time to try the different options under the Borders tab and also the Shading tab within this dialog box. You can learn to draw boxes around specific bits of text, color the boxes, or even shade the backgrounds within the boxes.

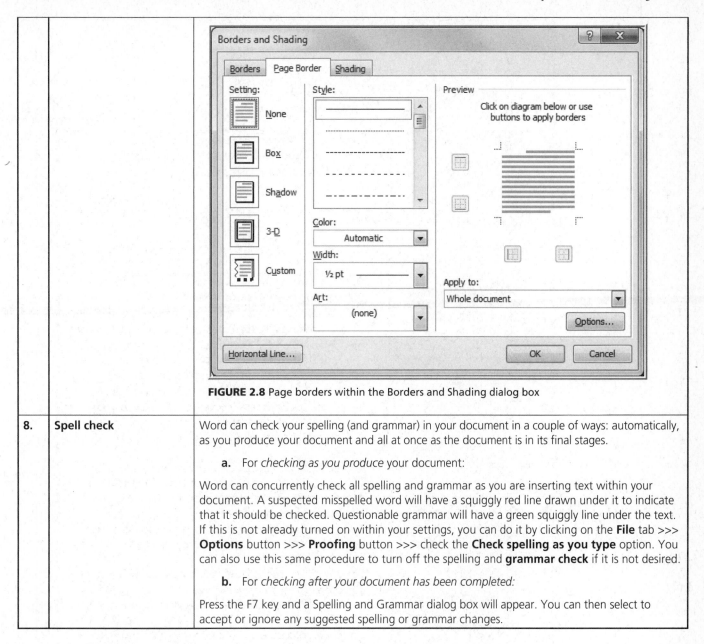

FIGURE 2.8 Page borders within the Borders and Shading dialog box

8.	Spell check	Word can check your spelling (and grammar) in your document in a couple of ways: automatically, as you produce your document and all at once as the document is in its final stages.
		a. For *checking as you produce* your document:
		Word can concurrently check all spelling and grammar as you are inserting text within your document. A suspected misspelled word will have a squiggly red line drawn under it to indicate that it should be checked. Questionable grammar will have a green squiggly line under the text. If this is not already turned on within your settings, you can do it by clicking on the **File** tab >>> **Options** button >>> **Proofing** button >>> check the **Check spelling as you type** option. You can also use this same procedure to turn off the spelling and **grammar check** if it is not desired.
		b. For *checking after your document has been completed*:
		Press the F7 key and a Spelling and Grammar dialog box will appear. You can then select to accept or ignore any suggested spelling or grammar changes.

Scenario 2: The story continues

Remember, Brinna from the opening scenario had actually given Sally three different documents to take home. The second document is shown as Figure 2.9. This figure also has various formatting features highlighted for easy identification.

One thing that an experienced teacher like Brinna knows is that the use of examples can be critical. In this case, the document is a lesson plan about blubber. Sally may not need this specific content, but the example of how to use the word processor to help in the creation of similar documents may be invaluable. Look closely at Figure 2.9 and note the key features we have included: **tables**, footnotes, **headers** and **footers**, page numbers, borders, **hyperlinks**, and **shading**. Are these features critical for you to become a good teacher? Probably not. But they'll help you organize your documents and make them more readable for those who may be reviewing them. That's important for your students.

Note: For the full blubber lesson plan, go to the website that accompanies this book and open the Blubber file. If you find this a useful template, select and cut the content and add your own content to the structure already designed for you.

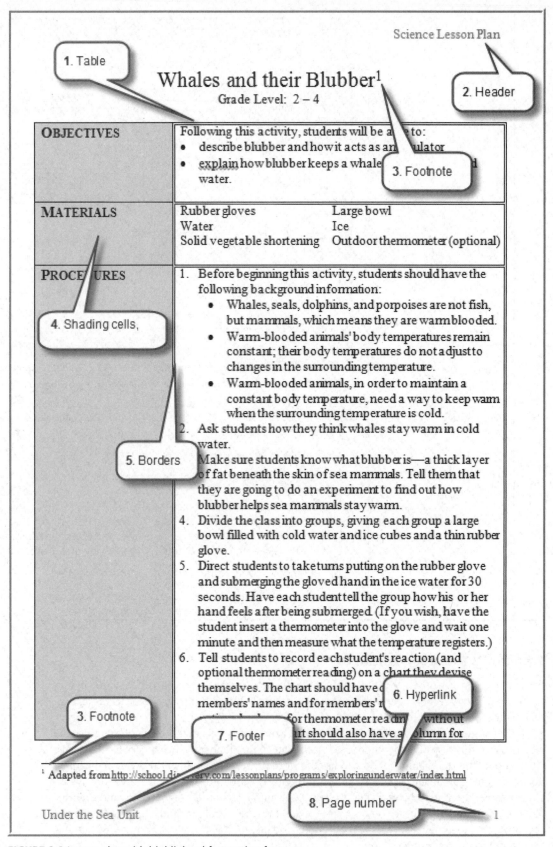

FIGURE 2.9 Lesson plan with highlighted formatting features

No.	Feature	Steps to Get It Done
1.	**Tables:** creating and formatting	1. Place your cursor in the document where you want the table to be inserted. 2. Click **Insert** tab >>> **Tables** group >>> **Table**. 3. Pull the mouse over the revealed grid to preview the creation of your table and click on the desired size (e.g., number of rows and **columns**). 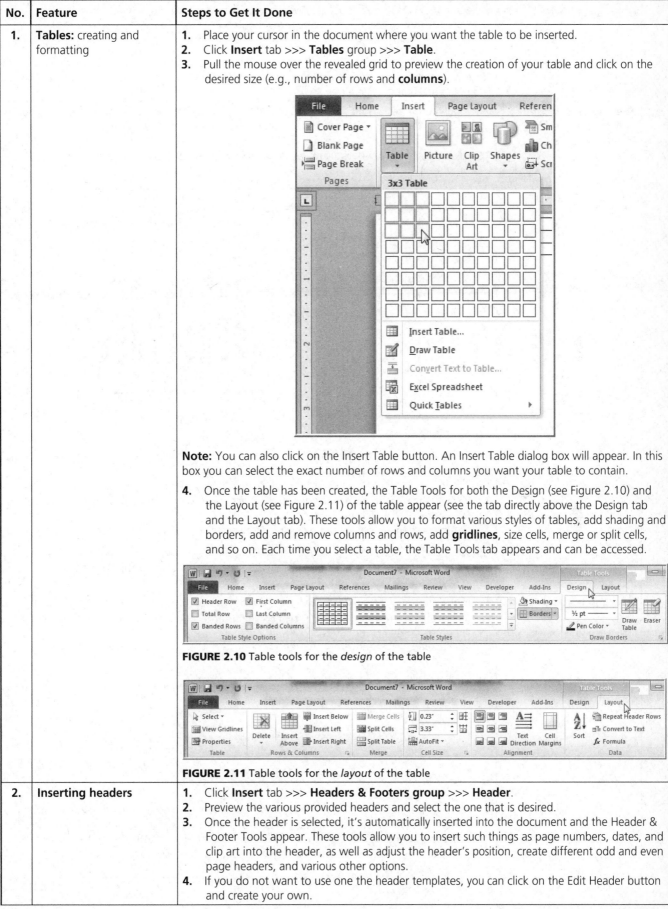 **Note:** You can also click on the Insert Table button. An Insert Table dialog box will appear. In this box you can select the exact number of rows and columns you want your table to contain. 4. Once the table has been created, the Table Tools for both the Design (see Figure 2.10) and the Layout (see Figure 2.11) of the table appear (see the tab directly above the Design tab and the Layout tab). These tools allow you to format various styles of tables, add shading and borders, add and remove columns and rows, add **gridlines**, size cells, merge or split cells, and so on. Each time you select a table, the Table Tools tab appears and can be accessed. **FIGURE 2.10** Table tools for the *design* of the table **FIGURE 2.11** Table tools for the *layout* of the table
2.	**Inserting headers**	1. Click **Insert** tab >>> **Headers & Footers group** >>> **Header**. 2. Preview the various provided headers and select the one that is desired. 3. Once the header is selected, it's automatically inserted into the document and the Header & Footer Tools appear. These tools allow you to insert such things as page numbers, dates, and clip art into the header, as well as adjust the header's position, create different odd and even page headers, and various other options. 4. If you do not want to use one the header templates, you can click on the Edit Header button and create your own.

(continued)

3.	**Adding footnotes**	1. Place your cursor in the document where you want the footnote number to be located. 2. Click the **Reference** tab >>> **Footnotes** group >>> **Insert Footnote**. 3. Enter the information for the footnote and it will be automatically entered at the designated place at the bottom of the page. **Note:** You can alter the appearance and location of the footnote (and endnotes) by accessing the Footnote and endnote dialog box.
4.	**Shading cells, columns, or rows (or anything inside and outside of a table)**	1. Highlight the section that you want shaded (e.g., a row, column, or set of cells within a table; or within the usual document this can be used on an individual word, sentence, paragraph, graphic, and so forth). 2. Click **Home** tab >>> **Paragraph** group >>> **Shading** icon. A shading gallery will appear. 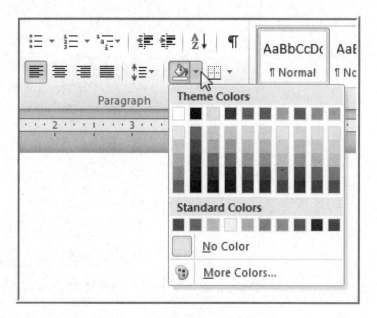 3. Preview the shading colors by moving your cursor slowly over the various color alternatives within the shading gallery. 4. Select the shading desired and click on it. Your selected area should now be shaded. **Note:** Specifically within that table, you can follow the previous procedures or you can also find a similar shading gallery by clicking Design tab (directly under the **Table Tools** tab) >>> **Table Styles** group >>> **Shading** button.
5.	**Inserting borders**	1. Highlight the section you want to have a border around (e.g., a row, column, or set of cells within a table or within the usual document this can be used on an individual word, sentence, paragraph, graphic, and so forth). 2. Click **Home** tab >>> **Paragraph** group >>> **Border** icon (down arrow for the various options). 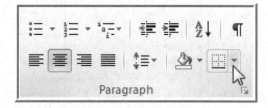 3. Review the different border options. If you don't see the option that you desire (e.g., you want to change the border color, style, width), then select the Border and Shading option and the Border and Shading dialog box will appear (see Figure 2.12). Select the Border tab and then this window will allow you to specify exactly the style, color, and width of the border you desire.

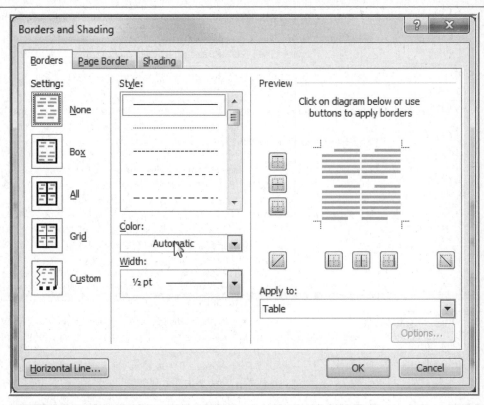

FIGURE 2.12 Selecting borders within the Borders and Shading dialog box

Note: If you are working directly within a table, you can also select the portion of the table where you want a border to be and then click **Design** tab (directly under the Table Tools tab) >>> **Draw Borders** group. Color, size, and type of border can also be selected from these alternatives.

6.	Adding hyperlinks	1. Type the text you would like to serve as the link. If you choose to use the **web** address as the text that appears, simply type in the address and press the space bar. The link is automatically created and the font and style changes to indicate its link to the web. 2. If you would prefer to use customized text for the link, insert the text, select it, click **Insert** tab >>> **Links** group >>> **Hyperlink** button. The **Insert Hyperlink** window (see Figure 2.13) will appear.

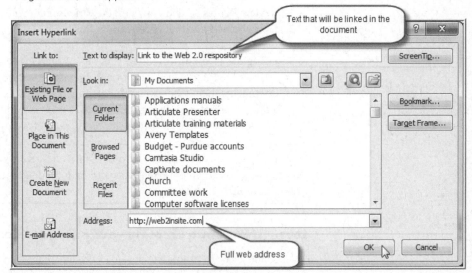

FIGURE 2.13 Creating hyperlinks within a document through the Insert Hyperlink dialog box

3. In the Text to display section of this same window, you may also modify the text you have chosen to display in your document.

(continued)

		4. In the Address section of the window, type in the web address of the website you want linked. **Note:** This is one case where spelling counts! In either method of creating a hyperlink, be sure to type in the web address accurately and completely (don't forget the http://)! **Another note:** With the use of this window, you can also link to more than just websites (e.g., specific documents, an e-mail address).

7.	**Adding page numbers**	1. Click **Insert** tab >>> **Header & Footer** group >>> **Page Number** icon. A gallery of options for the placement of the page number will appear. Click on the position that you desire.
		2. Page numbers can also be placed within the header or footer of a document. For example, to include it within the footer (the header page number also works in this same fashion):
		  • Click **Insert** tab >>> **Header & Footer** group >>> **Footer** icon and select the type of footer that you desire for your document. (**Note:** If you already have a footer within the document simply open your current footer.)
		  • Once the footer has been inserted or opened, click **Header & Footer Tools** tab (above the Design tab) >>> **Header & Footer** group >>> **Page Number**.
		  • As you select the page number placement, you will also notice an alternative to Format page number. . . . Selecting this alternative will display a Page Number Format window that will allow you to select the various ways to present your page numbers (e.g., 1, 2, 3; i, ii, iii; a, b, c, and so on.). This window will also allow you to select alternative page number starting points (e.g., if you desire to start on page 32—(or whatever)—instead of page 1).

8.	**Inserting footers**	1. Click **Insert** tab >>> **Headers & Footers** group >>> **Footer**. 2. Preview the various provided footers and select the one that is desired. 3. Once the footer is selected, it is automatically inserted into the document and the Header & Footer Tools appear. These tools allow you to insert such things as page numbers, dates, clip art, and so forth into the footer, as well as adjust the footer's position, create different odd and even page footers, and various other options.

Level 1a Workout: Practice using the basic Word features

To actually acquire the needed skills with word processing, you need to practice using Word. It generally isn't good enough to just read and watch how these features are developed. One way for you to accomplish this is by creating and formatting your own documents. As these documents are created, select and integrate the different features within your own work.

Here's a basic outline of what you need to do:

PDToolkit
for
*Teaching and Learning with
Microsoft® Office 2010 and
Office 2011 for Mac*

Go to PDToolkit for **Teaching and
Learning with Microsoft® Office 2010
and Office 2011 for Mac** to locate these
files within Workout Level One for Chapter Two.

1. Review Figures 2.5 and 2.9 and all the various highlighted features that are within those figures.
2. Go to the website that accompanies this book and open the unformatted versions of these two figures.
3. Using the given unformatted versions of the newsletter ("The Happenings …") and the lesson plan ("Blubber"), go through the list of features and practice adding those to your documents. Don't worry about matching the example figures exactly—that isn't the point. You can adapt and change the features as you add them. Remember this is a practice Workout—*practice integrating as many features as possible.*

Note: Refer to specific feature numbers and the given step-by-step procedures as needed. Additionally, use the mentoring videos to help guide you through any specific procedure that needs additional clarification.

Level 1b Workout: Creating your own document

The benefits of word processing become very apparent when you begin to create and format your own documents. Think about all the documents that you will need to create for your work, home, or school. Select one or two of those that are currently in need of being completed and do the following:

1. Generate a simple draft copy of the content of the document. If you have difficulty thinking of a topic, go to the Level 3 section of this chapter (subsection on further ideas on using word processing as a learning tool) and review all the various example topics given (e.g., write your teaching and technology-**integration** philosophy; write answers to questions posed

Table 2.1 Level 1 Workout and Practice Checklist: Creating and formatting a document

Document Content	___ Content is accurate and current.
	___ Content is relevant and cohesive throughout the document.
	___ Content achieves the proper level for the intended audience.
	___ Content is free from spelling and grammatical errors.
Document Format	___ A new document was created.
	___ Font size, style, and type were varied within the document to add emphasis to headings, and so on.
	___ Paragraph margin settings were adapted using the margin markers on the ruler.
	___ Appropriate graphics (e.g., clip art, pictures, images) were properly selected, sized, and placed within the document.
	___ A table was incorporated within the document.
	___ Borders were employed to add highlights to specific parts (page, paragraph, words, and so forth) of the document.
	___ Shading was used to add highlights and variety to specific parts (words, paragraphs, parts of a table, and so on).
	___ Automatic page numbers were employed within multipage documents.
	___ Live hyperlinks to specific Internet sites or other documents were incorporated.
	___ Headers and footers have been incorporated.
	___ Footnotes or endnotes were used to add reference material or additional clarity to the material.

for a scholarship application; create documents for work—such as work schedules, safety procedures, or letters to new customers; compose a written itinerary of your next vacation and all that you plan to do and see). If you can find something that needs to be done anyway, then the effort invested has greater value and what is learned will be retained longer.

2. Review the features demonstrated within Figures 2.5 and 2.9 from Scenarios 1 and 2.
3. Format your new document with as many of the features demonstrated in those figures as possible. Use Table 2.1 as a checklist to guide your efforts.

Note: Remember and implement the first rule to live by: *Save, save, save*, and then *save* your work again. Make sure you do that—or it will return to haunt you sometime down the road.

Also think about Rules 3, 4, and 5. Keep things simple, watch for how others accomplish what we have previously described, and make sure you think about saving the lesson plan as a template that can be adapted and used later as needed.

LEVEL 2: TABLES, TEMPLATES, AND OTHER GOOD STUFF

What should you be able to do?

You should learn to recognize additional word processing features and gain confidence using Help to create, edit, and format several original documents.

The key here is not to memorize all that the word processor is capable of—it is better to know some of the basics and when, where, and how to find assistance for everything else.

Getting some Help

Similar to Help in Windows, there is also Help in MS Word and most other sophisticated word processing software. To use Help, click the Help button on the tab bar of the main ribbon.

Clicking the Help button opens the Help window (see Figure 2.14). From here you can browse general Help topics, bring up a general table of contents of all help topics, complete a search for a specific question that you might have, and so on.

When you type in key words or even a full question, Help will respond with a variety of potential answers for you to investigate. Help generally does not have all of the answers but it will have a lot of them. Make sure you get a good sense for how it works and how often it can be of assistance. Don't forget to go to the website that accompanies this book and review the mentoring video that has been created to demonstrate Help and its various functions.

PDToolkit
for
Teaching and Learning with
Microsoft® Office 2010 and
Office 2011 for Mac

Go to PDToolkit for **Teaching and Learning with Microsoft® Office 2010 and Office°2011 for Mac** to locate the mentoring videos for Chapter Two.

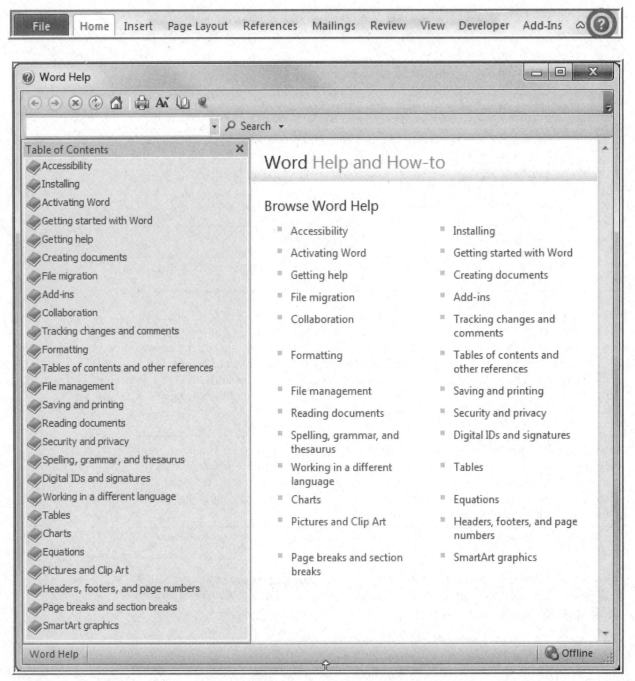

FIGURE 2.14 Word Help window

Scenario 3: "The Station"

The final document that Brinna gave Sally was "The Station" by Robert J. Hastings. For us, this word-processed document shows other formatting features that will be beneficial. Figure 2.15 shows the printed document and highlights the key formatting things that have been done to it.

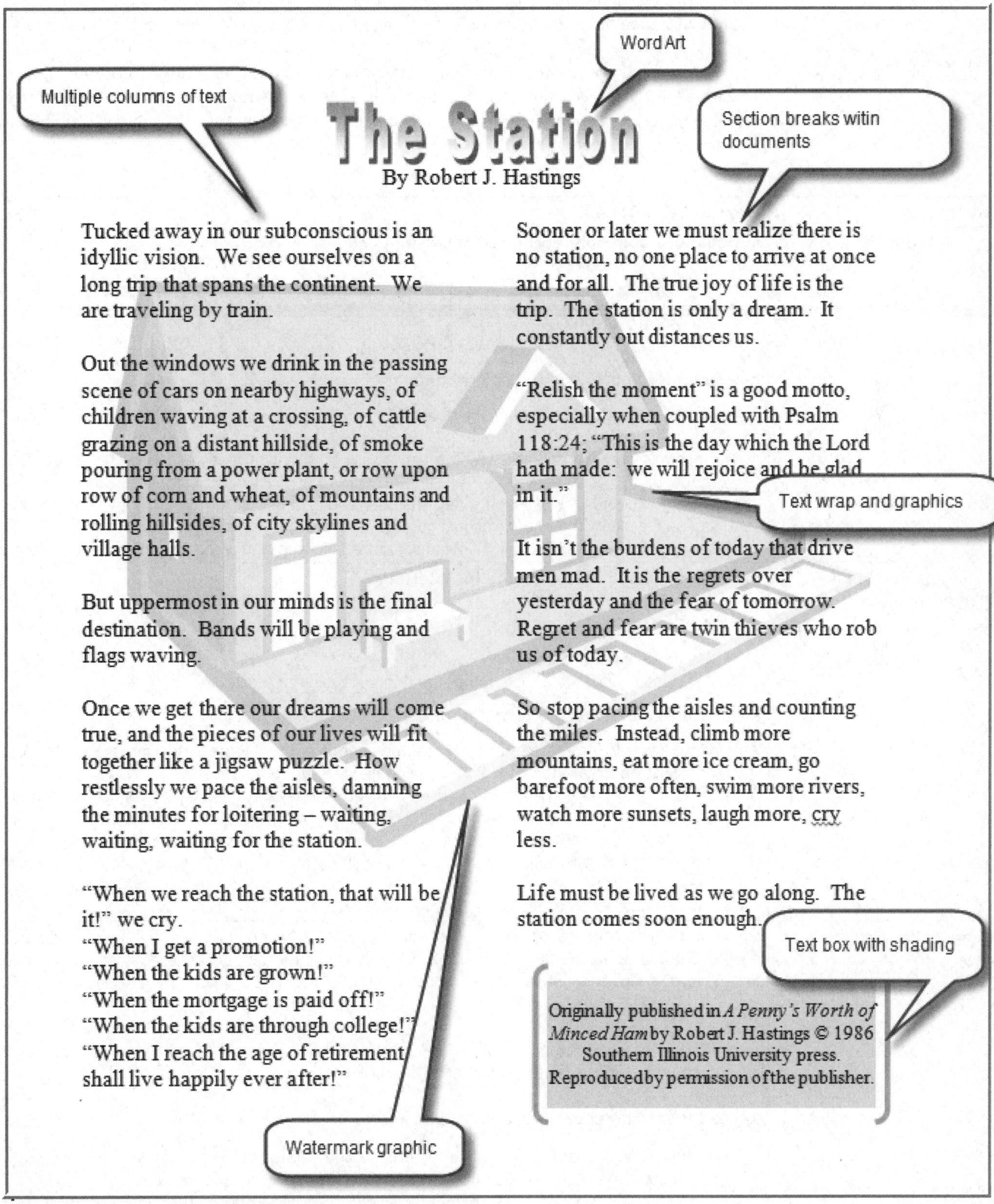

Word Art

Multiple columns of text

Section breaks witin documents

The Station

By Robert J. Hastings

Tucked away in our subconscious is an idyllic vision. We see ourselves on a long trip that spans the continent. We are traveling by train.

Out the windows we drink in the passing scene of cars on nearby highways, of children waving at a crossing, of cattle grazing on a distant hillside, of smoke pouring from a power plant, or row upon row of corn and wheat, of mountains and rolling hillsides, of city skylines and village halls.

But uppermost in our minds is the final destination. Bands will be playing and flags waving.

Once we get there our dreams will come true, and the pieces of our lives will fit together like a jigsaw puzzle. How restlessly we pace the aisles, damning the minutes for loitering – waiting, waiting, waiting for the station.

"When we reach the station, that will be it!" we cry.
"When I get a promotion!"
"When the kids are grown!"
"When the mortgage is paid off!"
"When the kids are through college!"
"When I reach the age of retirement, shall live happily ever after!"

Sooner or later we must realize there is no station, no one place to arrive at once and for all. The true joy of life is the trip. The station is only a dream. It constantly out distances us.

"Relish the moment" is a good motto, especially when coupled with Psalm 118:24; "This is the day which the Lord hath made: we will rejoice and be glad in it."

It isn't the burdens of today that drive men mad. It is the regrets over yesterday and the fear of tomorrow. Regret and fear are twin thieves who rob us of today.

So stop pacing the aisles and counting the miles. Instead, climb more mountains, eat more ice cream, go barefoot more often, swim more rivers, watch more sunsets, laugh more, cry less.

Life must be lived as we go along. The station comes soon enough.

Text wrap and graphics

Text box with shading

Originally published in *A Penny's Worth of Minced Ham* by Robert J. Hastings © 1986 Southern Illinois University press. Reproduced by permission of the publisher.

Watermark graphic

FIGURE 2.15 "The Station" with highlighted formatting features
Source: Originally published in *A Penny's Worth of Minced Ham* by Robert J. Hastings © 1986 Southern Illinois University Press. Reproduced by permission of the publisher.

It is given here as an example of some of the possibilities available to you or your students with word processing software.

As you explore this example, note how the title and author's name are centered at the top of the page but directly underneath all lines of the text are placed within two columns. This requires the document to be divided into **sections** so that in one section something can occur that you may or may not want to occur in other sections. Also note that we have inserted a picture of a railroad station but in this case we have created it as a **watermark**, enlarged it, and used it as a background to the words in the quote.

Once you have examined this figure, review how to find the key information about implementing these features within your documents. In addition, mentoring videos have been created and can be accessed on the website that accompanies this text that will guide you through the use of each of these features.

Feature	Steps to Get It Done
Inserting WordArt	**Information about and procedure for creating and inserting:** Word Help ? • Key word: **WordArt** • Select Add, change, or delete WordArt and follow the given procedure **Key features to note, explore, and try out:** • A quick way to get to WordArt is **Insert** tab >>> **Text** group >>> **WordArt** >>> select from the gallery of options and types. • Once your option is selected, a dialog box will ask for specific size, type, and exact words to be included. • Once your WordArt is selected, WordArt Tools will appear (look for the tab above the Format tab on the main ribbon) and you can edit the style, effects, size, and how it is arranged. • You can move and position your WordArt by clicking, holding, and dragging it to the new location.
Creating section breaks within documents	**Information about and procedure for inserting:** Word Help • Key words: **Section break** • Select Insert or delete a section break and follow the given procedure. **Key features to note, explore, and try out:** • A quick way to insert a section break is **Page Layout** tab >>> **Page Setup** group >>> **Breaks** >>> **Section Breaks** (pick the type that you need—e.g., continuous). • Section breaks allow you to cut your document into parts and each part can be formatted in a different manner. For example, you want a different header for a specific part of your document, you want the pages of your document to be vertically oriented in some areas but horizontally oriented in other sections. As an example, look at Figure 2.15 and see how the heading is within a one-column section of the page but the rest of the reading is in a two-column section of the page. This was completed using this section break function.
Adding multiple columns of text	Creating multiple columns of text is a common formatting technique used within newspapers, newsletters, and so on. Multiple columns allow for shorter, easier-to-read lines. As it is entered, the text generally wraps continuously from one column to the next (unlike columns in tables). **Online help:** www.office.com • Key words: Text columns • Select the article "Create newsletter columns" (Word 2010) **Key features to note, explore, and try out:** • To create columns of text, go to the following: **Page Layout** tab >>> **Page Setup** group >>> **Columns**. Make your selection from the different alternative types of columns. • In some cases, a break in the column is needed to equalize the columns' length or to insert a graphic and so forth. This can be quickly accomplished by inserting a column break (**Page Layout** tab >>> **Page Setup** group >>> **Breaks** >>> **Page Breaks** >>> **Column**).

Creating a watermark picture	**Information about and procedure for creating and inserting:** **Online help:** www.office.com • Key word: Watermark • Select the article "Insert a watermark or change a watermark" (Word 2010) **Key features to note, explore, and try out:** • The standard way of producing a watermark is **Page Layout** tab >>> **Page Background** group >>> **Watermark**. At this point, you can select from the gallery of watermarks or you can select a Custom Watermark and select a picture or other text to include. **Note:** Using some text (e.g., Urgent) as a watermark, would be the easiest and most efficient route; however, if you want to use a picture as a watermark, it may be easier—and allow better control—to insert a picture, adapt that picture (e.g., alter the contrast, color, and brightness, as well as the size), and then arrange it by sending it behind the text. Refer to Feature 6 from Scenario 1 (add, size, and place a graphic—see Figure 2.5) to review how to adapt pictures and graphics.
Text wrapping with graphics	**Text wrapping** allows you to insert a picture or object within your document and then control how the text is formatted in relationship to that object (e.g., above, below, around, on top of, or behind the object). **Information about and procedure for creating and inserting:** **Online help:** www.office.com • Key words: Wrap text • Select the article "Wrap text around a picture" (Word 2010) Word Help • Key words: Wrap text • Select Wrap text around a picture or drawing object and follow the given procedure. **Key features to note, explore, and try out:** • After inserting your graphic, make sure the graphic is selected and then click **Format** tab >>> **Arrange** group >>> **Wrap Text** and make your selection of the type of wrapping you desire **Note:** It may take a few attempts to get the text to wrap in the manner that is most desirable. Try different alternatives. **Another note:** You may also need to change the placement of the graphic (refer to Scenario 1, Feature 6). A little change to its location on the page often significantly changes how the text is wrapped.
Adding a text box	A text box is a specialized container of text within a document. It can add interest and break up the usual flow of the text. This container can be sized, colored, and positioned on a page. It is frequently used to highlight a special quote, place information in a side bar, or add some point of interest. Text boxes are both predesigned and custom created. Word Help • Keyword: **Text box** • Select Add, copy, or delete a text box **Key features to note, explore, and try out:** • A quick way to get to the action buttons is **Insert** tab >>> **Text** group >>> **Text Box.** **Note:** You can position the text box by selecting it, placing your cursor over one of the outline box lines, and clicking, holding, and dragging it to its new location. **Another note:** After selecting the text box, **Text Box Tools** are accessible (above the Format tab). These tools allow you change text direction, add box styles, effects, size, and arrange the position and the text wrapping.

Note: Each of these key features is demonstrated on the mentoring videos within the website that accompanies this book.

PDToolkit for *Teaching and Learning with Microsoft® Office 2010 and Office 2011 for Mac*

Go to PDToolkit for **Teaching and Learning with Microsoft® Office 2010 and Office 2011 for Mac** to locate the mentoring videos for Chapter Two.

Document Content	___ Content was accurate.
	___ Content was free from spelling and grammatical errors.
Document Format	___ A new document was created.
	___ Font size, style, and type were varied within the document to add emphasis to headings, and so on.
	___ WordArt has been incorporated.
	___ Paragraph margin settings were adapted using the margin markers on the ruler.
	___ Appropriate graphics (e.g., clip art, pictures, images) were properly selected, sized, and placed within the document.
	___ A watermark graphic was included and properly positioned and arranged.
	___ Text was incorporated and highlighted with appropriate shading.
	___ Text boxes were appropriately positioned and arranged with proper text wrapping.
	___ The document was divided into multiple sections.
	___ Multiple columns were incorporated within specific sections of the document.

Table 2.2 Level 2 Workout and Practice Checklist: Using additional formatting features within a Word document

Level 2 Workout: Practice using additional Word features

Now you try it.

1. Find a favorite quote, poem, newspaper article, or short essay that you have wanted to give to someone, hang up in your room, or whatever.
2. Enter the document into the word processor.
3. Divide it into appropriate sections.
4. Put some of the document into multiple columns.
5. Align and format the title and all key headings.
6. Insert an appropriate picture, clip art, or graphic and place it within the document so that the words are wrapped correctly.
7. Pull out salient quotes of interest and include within a text box.
8. Use Table 2.2 as a checklist to make sure you have included a number of key features that have been highlighted within Scenarios 1, 2, and 3 of this chapter (see Figures 2.5 and 2.8).

Note: Invoke Rule 1: Save your work.

LEVEL 3: INTEGRATION AND APPLICATION

What should you be able to do?

Here you need to think of how to use word processing in terms of yourself and your students. You should be able to apply the examples given to generate ideas on how to integrate and apply the word processor to improve personal productivity as well as student learning.

Introduction

Within Levels 1 and 2 of this chapter, we focus on word processing from the perspective of learning to use it. However, to extend its use, you need to think about word processing as a means to enhance the learning experience of students. There are times when integrating word processing within a learning situation may improve the learning opportunities and possibilities of the learners. However, there are other times when such integration would be more of a hassle than potential benefits may warrant. Learning to tell the difference can help you be successful in what you develop and use in your classroom.

Word processing integration

Creating the enhanced learning experience: A partial lesson plan

TOPIC:

A study of the people, places, and culture of an African country

OVERVIEW:

Mr. Carpenter is an eighth-grade social studies teacher at Lowell Middle School. He constantly searches for ways to increase his students' interest in the topics they explore and learn in his classes. Recently he had the opportunity to speak with one of his past students, Jonathon Rogers, who had attended Lowell a number of years ago. Jonathon is now a graduate student at a nearby university.

During their discussions, Jonathon explained to Mr. Carpenter that during the coming school year he was going to work on an internship for an international health organization. He would be traveling to the country of Zimbabwe in southern Africa to help with the organization's distribution of health supplies and educational materials. He would live and work with the Zimbabwean people throughout the next school year.

Through a little brainstorming, Mr. Carpenter and Jonathon determined that using mail, e-mail, and the Internet with applications like Skype, they could establish a connection between Mr. Carpenter's social studies classes with some of the culture, politics, education, and geography that Jonathon would be experiencing. The students at Lowell could perhaps come to vicariously learn through the eyes and ears of Jonathon as he explored another country halfway around the world.

SPECIFIC LEARNING TASK:

To begin the course of study on Zimbabwe, the students in Mr. Carpenter's classes were to make simple comparisons between Zimbabwe and the United States. Members of the classes were divided into smaller cooperative research groups. Each group selected a major topic of interest (e.g., education, geography, politics, health, culture) that they would investigate to make their comparisons.

SAMPLE LEARNING OBJECTIVES:

Students will be able to do the following:

1. Compare and contrast the key similarities and differences between the countries of Zimbabwe and the United States.
2. Identify and explain several common issues affecting the people of both countries as well as issues isolated within one country or the other.

PROCEDURE:

1. Break into the groups and brainstorm the key questions of inquiry to investigate about the selected topic.
2. Research answers for the questions from the view of both Zimbabweans and US citizens.
3. Create a comparison table that lists the questions and potential answers determined through research. Reference the answers to the questions that were found within the research.
4. Write a reflection paper about the key findings reported within the comparison table. Explain the major similarities and differences noted between the two countries.
5. Send the comparison tables to Jonathon and have him select several of the questions to ask people he encounters in Zimbabwe. Have him respond and enter those responses within a new column on the comparison table.
6. Based on the full findings of the group and the responses by Jonathon, the group will develop a final written executive summary of their findings to be distributed to all members of their class. The final version should include additional questions that the group now wishes to investigate if given the opportunity to do so.

QUESTIONS ABOUT WORD PROCESSING INTEGRATION:

Obviously, this lesson could be completed with or without the use of word processing software. Use these reflective questions to explore the value of potentially integrating word processing within such a lesson as outlined by Mr. Carpenter:

- Within this lesson, in what way could word processing be used by Mr. Carpenter, by Jonathon, and by the members of the social studies classes?
- How could word processing help with the development of the initial group brainstorming of the key questions?
- How could word processing be used to complete research on the selected topics? Could word processing increase the potential creativity and the breadth of the students' research?
- In what way could the use of word processing be helpful in the design and development of the comparison table? Would its value increase as information was input and periodically updated?
- How could word processing facilitate the development and production of the assigned reflective paper? Could word processing allow for additional insights and levels of creative thought and comparison?
- Could word processing facilitate increased levels of communication between Jonathon and the classes of social studies students?
- Could word processing affect the creation, production, and dissemination of the final executive summary report?
- Are there potential problems and pitfalls if word processing is integrated within this lesson and its respective assignments?

Level 3a Workout: Integrating word processing

Now it's your turn. Complete the following steps to this Workout as you think about the future use of word processing within an applied setting.

1. Read each of the following situations. Imagine being directly involved in the planning for each of these projects. Select one (or more if you wish) for further consideration.

Roller Park Proposal:

The mayor of Billingsburg has asked the city parks engineer to create a proposal for a park that would focus on rollerblade activities for the city youth. The park could be located on city land adjacent to the new city swimming pool. To accomplish this task, the city engineers have contacted the local middle schools and high schools and asked the students to make recommendations for the proposal. They want students to suggest layouts of the parks, types of jumps, obstacles, and activities that should be integrated, proposed fees for the use of the park, and so on. They have even asked the students to propose the types of safety features that should be included.

The Greatest Decade:

During the twentieth century many wonderful, sad, horrifying, and satisfying events occurred. But was there one decade that shines above the rest as making the greatest impact? How and why should one decade be selected over the others as being the most significant decade of the twentieth century? How can the strengths and weaknesses of each decade be effectively exposed, compared, and debated?

Senior Citizens and Young Mentors:

The activities chairperson at Heritage Retirement Center is constantly being asked for lessons on basic computer skills. Many residents of the Center desire to use the available computers to type letters, send e-mail, and surf the Internet. The activities chairperson contacts a neighborhood elementary class of fourth- and fifth-graders to come to Heritage and mentor the residents. Her thoughts are to have the children and the residents work together to produce a newsletter that could be published and distributed. The contents of the publication could be stories from the lives of the residents.

Making a Copy:

The high school media specialist is worried that many of her students may not fully understand the ramifications of copyright infringement. She notes that they seem to freely copy and distribute music CDs, pictures from the Internet, and even papers for various school class reports. She decides that perhaps a discussion is in order in which small groups of students will debate the pros and cons of such free media access and how it affects copyright law in today's digital world.

2. Based on your selected project, consider the following questions found within the integration assessment questionnaire (IAQ). Mark your response to each question.

Integration Assessment Questionnaire (IAQ)

Will using word processing software as a part of the project:	
Broaden the learners' perspective on potential solution paths or answers?	__Yes __ No __ Maybe
Increase the level of involvement and investment of personal effort by the learners?	__ Yes __ No __ Maybe
Increase the level of learner motivation (e.g., increase the relevance of the to-be-learned task, the confidence of dealing with the task, and the overall appeal of the task)?	__ Yes __ No __ Maybe
Decrease the time needed to generate potential solutions?	__ Yes __ No __ Maybe
Increase the quality and quantity of learner practice working on this and similar projects?	__ Yes __ No __ Maybe
Increase the quality and quantity of feedback given to the learner?	__ Yes __ No __ Maybe
Enhance the ability of the student to solve novel but similar projects, tasks, and problems in the future?	__ Yes __ No __ Maybe

3. If you have responded "yes" to one or more of the IAQ questions, you should consider using word processing to enhance the student's potential learning experience.
4. Using the example lesson plan, develop a lesson plan based on your selected project. Within the plan, indicate how and when the learner will use word processing. Additionally, list potential benefits and challenges that may occur when involving this software within the lesson.

Level 3b Workout: Exploring the NETS connection

PART A: Once you have an understanding of the features and applications of general word processing skills, it is important to provide a context for the professional purpose that these skills can have in the classroom. By using the National Educational Technology Standards (NETS) developed by the **International Society for Technology in Education (ISTE)**, the next few tasks will provide a foundation for the importance of integrating this chapter's skill set into any teacher's professional practice. There are two sets of NETS: one designed for the skills needed by teachers (NETS-T), the other for the skills needed by K–12 students (NETS-S). A complete listing of these standards can be found in the Appendix of this book.

PART B: The following chart provides examples of how the use of a word processing application can directly align with the NETS-T and the NETS-S. As you read these strategies, try to consider additional connections that could be made between these standards and this set of skills. Additionally, consider the answer to the focus questions presented for each unique standard.

NETS-T and NETS-S	Example Activities and Focus Questions
NETS-T 1. Facilitate and Inspire Student Learning and Creativity NETS-S 1. Creativity and Innovation	• Write an autobiography that includes digital images. • Develop a digital reflection journal to monitor student progress, questions, and insight. • Promote the use of visual components along with content-rich text when creating standard assessments such as book reports or essays. 1. How can the use of word processing help develop students' higher-order skills and creativity? 2. How might the use of word processing change the nature of student work? What benefits do you perceive? What challenges might be presented? How might this affect the role of the teacher?
NETS-T 2. Design and Develop Digital-Age Learning Experiences and Assessments NETS-S 4. Critical Thinking, Problem Solving, and Decision Making	• Create classroom contracts for extended or privileged activities. • Collect data to inform a classroom decision. • Identify a problem in the school, community, or world. Use a word processor to develop a written description of potential solutions or calls for assistance. 3. How could a word processor be used to organize data in the classroom for a teacher? 4. How could a word processor be used to organize data in the classroom for students? 5. How can word processing improve how the collection, analysis, and assessment of student work or data are completed? Could this increased information be used to improve the learning environment and experience?
NETS-T 3. Model Digital-Age Work and Learning NETS-S 2. Communication and Collaboration NETS-S 3. Research and Information Fluency	• Routinely publish classroom newsletters, reports, and so on. • Create advertising or informative packets for school events. • Critically evaluate and examine the resources and references being used as sources of factual information. • Prior to the start of a project, brainstorm the potential use of technology as a means to aid in its completion. 6. What effect does a teacher's attitude toward or use of technology have on the students' perceptions of its usefulness? 7. Why is it important for a teacher to model the *efficient* use of technology? 8. In what ways could word processing be used to facilitate the communication and collaboration among teachers, students, parents, and subject matter experts on specific projects that ultimately affect student learning?

| NETS-T 4. Promote and Model Digital Citizenship and Responsibility

NETS-S 5. Digital Citizenship

NETS-S 3. Research and Information Fluency | • Discuss copyright and seek out copyright-friendly images to use in classroom projects.
• Practice the art of citation and appropriate use of the work of others.
• Develop correspondence between other peer groups (within the school, across the nation, or internationally).
• Analyze personal writing to determine if it is appropriate to share in a public manner. (Are there elements of this essay or story that should be modified prior to submission to a social networking site?)

9. Is the process of teaching students to limit the content they post on the Internet a form of censorship? Why or why not?
10. In the digital age, should elements of privacy, online, and the protection of personal information become components of a traditional writing curriculum? Explain. |
| NETS-T 5. Engage in Professional Growth and Leadership | • Develop and maintain a reflective journal on professional practice and strategy selection.
• Share and collaborate with colleagues outside of your school environment.
• Critique and comment on public policy and best practices.

11. Why is it important for teachers to continually contribute to the field of education?
12. How important is collaboration to curriculum development? How can the use of a word processor aid in this process? |

Collaborating and coauthoring in Word 2010

An important new feature of Word 2010 is the ability to share the workload through Internet connections. As highlighted by the NETS, collaboration is a key expectation in the twenty-first century and there is now a way to facilitate this process using MS Word. To do this, you and those that you want to involve in the joint team effort need to get Windows Live SkyDrive accounts (available at www.skydrive.live.com). This account is free and it gives you a large amount of storage space. In addition, it provides a place to organize your work into folders. This storage space, however, does not reside on your machine; it is saved on servers that you access via the Internet. It is actually a nice, simple, and free way to back up your work—just in case something were to happen to your computer and its main storage drives.

A nice feature of this storage space at SkyDrive is that you can set up specific folders to synch with the folders of others who also have SkyDrive accounts. Thus you can write on a document, save it to your SkyDrive storage place within one of your synched folders and that document becomes immediately available in the synched folder of those with whom you are collaborating. You have control over who can be synched to your work—thus you can create small (or large) working groups that can access the work. This is not a real big deal if the person you are working with is sitting right next to you in your office; however, if that person is across town in another school or across the country or even on the other side of the world, the document is immediately available. This allows groups of individuals to work together on the same document. Word actually notifies you when one of your group members is currently working on the document. This helps to ensure you don't make changes while someone else is making the same changes.

Think of how this coauthoring function could be used for class projects that involve word-processed documents. For example:

• A book report that needs to be created by a small team of students. Each subsection of the book is summarized by a different author and combined together into a single document that is quickly created and reviewed by all team members—even when they go to different schools in different cities.
• A research project that has several individuals developing the procedures for collecting the needed data. A single document of the procedures is co-developed by starting the list and having each member add, evaluate, adapt, and adjust the list even though they are not meeting in the same time and location.
• Five lifelong friends create a bucket list of adventures they want to experience before graduating from college. The list is constantly evolving and changing as items are accomplished and new items are added. Each member always has access to the most up-to-date list.
• Family members that now live all over the world write a holiday family newsletter. Each contributes his or her perspective and insights by accessing the newsletter that is synched across all family members.

Further ideas on using word processing as a learning tool

When students use a word processor, they frequently are asked to generate a written report of some kind. The word processor is a great tool to facilitate reflection, generation, and editing of materials.

Note: These ideas are to help you generate your own ideas of what can be done. Don't let it bother you if they're not the right content or grade level; use the idea and adapt it to be helpful within your own situation. These are meant to be stimuli for additional ideas.

Here are a few ideas that may help you see how the word processor might be beneficial:

1. Create a table and have the students fill in the blanks or have them create the frame for themselves. For example, on the axis on the left side include different types of Native Americans and where they lived. Along the top table row or axis, put categories of clothing, shelter, tools, or food sources. Have the students fill in the cells of the table and make predictions about the relationships between climate and their tools, shelter, and so forth.
2. Compose and format different types of letters (e.g., business, personal, memo, cover letter, persuasive communication, and letter to the editor) and then compare the different styles of writing.
3. Have students conduct research by generating data-gathering instruments (e.g., questionnaires), describing procedures, and then summarizing the results.
4. Have learners create an assessment rubric that outlines all criteria for a group project presentation.
5. Have students write a group report using comments and track changes in the word processor to monitor who makes which comments and suggestions within the document.
6. Have students develop a brochure about a specific historical topic (e.g., colonial America), their personal work history and skills (e.g., jobs they have worked and what they have done), or places they may someday travel (e.g., Australian Outback).
7. Have learners use the word processor's outlining function and brainstorm and design a required group presentation.
8. Given specific paragraphs from the writings of famous authors, have students identify and highlight nouns, verbs, adjectives, and so on, in various electronic highlighter colors.
9. Have students review a paragraph or document that contains highlighted target words. Have them use the thesaurus and change the words to add clarity to the document.
10. Have students work in groups to develop divergent viewpoints about historical controversies (e.g., US Japanese internment camps; Iraq War; Antitrust settlements of AT&T or Microsoft). Their written points and counterpoints can then be summarized, shared, and discussed within a single document.
11. Have students evaluate a set of instructional materials (e.g., a biology CD) and give their opinions on its value, what they felt was worthwhile, and what they felt could have been improved to make it more effective.
12. Have students develop (or complete) a matching game that consists of a table of anatomy terms in one column and a picture of various anatomical structures in the other column.
13. Have learners create original poetry and combine it with an inspirational photo as a background to their written work.
14. Have students use voice recognition software and compose a short story about living in a world without the use of one's eyes or hands.
15. Have students identify three college scholarship applications that require short essays as part of the application process. Have them create word-processed responses to those essay questions.

Additional ideas on using the word processor as an assistant

1. *School conduct report.* Create a table that highlights all of the rules of class conduct and cells to report when the rule is not followed.
2. *Communication report.* Create a template that allows you to monitor how often notes are sent to parents or supervisors about a student.

3. *Certificates.* Create of certificates for extra effort and merit.
4. *Progress reports.* Develop reports to keep students (and parents) informed of what has been accomplished and what is still needed.
5. *Work sheets.* Construct various types of worksheets and directions for projects.
6. *Individual education plans (IEPs).* Develop IEP templates that can be altered and adjusted for each individual student.
7. *Calendars.* Develop and use daily, weekly, and monthly assignment or work calendars.
8. *Weekly lesson planning.* Develop a table template of all weekly planning for lessons and subjects.
9. *Badges and labels.* Produce name badges for students, class helpers, and parents, and create labels for files, folders, and so forth.
10. *Programs.* Develop programs and handouts for school productions.
11. *Newsletters.* Write weekly or monthly classroom newsletters containing relevant information for students and parents.
12. *Permission slips.* Develop permission slips for events such as field trips, bus rides, and authorized school activities.
13. *Makeup work assignments.* Develop a template for helping students who have missed school so they know what was missed and when it is to be completed.
14. *Volunteer schedules and job responsibilities.* Create a document that explains job responsibilities and schedules for individuals who volunteer at the school.
15. *Reminders.* Write memos to remind students about their assignments or to sign up to complete tasks (e.g., bring snacks or give a report).
16. *Class activities.* For example, develop a short script for a play that includes text columns for sets, narration, different pictures, and scenes. Use graphics to draw basic areas of the stage and where actors and scenery will be placed.

MS Word for Mac 2011

Terms to Know
Contextual tabs

ORIENTATION

This section assumes you have previewed the full Chapter 2 and have a grasp of the general workings of the word processor. This section of the chapter focuses specifically on the use of MS Word that has been created to work on the Macintosh operating system. In most cases, there is a close similarity to how MS Word for the PC (Word 2010) functions, but there are some unique differences that we will highlight within this addendum.

What's the MS Word for Mac 2011 workspace look like?

Figure 2.16 is an example of MS Word for Mac 2011.

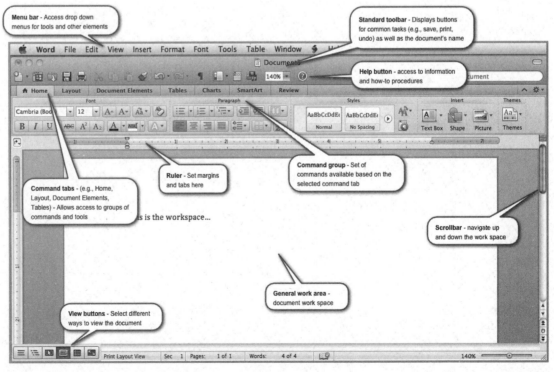

FIGURE 2.16 View of a Microsoft Word for Mac word processing work area

FIGURE 2.17 View of the menu bar with drop-down Insert menu revealed

What commands can be used?

Within the Mac version of MS Office, there are drop-down menu options (see Figure 2.17) and a ribbon of tools that runs across the top of the work screen. So, for example, if you wished to insert a picture into your document, you could accomplish that by going to the **Menu bar** >>> **Insert** drop-down menu >>> **Photo**.

Note: The menu bar provides quick access to a variety of relevant dialog boxes. For example, when you choose to insert a footnote via the menu bar, a dialog box will appear that will give you a number of options of how that footnote could be formatted. As shown in Figure 2.17 you can explore these menu bar options to see all of the different dialog boxes (e.g., Page Numbers, Date and Time, Watermark, Table, Chart) that can be accessed.

Likewise, you could use the ribbon as shown in Figure 2.18 and click on the **Home** tab >>> **Insert** command group >>> **Picture** button. To remain consistent with the MS Office 2010 PC

FIGURE 2.18 The ribbon holds the command tabs, command groups and sets, and individual commands

FIGURE 2.19 Selecting a specific item (e.g., graphic, picture) in the workspace reveals contextual tabs and associated contextual commands that can be accessed and used with the selected item.

version, we will focus most of our comments on using the ribbon to accomplish the tasks within this text. Some basic things to note about the use of the ribbons:

- The command groups change based on the command tab selected.
- Many of the selected tool buttons within the command groups can be opened to reveal galleries of options (e.g., review the gallery for themes by selecting the **Home** tab >>> **Theme** group >>> **Themes** button).
- **Contextual tabs** with associated contextual command groups appear when a specific object like a picture, graphic, table, or chart is selected in the document (see Figure 2.19).

Orientation Workout

Return to the Orientation Workout on page 40 of this text and complete it as it is designed. The main purpose of this Workout is to get you familiar with how to enter text, graphics, and so on within the workspace as well as accessing and using the various tools on the menu bar and ribbons.

LEVEL 1: DESIGNING, CREATING, AND PRODUCING WRITTEN DOCUMENTS

Scenario 1

To accomplish this Level 1 task, review Scenario 1 (page 43), specifically focusing on Figure 2.5 and the text formatting features highlighted by the callouts within that figure. Using Figure 2.5 as a guide, re-create that document by following these steps:

No.	Feature	Steps to Get It Done
1.	**Enter the text**	1. Start Word and create a new document (**File** menu >>> **New Blank Document**). 2. Enter the content as shown in Figure 2.4. More options: **File menu** >>> **New From Template . . .** and the document gallery will open. Here you can select from all types of professionally developed templates to help set up your new document.
2.	**Alter font type, size, and style**	1. Select (highlight) the title of the newsletter "The Happenings. . . ." 2. Review the Font set of commands (**Home** tab >>> **Font** group) as shown in Figure 2.6. 3. Click on the down arrow to reveal the gallery of different font types (e.g., Times New Roman). Click on your preferred type. 4. Use the down arrow on the font size (e.g., 12) to reveal selected font sizes that can also be previewed in a similar fashion. Follow the same procedure to preview and select the size of the font you desire. 5. Using this same font group of tools, you can change the font style (e.g., **bold**, *italic*, underline), font color, and background highlighting within the document. **Note:** You can also use the Quick Styles feature (**Home** tab >>> **Styles** group) as shown in Figure 2.20. More options: **Format** menu >>> **Font . . .** or **Font** menu

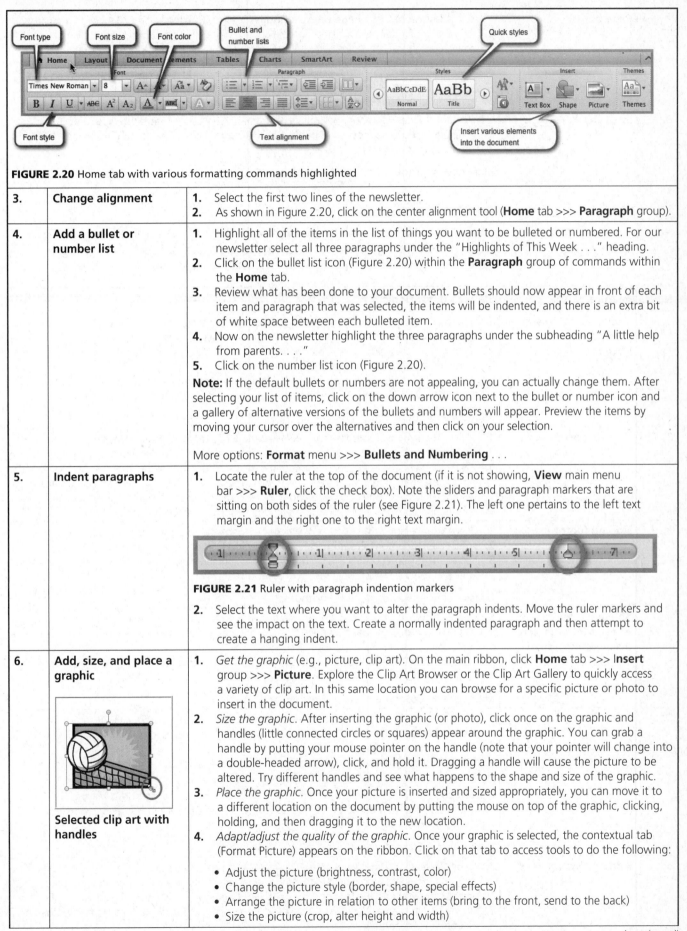

FIGURE 2.20 Home tab with various formatting commands highlighted

3.	Change alignment	1. Select the first two lines of the newsletter.
		2. As shown in Figure 2.20, click on the center alignment tool (**Home** tab >>> **Paragraph** group).
4.	Add a bullet or number list	1. Highlight all of the items in the list of things you want to be bulleted or numbered. For our newsletter select all three paragraphs under the "Highlights of This Week . . ." heading.
		2. Click on the bullet list icon (Figure 2.20) within the **Paragraph** group of commands within the **Home** tab.
		3. Review what has been done to your document. Bullets should now appear in front of each item and paragraph that was selected, the items will be indented, and there is an extra bit of white space between each bulleted item.
		4. Now on the newsletter highlight the three paragraphs under the subheading "A little help from parents. . . ."
		5. Click on the number list icon (Figure 2.20).
		Note: If the default bullets or numbers are not appealing, you can actually change them. After selecting your list of items, click on the down arrow icon next to the bullet or number icon and a gallery of alternative versions of the bullets and numbers will appear. Preview the items by moving your cursor over the alternatives and then click on your selection.
		More options: **Format** menu >>> **Bullets and Numbering** . . .
5.	Indent paragraphs	1. Locate the ruler at the top of the document (if it is not showing, **View** main menu bar >>> **Ruler**, click the check box). Note the sliders and paragraph markers that are sitting on both sides of the ruler (see Figure 2.21). The left one pertains to the left text margin and the right one to the right text margin.

FIGURE 2.21 Ruler with paragraph indention markers

		2. Select the text where you want to alter the paragraph indents. Move the ruler markers and see the impact on the text. Create a normally indented paragraph and then attempt to create a hanging indent.
6.	Add, size, and place a graphic	1. *Get the graphic* (e.g., picture, clip art). On the main ribbon, click **Home** tab >>> **Insert** group >>> **Picture**. Explore the Clip Art Browser or the Clip Art Gallery to quickly access a variety of clip art. In this same location you can browse for a specific picture or photo to insert in the document.
	Selected clip art with handles	2. *Size the graphic.* After inserting the graphic (or photo), click once on the graphic and handles (little connected circles or squares) appear around the graphic. You can grab a handle by putting your mouse pointer on the handle (note that your pointer will change into a double-headed arrow), click, and hold it. Dragging a handle will cause the picture to be altered. Try different handles and see what happens to the shape and size of the graphic.
		3. *Place the graphic.* Once your picture is inserted and sized appropriately, you can move it to a different location on the document by putting the mouse on top of the graphic, clicking, holding, and then dragging it to the new location.
		4. *Adapt/adjust the quality of the graphic.* Once your graphic is selected, the contextual tab (Format Picture) appears on the ribbon. Click on that tab to access tools to do the following:
		• Adjust the picture (brightness, contrast, color)
		• Change the picture style (border, shape, special effects)
		• Arrange the picture in relation to other items (bring to the front, send to the back)
		• Size the picture (crop, alter height and width)

(continued)

7.	Page border	1. Click **Layout** tab >>> **Page Background** group >>> **Borders**
		2. The Borders and Shading dialog box will appear. Click the Page Border tab if it isn't already selected and use the various alternatives to create a page border for your document.
		3. With the use of the Border and Shading dialog box you can learn to draw boxes around specific bits of text, color the boxes, or even shade the backgrounds within the boxes.
		More options: **Format** menu >>> **Borders and Shading . . .**
8.	Spell check	To turn on the automatic spelling and grammar check (or to turn it off), **Word** main menu >>> **Preferences** >>> **Spelling and Grammar** >>> **Check spelling as you type** (make sure it is checked).
		More options: **Tools** menu >>> **Spelling and Grammar . . .**

Scenario 2

To accomplish this Level 1 task, review Scenario 2 (page 49), especially focusing on Figure 2.9 and the specific text formatting features highlighted by the callouts within that figure. Using Figure 2.9 as a guide, re-create that document by following the steps.

No.	Feature	Steps to Get It Done
1.	**Tables: creating and formatting**	1. Place your cursor in the document where you want the table to be inserted.
		2. Click **Tables** tab >>> **Table Options** group >>> **New.**
		3. Pull the mouse over the revealed grid to preview the creation of your table and click on the desired size (e.g., number of rows and columns).
		4. Once the table has been created, the Table Layout contextual tab will appear and you can use its tools to format the rows, columns, cells, and so on within your table.
		More options: Table menu on the menu bar
2.	**Inserting headers**	1. Click **Document Elements** tab >>> **Headers & Footers** group >>> **Header.**
		2. Preview the various provided headers and select the one that is desired.
		3. Once the header is selected, it is automatically inserted into the document and the Header and Footer contextual tab appears. The tools on this tab allow you to insert such things as page numbers, dates, clip art, and so on into the header, as well as adjust the header's position, create different odd and even page headers, and various other options.
3.	**Adding footnotes**	1. Place your cursor in the document where you want the footnote number to be located.
		2. Click the **Document Elements** tab >>> **Citations** group >>> **Footnote.**
		3. Enter the information for the footnote and it will be automatically entered at the designated place at the bottom of the page.
		More options: **Insert** menu >>> **Footnotes . . .**
4.	**Shading cells, columns, or rows (or anything inside or outside of a table)**	1. Highlight the section that you want shaded (e.g., a row, column, or set of cells within a table—or within a usual document this can be applied to an individual word, sentence, paragraph, graphic, and so forth).
		2. Click on the **Tables** tab >>> **Table Styles** group >>> **Shading** icon. Click to open the shading gallery and select the color preferred.
		More options: **Format** menu >>> **Borders and Shading . . .**
5.	**Inserting borders**	1. Highlight the section you want to have a border around (e.g., a row, column, or set of cells within a table—or within a usual document this can be used on an individual word, sentence, paragraph, graphic, etc.).
		2. Click on the **Home** tab >>> **Paragraph** group >>> **Border** button (down arrow for the various options) and select your preferred border option.
		Note: If you are working directly within a table, you can also select the portion of the table where you want a border to be and then click on the **Tables** tab >>> **Draw Borders** group >>> **Borders** button.
		More options: **Format** menu >>> Borders and Shading . . .
6.	**Adding hyperlinks**	1. Type the text you would like to serve as the link. If you choose to use the web address as the text that appears, simply type in the address and press the space bar. The link is automatically created for you and the font and style changes to indicate its link to the web.
		2. If you would prefer to use customized text for the link, insert the text, select it, click **Insert** menu >>> **Hyperlink . . .** The Insert Hyperlink dialog box will appear.

7.	Adding page numbers	1. Click **Document Elements** tab >>> **Header & Footer** group >>> **Page #** icon. A page number dialog box will appear and you can select the formatting for the page number.
		2. Page numbers can also be placed within the header or footer of a document. For example, to include it within the footer (the header page number also works in this same fashion):
		• Click **Document Elements** tab >>> **Header & Footer** group >>> **Footer** icon and select the type of footer you desire for your document. The page number will be included in the footer
8.	Inserting footers	1. Click **Document Elements** tab >>> **Headers & Footers** group >>> **Footer**.
		2. Preview the various provided footers and select the one that is desired.
		3. Once the footer is selected, it is automatically inserted into the document and the Header & Footer contextual tab appears. These tools allow you to insert such things as page numbers, dates, clip art, and so on into the footer as well as adjust the footer's position, create different odd and even page footers, and various other options.

Level 1a and 1b Workouts

Return to the Level 1a and 1b Workouts found on pages 54 and 55, respectively. Complete the Workouts using Figures 2.5 and 2.9 as guides for your work.

LEVEL 2: TABLES, TEMPLATES, AND OTHER GOOD STUFF

What should you be able to do?

The focus within Level 2 is to help you use Help and other resources to access and use various other features of the MS Word application.

Similar to Help in Windows, there is also Help in MS Word and most other sophisticated word processing software. To use Help, click the Help button on the on tab bar of the standard toolbar (see Figure 2.16).

As shown in Figure 2.22 you can also access the help function through the Help drop-down menu on the menu bar.

Clicking the Word Help button opens the Help window (see Figure 2.23). From here you can browse general Help topics, enter key words to search for a specific question that you might have, explore additional online Help topics, review tutorials to help you get started, and so on.

FIGURE 2.22 Accessing Help through the main menu bar in MS Word for Mac

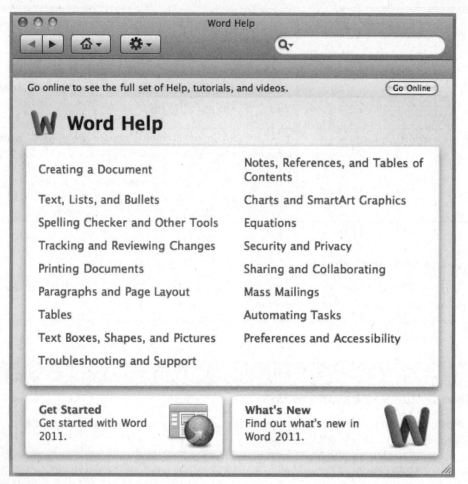

FIGURE 2.23 Word Help window for Mac

Scenario 3

To expand your capabilities and begin to see how Help can be accessed and used to find additional features, review Scenario 3 on page 57, paying close attention to Figure 2.15 and the call-outs of its various features. Using Figure 2.15 as a guide, practice using the highlighted features by accessing and using each of the following word processing features.

Feature	Steps to Get It Done
Inserting WordArt	Within Word Help • Keyword: WordArt • Select: Add effects to text and explore the various topics. WordArt can be directly accessed by **Document Elements** tab >>> **Text Elements** group >>> **WordArt** >>> select from the gallery of options and types.
Creating section breaks within documents	Within Word Help • Keywords: Section break • Select: insert, delete, or change a section break and follow the given procedure. A quick way to insert a section break is **Layout** tab >>> **Page Setup** group >>> **Breaks** >>> **Section Breaks** (pick the type that you need, e.g., continuous).
Adding multiple columns of text	Within Word Help • Keyword: Columns • Select: Lay out a page by using columns To create columns of text, **Layout** tab >>> **Text Layout** group >>> **Columns.** Make your selection from the different alternative types of columns.

Creating a watermark picture	Word Help
	• Keyword: Watermark • Select: Add a watermark The standard way of producing a watermark is **Layout** tab >>> **Page Background** group >>> **Watermark.**
Text wrapping with graphics	Text wrapping allows you to insert a picture or object within your document and then control how the text is formatted in relationship to that object (e.g., above, below, around, on top of, or behind the object). Word Help • Keywords: Wrap text • Select: Control text wrapping around objects and then select whether you want to wrap around pictures, objects, or a table. After inserting your graphic, make sure the graphic is selected and then click on the **Format Picture** contextual tab >>> **Arrange** group >>> **Wrap Text** and make your selection of the type of wrapping you desire
Adding a text box	A text box is a specialized container of text within a document. It can add interest and break up the usual flow of the text. This container can be sized, colored, and positioned on a page. It is frequently used to highlight a special quote, place information in a side bar, or add some point of interest. Text boxes are both predesigned and custom created. **Information about and procedure for creating and inserting:** Word Help • Keywords: Text box • On the Word Help home page, select Text Boxes, Shapes, and Pictures. A quick way to get to the action buttons is **Home** tab >>> **Insert** group >>> **Text Box.** Another way: **Document Elements** tab >>> **Text Elements** group >>> **Text Box.** **Note:** You can position the text box by selecting it, placing your cursor over one of the outline box lines, and clicking, holding, and dragging it to its new location. **Another note:** After selecting the text box, Text Box Tools are accessible (click the Format contextual tab). These tools allow you change text direction, add box styles, effects, size, and arrange the position and the text wrapping.

Level 2 Workout

Return to the Level 2 Workout found on page 60. Complete the Workout using Figure 2.15 as a guide.

3 SPREADSHEETS

MS Excel: The Basics of a "Number Cruncher"

INTRODUCTION

What should you know about spreadsheets?

Spreadsheets are designed to help you work with numbers—not just the usual adding, subtracting, and so forth, but also for comparing, making predictions, and evaluating. Beyond numbers, this software deals with text in a way that teachers can find very helpful. Within this introduction to spreadsheets, we want you to discover the following:

- What a spreadsheet is, what it can do, and how it can help in teaching and learning
- How to justify the use of the spreadsheet as an effective tool—knowing when and why it should or shouldn't be used

Terms to know			
cell	fill	page orientation	workbook
cell reference	fill handle	rows	worksheet
charts	formula	split pane	
column	functions	what if?	
dialog box expander	Microsoft Excel	word wrap	

What is a spreadsheet and what does it do?

Spreadsheets are remarkable tools that allow you to organize, calculate, and present data (generally, this data has something to do with numbers but not always). These tools organize the world into a grid of rows and columns.

A grade book is a familiar example for most teachers. Within an electronic spreadsheet grade book, you not only can quickly find and organize data for each student, but the spreadsheet can also be set up to do the needed calculations automatically for you. Just as quickly, you can rearrange how the grade book looks and how grades are calculated. Figure 3.1 shows a very simple form of such a grade book.

Student's Name	Project 1	Project 2	Project 3	Total
Anderson, Timbre	13	14	13	40
Butler, Landon	14	15	15	44
Jersey, Alexis	12	11	13	36
Johnson, Brayden	15	14	15	44
Nesbit, Max	11	10	9	30
Rendolf, B. Jane	15	15	15	45

FIGURE 3.1 Simple grade book spreadsheet

What are some commonly used spreadsheets?

Standard software varieties:

- **Microsoft Excel**
- Lotus 1-2-3
- Corel Calculate
- Sun Microsystems StarOffice/OpenOffice Calc
- The spreadsheet program within Microsoft Works

Web 2.0 varieties:

- Google Docs (spreadsheet program)
- Zoho Sheet

Note: We focus on Microsoft Excel in this book. However, *what we present can be done in any of the other spreadsheets listed.* So if you don't have access to MS Excel at home, don't be alarmed—you can still complete the projects and learn the basic skills.

Another note: Web 2.0–based applications are found on the web and generally can be used for greater collaboration and for little if any cost for the basic application. For these suggested spreadsheets see www.docs.google.com or www.sheet.zoho.com.

Why bother learning how to use a spreadsheet?

- *To cut your time.* Just think about it—if you have six class periods in a day with twenty to twenty-five students in each period, and over the course of the grading period you record a dozen assignments, three quizzes, and two tests, you have over two thousand scores to record! Think of the time it takes to calculate totals, subtotals, averages, and so on during the course of a semester. The spreadsheet can calculate automatically for you.
- *To cut your mistakes.* If you are continually entering and reentering the same data over and over, you'll eventually punch in the wrong number. Having the computer do the calculations for you can be a way of overcoming many of the little problems that creep in because of fat fingers, tired eyes, and low power cells (yours and the calculator's).
- *To use the work of experts.* Maybe you don't know much about certain statistical, accounting, or other formulas and functions. Many of these are built into an electronic spreadsheet. Instead of creating the **formula**, you just make a selection and the computer completes the calculation.
- *To allow predictions.* This software allows you to imagine what the possibilities are if the current course of action continues or if some changes are made (what if?).
- *To allow for quick repurposing.* Instead of constantly rebuilding from scratch (e.g., creating a new grade book for next semester's class), you can use a spreadsheet that is similar and just make some quick adaptations. This is often faster than starting over.
- *To help you see things differently.* Through the use of **charts** that can be quickly and easily generated from the spreadsheet, what was once a bunch of rows and columns of numbers may now be seen as simple, understandable trends and answers to problems that were unnoticed before.

How can spreadsheets be used at school? A brief list of ideas

By the teacher:	By the student:
• Grade books	• Math assignments
• School class expense budget	• Assignment planners
• Track fundraiser sales	• Personal budgets
• Highlight relationships and trends graphically	• Science reports for calculating and reporting results
• Create class seating charts	• Chart personal goals and progress
• Track and monitor assessments	

ORIENTATION

What's the workspace look like?

Figure 3.2 depicts the workspace of a common spreadsheet (MS Excel). Note that the workspace consists of designated **rows** and columns (where a row and a column intersect is known as a **cell**). Similar to other programs, there is the ribbon with various tabs, galleries, and tools as well as scroll bars and ways to view the workspace.

What commands can be used?

As in all MS Office applications (e.g., MS PowerPoint, MS Word), there's a ribbon (see Figure 3.3) of tools that runs across the top of the work screen. Within each ribbon the actual tools that can be used to input, format, and edit the numbers to be analyzed are grouped together under the various command tabs (e.g., File, Home, Insert, Page Layout, Formulas).

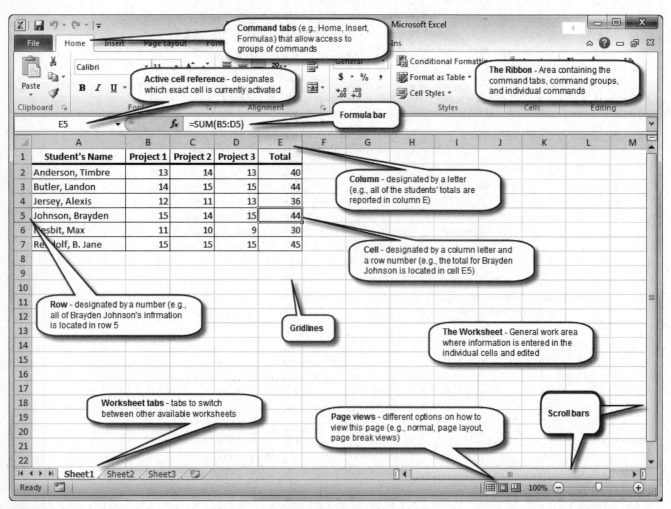

FIGURE 3.2 View of Microsoft Excel spreadsheet work area with simple grade book

FIGURE 3.3 The ribbon holds the command tabs, command groups or sets, and individual commands

FIGURE 3.4 The ribbon with the Insert tab selected revealing items that can be inserted

Selecting a specific tab reveals an associated command set or group. Once a command tab has been selected, this specific group remains visible and ready for use. Items within the set may appear as individual items or as a gallery of related items. For example, selecting the Insert tab (see Figure 3.4) in Excel reveals a group of commands that deal specifically with the insertion of, for example, tables, illustrations, charts, links, Word art, and text boxes.

The tabs have been developed to make your life easier. They allow you quick access to related groups of commands.

Note that there are additional commands that will occasionally be needed. As shown in Figure 3.5 (Chart Tools), these contextual commands appear when a specific object like a **chart**, picture, graphic, or table is selected.

For more information about Excel ribbon and command tabs, please review the Excel Orientation video on the website that accompanies this book.

Those grids of rows, columns, and cells

Spreadsheets are designed to maximize organization. Think about it. Everything on the sheet can be identified based on which row and column in which it resides.

For convenience, numbers generally designate rows and the columns are referred to by letters. So if in your grade book you want to know how well Brayden Johnson did on his third project, you can look for Brayden's name under the student name column, then locate the column that lists the third project. Where the row with Brayden's name (row 5) and the column with the Project 3 scores (column D) intersect, that's where Brayden's third project score (cell D5) will be located.

A spreadsheet is a great way to organize certain parts of your world. Mapmakers use this system to help you find exact locations—city planners may call them streets, avenues, and blocks—but they have the same idea. And, of course, accountants know all about such grids for keeping track of income, expenses, and totals.

What can go in the cells?

In an electronic spreadsheet, something interesting happens. Within any one cell you can insert words (project 1, student's name, and so forth), numbers (actual scores on projects), variables (=B5, which tells the spreadsheet to find cell B5, copy what it finds there, and insert whatever it finds into the current cell), or even mathematical formulas or **functions** (=B5+D5, which instructs the spreadsheet to add the number found in cell B5 to that found in cell D5 and place the sum in the current cell).

This opens up all kinds of possibilities. Soon you can envision a grade book that has your students' names in one column as well as a set of cells that includes scores for all of their assignments, projects, and so forth. Additionally, you should begin to see that there may be cells

FIGURE 3.5 Selecting a specific item (e.g., graphic, picture) in the workspace reveals contextual commands that can be accessed and used with the selected item

containing formulas that add up all of the scores for individual students, provide averages, show high and low scores, and so on. All of these can be accomplished simply by controlling what happens in the cells.

The "power of manipulation": Using functions and formulas

The power of the spreadsheet is in how it manipulates the data found in its cells. Within those cells it is possible to write formulas or equations that complete calculations on the data recorded in the spreadsheet. So not only does the spreadsheet organize, it can also manipulate data through addition, subtraction, and so forth.

Look at the simple grade book example in Figure 3.2. In cell E5 we have inserted a simple addition formula to add up all of Brayden Johnson's scores. When the cell is highlighted, a formula (=B5+C5+D5 or stated another way =Sum(B5:D5)) can be inserted on the formula bar line, however, once activated, cell E5 automatically (and very quickly) reveals the total of those scores. Once that formula is inserted, if a change to any of Brayden's scores occurs, the total found in cell E5 *automatically updates*.

The power of what if?

Sometimes it helps if you can imagine what would happen if _____ (you fill in the blank). What if . . . I had married my high school boyfriend? What if . . . I decreased my calorie intake of food by 20% for the next two months? What if . . . I made 10% more than I do now? What if . . . Brayden Johnson had scored a 15 on Project 2?

We doubt that the first what if? will be helped by a spreadsheet; however, for the last three it can play an important part. Because it can calculate so quickly and with such relative ease, you can plug in formulas and then readjust those formulas to immediately see different types of results based on certain variable factors. That is, you can make projections or estimations of how things would be "if . . . ."

Imagine what you can do with your students, then, when you discuss world populations and the effect of a population growth that increases by 6% instead of 3% over the next ten years. Perhaps you could get them to understand the mind-set of those in a third-world nation who attempt to leave their country when inflation hits an all-time high and the value of their country's money drops by 30% over a short period of time.

It's very powerful to be able to see into the future. Most individuals can't do this with consistent accuracy; however, with a spreadsheet some different scenarios can be played out so that predictions can be accurately made if specific situations occur.

Seeing the possibilities

Spreadsheets are the darlings of number manipulators. However, some of us can't see everything we need when given a big grid of numbers. Another wonderment of spreadsheets is that they can take the numbers and convert them to various graphs and charts with relative ease. In this way, instead of seeing a column of numbers you can see a bar, line, pie, or column chart. Magically, the numbers turn into revealing pictures.

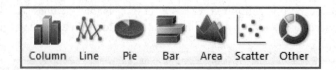

Column   Line   Pie   Bar   Area   Scatter   Other

Sometimes looking at data differently allows important correlations to stand out. For example, for a middle school student listing all of the average weekly temperatures for Indianapolis, Indiana; Bahrain, Saudi Arabia; and Santiago, Chile, may not mean much other than a big bunch of numbers. Showing those same numbers but as overlapping different colored line graphs, however, may suddenly turn on light bulbs about how temperatures vary across these widely dispersed cities. You could easily do the same for personal budgets, speeds on the 100-meter, cars crossing various bridges over the same river in downtown Chicago, and the growth of a classroom of students over the course of a semester.

Note: By combining the what if? function with the graphing function, you can start to readily visualize the potential relationships and how you can prepare for those possibilities.

Orientation Workout: Explore the territory

Turn on your computer and attempt the following:

1. Launch Microsoft Excel (or a similar spreadsheet software).
2. Create a new Excel spreadsheet.
3. Explore the various tabs on the ribbon and examine the different command groups.
4. On the new spreadsheet, attempt the following:
   - Click on a cell and enter a word or a number.
   - Highlight the words or numbers you have entered in the cell and change its formatting in some way (e.g., with the Home tab selected, try clicking on various font commands).
   - With the same cell selected, note its location identified in the active **cell reference** (see Figure 3.2) and also note what's listed in the formula bar.
   - Practice cutting and pasting from one cell to another.
   - In column A of your spreadsheet, insert the number 10 in cell A2, put the number 12 in cell A3, the number 9 in cell A4, and the number 11 in cell A5. Once that is completed, do the following:
     a. Select cells A2, A3, A4, and A5.
     b. Click on the Insert tab and select one of the charts from the chart commands (e.g., Pie).
     c. Examine what you have created.
     d. Click on the Change Chart Type button and try some of the other potential chart types (e.g., line, column, bar).
     e. Change some of the numbers in A2 through A5 and watch your chart as you input the new number. This is just a preview of things to come.

LEVEL 1: DESIGNING, CREATING, AND PRODUCING A USEFUL DATA-BASED CLASS PROJECT

What should you be able to do?

At this level, the emphasis is on using various tools and techniques of the spreadsheet software to create a document given specific guidelines and step-by-step procedures.

What resources are provided?

Basically, Level 1 is divided into common teaching scenarios, selected solutions, and practice exercises (i.e., Workouts). The scenarios have been constructed to allow you to examine common problems and how they can be addressed through the use of this software. To do this we have provided the following:

1. Draft spreadsheet documents that you can use to practice and review how the features can address the problems presented within each scenario.
2. Quick reference figures (see Figure 3.7 and 3.11) that identify (via visual callouts) all of the key features that have been incorporated within the solution presentations. These allow you to rapidly identify the key features and reference exactly how to include such features within your own work.
3. Step-by-step instructions on how to incorporate all highlighted features within your work.
4. Video mentoring support that guides you through the integration of each of the highlighted features.
5. Workout exercises that allow you to practice identifying and selecting which software features to use, when to use those features, how they should be incorporated, and to what degree they are effective.

PDToolkit
for
Teaching and Learning with Microsoft® Office 2010 and Office 2011 for Mac

Go to PDToolkit for **Teaching and Learning with Microsoft® Office 2010 and Office 2011 for Mac** to locate Workout Level One for Chapter Three.

PDToolkit
for
Teaching and Learning with Microsoft® Office 2010 and Office 2011 for Mac

Go to PDToolkit for **Teaching and Learning with Microsoft® Office 2010 and Office 2011 for Mac** to locate the mentoring videos for Chapter Three.

How should you proceed?

If you have *little or no experience* with MS Office 2010, particularly Excel, then we suggest you do the following:

1. Read and review Scenario 1.
2. Examine the quick reference figure (Figure 3.7) and all of the highlighted features.
3. Using the step-by-step directions, use the software and practice using each of the highlighted features.
4. If you have any confusion or difficulty with these features, access the videos and monitor the features as they are demonstrated and discussed within the short video clips.
5. Once you feel comfortable with these features, go to Scenario 2 and repeat these same steps with the new features introduced for that scenario. Monitor the quick reference figure (Figure 3.11) closely.
6. After both scenarios have been reviewed, go to the Workout and work through the problems and exercises it outlines.

If you have *experience* with Excel 2010, you may want to review the scenarios and the quick reference figures first. If any of the features are unfamiliar, then you may wish to access and use the step-by-step procedures as well as the mentoring support videos. Once the review has been completed, then move directly to the Workout exercise and create your own worksheet by incorporating many of the highlighted features.

Scenario 1: Trying to make a difference

John Rena is trying to get his middle school science students to be more environmentally conscious. Even though many of them complain that their efforts really don't add up to too much, John wants to help them understand that they each can make a significant impact. To accomplish this, he has initiated an aluminum can recycling project. He begins by challenging each of his five classes to bring to school the empty aluminum beverage cans that they get from their own homes. Each class then counts, crushes, and stores the cans for pickup by the local recycling company. John has each class create a simple spreadsheet to keep track of how many cans are collected each month and he keeps a master spreadsheet of the totals for all classes. At the end of each month, the totals are tabulated and posted for all classes to see. In addition, money earned from the sale of the cans is then used for some needed school science equipment.

Take a close look at Figure 3.6. This is a very simple, incomplete spreadsheet of the results of Mr. Rena's science class's five-month recycling project. Figure 3.7 is the same thing; however, it highlights all of the unique features that have been done to the spreadsheet to get it to look and work as a finished product. Within Figure 3.7, callout bubbles have been

	A	B	C	D	E	F	G
1	Class	Jan	Feb	Mar	April	May	Total per class
2	1st hour	923	1243	1198	1463	1507	
3	2nd hour	540	832	927	1103	1097	
4	3rd hour	752	647	527	1054	1209	
5	4th hour	621	845	829	995	1056	
6	5th hour	1105	1267	1015	1513	1483	
7	Total by month						
8	Class average						

FIGURE 3.6 A draft spreadsheet (incomplete and unformatted) showing the number of empty aluminum beverage cans donated by Mr. Rena's science classes during the spring semester

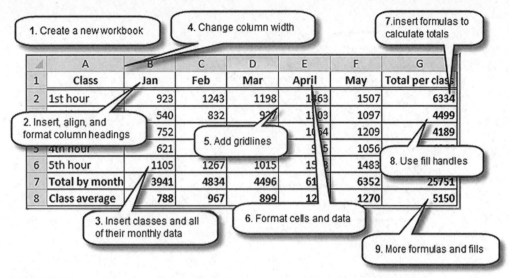

FIGURE 3.7 A complete spreadsheet with finishing and formatting steps highlighted

inserted to identify the key features that were incorporated to enhance the formatting of the document.

- Using Figure 3.7 as the guide, follow the numbered features in the step-by-step procedure to learn how each is employed.
- If additional guidance is needed, go to the mentoring videos on the website that accompanies this book and select the short clip that demonstrates the use of the needed feature.

for
Teaching and Learning with Microsoft® Office 2010 and Office 2011 for Mac

Go to PDToolkit for **Teaching and Learning with Microsoft® Office 2010 and Office 2011 for Mac** to locate the mentoring videos for Chapter Three.

No.	Feature	Steps to Get It Done
1.	**Create a new workbook (worksheet and templates)**	1. Launch Excel. If a new worksheet doesn't appear, click on the ribbon's File tab and select New from the drop-down menu. 2. Select the Blank **Workbook** (it may already be selected) and click on the Create button. A new, blank **worksheet** should appear and you can begin entering data. **Note:** When you have the New Workbook dialog box open, you can also select from various Excel spreadsheet templates. Some may be currently available on your machine and others may be acquired by clicking on the preferred template and downloading it from the Office.com site on the Internet. Such templates may help to speed up your work by providing much of the initial design and formatting.
2.	**Insert, align, and format column headings**	1. To insert a column heading, click on the cell where you want the heading to be inserted. For our example, click on cell A1 and then type the word *Class*. Hit the tab key and cell B1 will be highlighted. Type in *Jan*. Hit the tab key and continue until all of the headings have been entered. **Note:** It is not necessary to leave blank rows at the top of the spreadsheet workspace. Adding or deleting rows (or columns) at a later time can be easily completed. 2. To align the contents of a cell (column or row), highlight the cell you wish to align and then click on the Home tab and select your preferred alignment from the Alignment group (e.g., left, center, right) as shown in Figure 3.8. 3. To format items in a cell (row or column), select what you wish to format and then click the type of formatting (e.g., font type, size, boldface, italic) that you desire (**Home** tab >>> **Font** group). See Figure 3.8 for examples of the highlighted formatting features. **Note:** If you make a mistake, don't panic. Click on the cell you want to change and then enter the corrected data. Once you have clicked on the cell, you can also make the change by going to the Formula bar at the top of your spreadsheet (just under the command ribbon) and make your changes there. **Another note:** Copy, cut, and paste work fine in this application. If you find that you need to enter similar headings (e.g., Assignment 1, 2, 3, 4, . . .) and you don't want to type the same words over and over, you can copy the heading and then continually paste it into the cells as needed.

(continued)

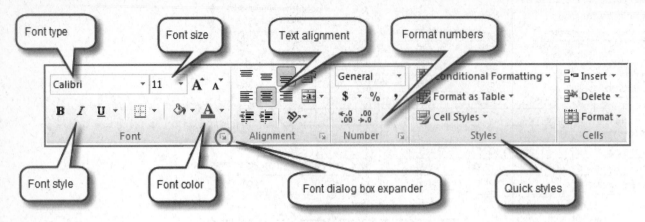

FIGURE 3.8 Home tab with various formatting commands highlighted

3.	**Enter classes and the main data of the spreadsheet**	1. Click on a cell (e.g., A2) and enter in the name of the first class of Mr. Rena. Click on the tab key and enter that class's total cans donated during the month of January, click the tab key and enter the total for the second month of the project, and continue until all classes and their respective data have been entered. Leave the Total per class column empty of all data. Additionally, don't put any data in for the Total by month row. We'll do that in just a minute. 2. If any entry errors are made, click on the cell and go to the Formula bar and make the needed editorial changes. Once finished with the editorial change, click the Enter key and the change will have occurred within the proper cell.
4.	**Adjust column width (or row height)**	1. Directly beneath the Formula bar, each column is labeled with a letter. Click on the letter of the column that you wish to adjust (e.g., A). The whole column will be highlighted. Then move your mouse pointer to the line that divides the target column and the next adjoining column. The pointer will change into a two-headed arrow. 2. With the two-headed arrow showing, click and hold the mouse and drag it to the right or left. You'll notice that as long as you have the mouse button held down, the width of your target column will change based on your mouse movement. 3. When you have determined the correct size, release the mouse and the column size has been altered. If you don't like it, you can immediately repeat the process and produce a different size. **Note:** This same procedure works for adjusting the height of rows. Click on the targeted row number and then move the cursor to the line between the adjoining row and your target and the two-headed arrow will appear. **Another note:** If you need to be precise, you can actually set a column width or a row height to an exact measurement. To do so, place your cursor in the proper row or column and then go to **Home** tab >>> **Cells** group >>> **Format** >>> select the option for column width or row height. A dialog box will appear that allows you to input the exact size you desire.
5.	**Add gridlines**	1. Select all of the cells, rows, or columns where you want the gridlines or borders to be displayed. 2. Go to the Font group of tools (**Home** tab >>> **Font** group) and click on the Border button. 3. From the drop-down gallery, select the type of gridline you desire (check out the different line styles, colors, thicknesses, and placements available). **Note:** You can also return to the Format Cell dialog box (**Home** tab >>> **Font** group >>> **Font dialog box expander**) and select the Border tab (see Figure 3.7) for additional options.
6.	**Formatting cells (and the things in them)**	1. To change the alignment of column headings, cell data, and so on, select the cells you want to format. For example, select all of the headings from cell A1 to G1. Refer to Figure 3.7 and Feature 2 (steps 2 and 3—formatting column headings). 2. Go to the **Home** tab >>> **Font** group and click on the **Font group dialog box expander** (see Figure 3.7). The Format Cells window opens. Examine all of the possibilities within this window (note the tabs along the top of this dialog box—click on a tab and it will show you additional functions that can be used). See Figure 3.9 for a peek at what you can play with. 3. To change font style, click the Font tab and select the type, style, size, color, and any other effects that you desire. Click the OK button and what you selected will be applied to all selected cells. 4. To change the alignment (center, left, right, and so on) or to change the direction of the words within your selected cell(s), click on the Alignment tab within the Format Cells window.

Note: At times you may wish to have certain cells (e.g., column headings) insert the words vertically or at a slant. This Format Cells window is where you make such changes.

5. Other cell formatting functions include choosing borders for the cells, adding patterns to the cells, and protecting the cells in certain ways. All of these functions are completed through this Format Cells window.

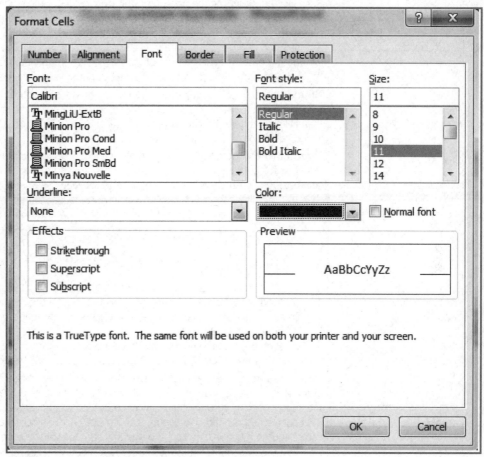

FIGURE 3.9 Format Cells dialog box (Font tab selected)

Note: Excel also has predefined styles that can be readily accessed (**Home** tab >>> **Styles** group >>> **Cell Styles** and a grid layout gallery will appear) and used to format cells.

| 7. | **Inserting a formula to calculate a total** | 1. Click on cell G2. This is the cell where the overall total for the first-hour class (sum of all cans collected over the spring semester by the first-hour class) should be calculated.
2. Instead of manually entering the total here, we'll enter a formula that tells the spreadsheet how to complete the calculations and then to post the result in this cell.
3. On the Formula bar (see Figure 3.2) enter the following equation: =Sum(B2:F2). This translates into Sum up all of the totals found in cells B2 through F2 and put the total in cell G2.

Note: The equals sign (=) plays a key role. It tells the spreadsheet that what follows is an equation that needs to be calculated. If you forget this, it will treat the equation as a simple set of text and it won't do any calculations. This is a common mistake.
Another note: There are generally a number of ways to write these equations. A different way that also works is: =B2+C2+D2+E2+F2. |

8.	**Use the fill handle** 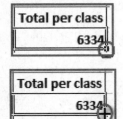	1. Once one formula has been constructed as in G2, you can use that same one for all of the other totals that need to be calculated in the Total per class column (G2 through G6). It's very simple and doesn't take much time. Click on cell G2.
		2. A box will be drawn around the total that now appears in that cell. Note that in the lower right-hand corner a small black square (known as a *handle*) appears. Place your cursor over that small handle and it will turn into a thin cross.
		3. Click and hold the mouse and drag it from cell G2 to G6. Release the mouse—and behold what you have done. Totals have now been calculated for each of the classes, using the correct scores. Actually, the formula that you created in G2 has been filled into all of the other cells below it relative to the data in each cell's respective row. That is, the total for the third-hour class is based on the number of cans they brought in (found in cells B4 through F4), but the fifth-hour class's total is based on their donated cans, which are found in B6 through F6.

Note: Another way of completing this **fill** command is to enter the formula (or whatever you want to fill) into the cell (e.g., G2 in our example), select that cell and all other cells that you want to fill, then **Home** tab >>> **Editing** group >>> **Fill** button. You'll note that you can also select to fill in various directions (e.g., right, up, left). This eliminates the need to use the **fill handle.**

Another note: The fill command can also be expanded in usefulness because it works with more than just formulas. For example, if you want to use the names of months as headers of your columns, type in the headers for January and February. Highlight both of those column headers and then use the fill button to pull across the ten successive columns. You will note that the fill button will fill in with each of the successive months of the year automatically.

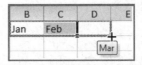

9.	**More formulas and fills**	1. Click on cell B8 and enter the following formula on the Formula bar: =Average(B2:B6). Hit the Enter key and see if the average of all classes for number of recycled cans for January is now reported in cell B8.
		2. Click on B8, find the handle, and click, hold, and drag to the right. This should efficiently fill in the averages for all of the rest of the months as well as the total-per-class columns.

Note: The spreadsheet has lots of built-in formulas. To view these click **Formulas** tab >>> **Functions Library** group. An embedded gallery of formula types will be displayed. In addition, you can click on the Insert Function button within that same Functions Library group and an Insert Function dialog box will be launched. As shown in Figure 3.10, this box allows you to search for a specific function. Once you select the function, you can also view the structure of the formula and if you desire you can access help that gives examples and procedures to walk you through the setup and use of the formula.

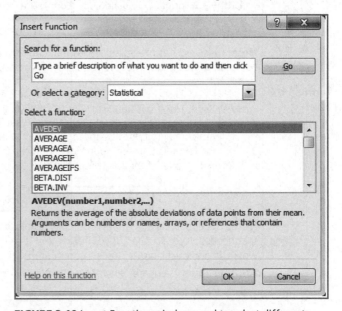

FIGURE 3.10 Insert Function window used to select different built-in functions and formulas

Scenario 2: The story continues

Through the efforts of Mr. Rena's science classes, a total of over 25,700 cans were collected and recycled. Receiving approximately 1 cent per can, the school received a payment of $257.51 for their science equipment. Because of the success of the program, Mr. Rena asked several of his students to use the data and make a presentation to the school principal, petitioning for a new schoolwide can recycling project to be started in the following school year.

Figure 3.11 represents a part of the visual presentation developed by the students. Notice that these data, when compared with that presented in Figure 3.7, have been changed for the presentation. For example, a title row and columns for number of students, student average, and money earned have all been added; at the same time, one row of data (class average) has been deleted.

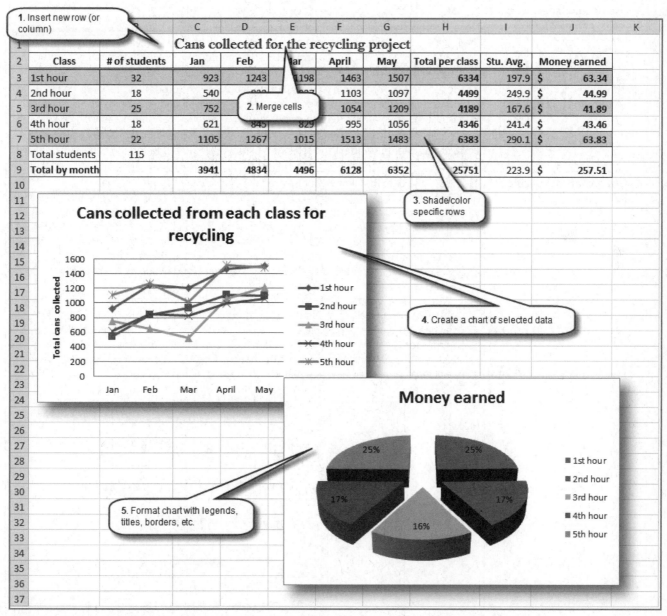

FIGURE 3.11 Mr. Rena's science class's expanded spreadsheet of data of recycled cans with added data charts

1.	**Insert a new row (or column)**	1. To insert a new row, place your cursor in the row (or column) immediately *after* where you want your new row (or column) to appear. 2. Go to **Home** tab >>> **Cells** group >>> **Insert** >>> select the option for **Insert Sheet Rows** (or **Insert Sheet Columns**). The new row is inserted into the sheet directly above (or to the left of) where your cursor was placed.
2.	**Merge cells**	At times it is appropriate to have several cells merge to display data that would usually go beyond the single cell size. In Figure 3.10 this is done to format a title to the data table. 1. Begin by selecting all of the cells that you want to merge. **Note:** The cells must be next to each other in the adjoining row(s) or column(s). 2. Go to **Home** tab >>> **Alignment** group >>> **Merge & Center** gallery button. The cells will be automatically merged. The **Merge & Center** drop-down gallery also allows you the option to merge without centering or to unmerge cells when needed. 3. To format the data in the cell, select the cell(s) and specific data you want to format, then go to **Home** tab >> **Font** group and make your selection from the given alternatives (see Figure 3.8).
3.	**Shade or color specific rows (or cells, columns)** 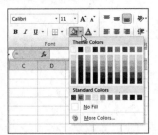	1. Select the row(s), column(s), or cell(s) you wish to shade. **Note:** To select a whole row (or column), click on the number associated with that row (or the letter for the column). The full row will highlight all at once. To select more than one row, press and hold the Control key as you select the various rows you wish to highlight. In this way, multiple rows can be selected at any time. 2. Return to the Font group of tools (**Home** tab >>> **Font** group) and click on the fill button. A grid layout of a color gallery will be displayed and you can make your selection. Select the color and pattern that you wish your selection to contain and then click OK. **Note:** You can also return to the Format Cell dialog box (**Home** tab >>> **Font** group >>> **Font dialog box expander**) and select the fill tab (see Figure 3.8) for additional options.
4.	**Create a chart of specific data**	1. Select the data that you want displayed within the chart. In the first chart of our example, we selected cells A2 through A7 (name of all of Mr. Rena's classes *and* the title of that column (Class). We did this by holding down the Control key and clicking and holding the mouse key down while dragging the pointer from cell A2 down to cell A7. With the Control key continuously held down, recycled can data from C2 to G7 were selected. Note that this included the column month titles as well as the data for each of classes across all of the months. At this point, selected data (and headings) in column A, C, D, E, F, and G were highlighted. 2. With the data selected, click on the Insert tab. Review the possible charts listed on the embedded chart gallery within the Chart group of tools. However, to see a full selection of chart types and the possible derivations of each, click on the Chart group **dialog box expander.** As shown in Figure 3.12, the Insert Chart dialog box will appear. Scrolling allows you to review all of the types of charts available. Select one and click OK. Your selected chart should now be created and inserted within your spreadsheet document. 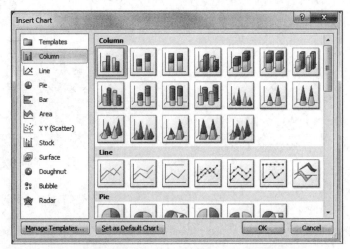 **FIGURE 3.12** Insert Chart dialog box used to select different built-in charts

		Note: If you decide you don't like your selected chart type—no problem. Simply click on the new chart and the Chart tools contextual tab will appear. Go to **Chart Tools/Design** tab >>> **Type** group >>> **Change Chart Type** button. Clicking that button will return you to the Insert Chart dialog box, where you can select a different chart type and start the process over.

Another note: Two mistakes frequently occur: (1) The title of the columns (e.g., *Class, Jan, Feb, Mar*) is not included as the rest of the data is being selected. The spreadsheet may still create the chart, but without the headings the chart will input its own set of titles that may or may not make sense to you. (2) If there is a title above the column headings, make sure you don't accidentally select it so that the chart wizard attempts to include it within the chart. Select only those relevant columns of headings and data.

5.	**Format changes on the chart**	Although charts can be quickly created, often changes to the overall design, layout, or format are needed for the charts to be optimally effective. Several of these possible adaptations have been highlighted in Figure 3.11. To alter charts after they have been created, consider the following steps:

1. For simple editing changes to elements (e.g., titles, legends) that already appear on the chart, simply click directly on the element that you want to change. A box and handles will appear around the element. Words within the box can then be selected and edited or the element's location can be changed by clicking and dragging it to the new location.

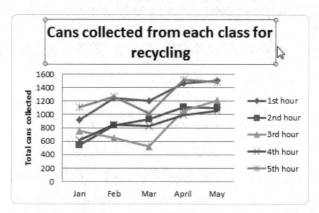

2. For more major changes to the chart (see those highlighted in Figure 3.13), click on the chart to select it. This will cause the Chart Tools contextual tab for Design, Layout, and Format to appear. Use these tabs to access the needed tools for the following changes:

   a. *Change from lines to pies.* If you need to change the overall type of chart (e.g., see Figure 3.11 to view the pie type), go to **Chart Tools/Design** tab >>> **Type** group >>> **Change Chart Type**. The Insert Chart dialog box will appear (see Figure 3.12) and you can select a different type for your data. This is one of the easiest, quickest, and most valuable major change you will ever attempt. *Do it a number of times to make sure your data is presented in the best possible way.*

   b. *Alter axis titles.* If the titles on your chart axis don't appear or are not in the correct position, you can change them by clicking **Chart Tools/Layout** tab >>> **Labels** group, or the **Axes** group of tools.

   c. *Add gridlines.* Play with the types and number of gridlines that can be added to a chart by going to **Chart Tools/Layout** tab >>> **Axes** group >>> **Gridlines** drop-down gallery.

   d. *Include a chart title.* Similar to changing an axis title, chart titles can be altered by going to **Chart Tools/Layout** tab >>> **Labels** group >>> **Chart Title**.

   e. *Include and adapt a legend.* To include a legend within the chart, go to **Chart Tools/Design** tab >>> **Chart Layouts** group >>> review the gallery of layouts and select one with a legend. To alter the position of the legend that has been included within the chart, go to **Chart Tools/Layout** tab >>> **Labels** group >>> **Legend** and select from the drop-down gallery options.

   f. *Add or alter chart border shading.* Border shading can add highlights and dimension to the chart on the spreadsheet page. To do this, go to **Chart Tools/Format** tab >>> **Shape styles** group >>> **Shape Effects** and try various shadow and three-dimensional (3D) alternatives for your chart.

Note: These are only a few of the design, layout, and format changes that can be included within your chart. Create a chart and explore the various options available for use.

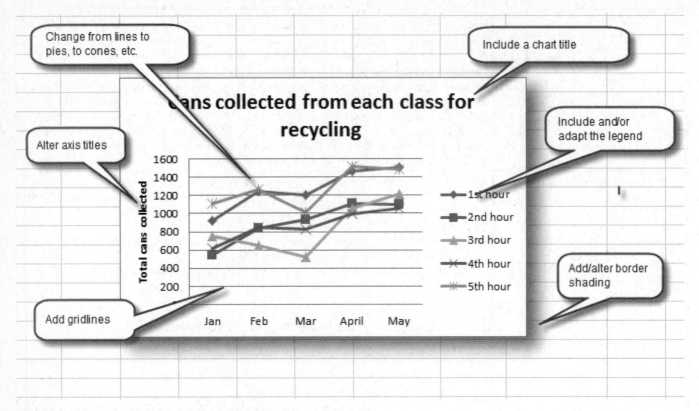

FIGURE 3.13 Example chart with highlighted elements that can be altered

Level 1a Workout: Practice using the basic Excel features

Now it's time for you to practice using this spreadsheet software. With this first Workout, we want you to review all that was presented within the step-by-step procedures. However, there are many other things that were not touched on within this chapter, so as you go about working on this exercise, please explore and experiment with some of the new things you encounter. Later, when you are working on a new project, you may find that those features you discovered are some of the features you find most helpful.

Here is a basic outline of what you need to do:

1. Review Figures 3.7 and 3.11 and all of the various features that have been highlighted within those figures.
2. Go to the text's accompanying website and open the unformatted version of these two figures.
3. Using the given unformatted version, go through the list of features and practice adding them to your spreadsheet. It really isn't that important for you to match the text's example with your product, but try the feature to see how it works and how it can be adapted for your use. Explore and have fun with this. Remember this is a practice Workout—*practice integrating as many features as possible.*

for
Teaching and Learning with Microsoft® Office 2010 and Office 2011 for Mac

Go to PDToolKit for **Teaching and Learning with Microsoft® Office 2010 and Office 2011 for Mac** to locate the mentoring videos for Chapter Three.

Note: Refer to specific feature numbers and the given step-by-step procedures as needed. Additionally, use the mentoring videos to help guide you through any specific procedure that needs further clarification.

PDToolkit
for
Teaching and Learning with Microsoft® Office 2010 and Office 2011 for Mac

Go to PDToolkit for **Teaching and Learning with Microsoft® Office 2010 and Office 2011 for Mac** to locate the mentoring videos for Chapter Three.

Level 1b Workout: Creating your own spreadsheet

To help you transfer the information from the text to something you'll actually use, it is time for you to use this software with some of your own data. You can use a spreadsheet to input and store important data as well as organize, analyze, and present it in new and important

Table 3.1	Level 1 Workout and Practice Checklist: Creating and formatting a spreadsheet
Spreadsheet Content	___ Data was organized (rows and columns) in a clear, logical manner.
	___ Cell content is free from spelling errors.
Document Format	___ A new worksheet within the spreadsheet program was created.
	___ Column and row headings were inserted, aligned, and formatted appropriately.
	___ Cells were populated with data.
	___ Column widths were sized appropriately so that titles and data could be easily read.
	___ Gridlines were incorporated.
	___ Formulas were incorporated to analyze the data.
	___ Selected rows, columns, or cells were colored or shaded.
	___ Charts of the data were created and included within the spreadsheet document.
	___ Charts were easy to read and included titles, a legend, and gridlines (if applicable).
	___ Charts were formatted to highlight the data and the chart itself (e.g., use of shading, colors).

ways. For the Workout, create a spreadsheet that includes your own data. You may get the numbers from your own data collection or you may get them from other sources such as the Internet, textbooks, magazines, and so on. What is important is for you to acquire some numbers that can be input into the spreadsheet, organized, formatted, analyzed, and output in some manner.

Some examples of data that you might use include the following:

- Statistics from some of your favorite sports teams (e.g., softball hitting or pitching statistics)
- Comparisons of birth and death rates for several countries
- Number of illegal downloaded songs on college campuses since 2000
- Boxes of Girl Scout cookies sold and profits made
- Gas prices from various areas of the country or the world at different times during the last few years
- Prices of several different common food or drug items from various stores
- Personal budget of income and expenses for the past six months

As you can see, a wide variety of data can be collected. After you have determined what data you will use, do the following:

1. Open your spreadsheet program and create a draft worksheet that includes columns and rows of your data. Include column and row titles.
2. Review the features demonstrated within Figures 3.7 and 3.11 from Scenarios 1 and 2.
3. Format your new document with as many of the features demonstrated in those figures as possible. Use Table 3.1 as a checklist to guide your efforts.

LEVEL 2: WHAT IFS? AND OTHER GOOD STUFF

What should you be able to do?

In this section we want you to learn to recognize and use additional spreadsheet features as well as to understand how to use the Help feature of the software effectively. With this instruction, you should be able to create, edit, and format several original data sets into a spreadsheet format and use formulas to compare, analyze, and summarize the data.

Getting some Help

Similar to the other Office programs, there is also Help in MS Excel and most other sophisticated spreadsheet software. To use Help, click the Help button on the tab bar of the main ribbon.

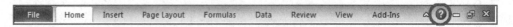

Clicking the Help button opens the Help window (see Figure 3.14). From here you can browse general Help topics, bring up a general table of contents of all Help topics, complete a search for a specific question that you might have, and so on.

By typing in key words or even a full question, Help will respond with a variety of potential answers for you to investigate. Help generally does not have all of the answers but it will have a lot of them. Make sure you become familiar with how it works and how often it can be of assistance.

Scenario 3: "The Store"

Barry Pfleger couldn't believe what he had just been "volunteered" for. As an assistant soccer coach, he was "asked" to take charge of the Woodrow High School Gotta Have It Spirit Store. Originally the store's inventory had been helpful in getting students to purchase and use items like pencils, paper, flags, and clothing—all with the school Whippoorwill logo engraved or embossed. Additionally, the extra revenue, although not great, had been used to purchase a few extra pieces of equipment for various "Fightin' Whipper" athletic teams.

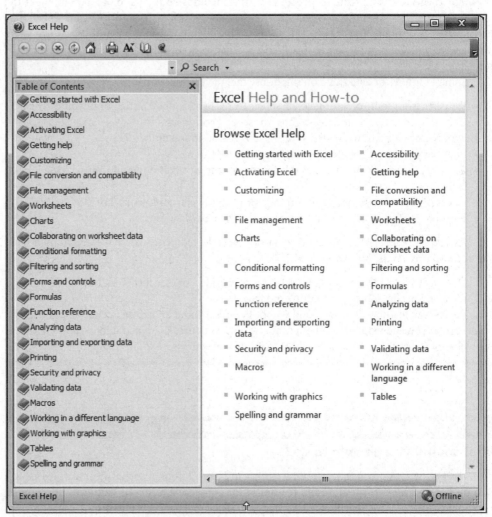

FIGURE 3.14 Excel Help window

Over the course of the last couple of semesters, however, the inventory had gotten old, products weren't ordered correctly, and the store hadn't been open for regular business. Barry was a pretty good English teacher, but he wasn't too sure about learning the retail business. Luckily, Olivia, one of his senior soccer players, noticed his anxiety and offered her help. She explained that her parents owned a small pet store and she was always helping her dad with his books.

"First," she began, "you really need to determine where you are. So, let's get a couple students into the Gotta Have It Store and together we can count everything that it contains. We'll need to get a record of what every item is, how many there are, and if possible the original cost of each." She quickly drew a grid on her coach's clipboard (see Figure 3.15) and labeled the rows Item and the columns Cost and Quantity.

After an afternoon of sorting, counting, and looking through old receipts, Coach Pfleger and Olivia reviewed their completed inventory sheet. Olivia then suggested that the next step would be to re-create it as an electronic spreadsheet. She explained that with the inventory in an electronic format, a formula could be used to calculate the wholesale subtotal. In addition, she suggested adding some columns, such as one for the subtotals for how much the inventory was worth now (wholesale price × the quantity of a specific

Item	Cost	Quantity	...
#1			
#2			
#3			

FIGURE 3.15 Starting of a simple inventory spreadsheet

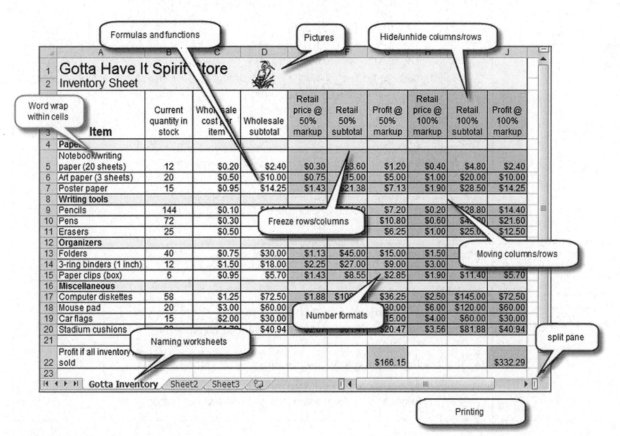

FIGURE 3.16 Gotta Have It inventory

PDToolkit for Teaching and Learning with Microsoft® Office 2010 and Office 2011 for Mac

Go to PDToolkit for **Teaching and Learning with Microsoft® Office 2010 and Office 2011 for Mac** to locate the mentoring videos for Chapter Three.

item) and columns for the subtotals if there were markups of 25%, 50%, or even higher. Olivia explained that as the inventory changed over the next few months, it would be easy to then update the changes on the electronic spreadsheet and the totals would automatically be calculated (see Figure 3.16).

We aren't going to explain exactly how to do each but we will give you the example of the feature and critical questions you can think about and investigate (via the Help feature) to find the needed answers. In addition, mentoring videos have been created, and can be accessed on the website that accompanies this book, which will guide you through the use of each of these features.

Feature	Steps to Get It Done
Using formulas and functions	**Information about and procedure for creating and inserting:** Excel Help • Key word: Formula • Select Quick start: Create a formula and follow the given procedure. • Select Create a formula with functions. **Key features to note, explore, and try out:** • As shown in Features 7, 8, and 9 in Scenario 1 of this chapter, you can create your own simple formula and insert it within a cell. For simple calculations, this is often the quickest and easiest method. • For more advanced calculations, it may be more efficient to click on the Formula bar button (see Figure 3.2) *fx* to produce the Insert Function dialog box (see Figure 3.10). Within this box you can select the functions that have already been developed within Excel. The function wizard will guide you through selecting the correct cells to reference.
Inserting graphics or pictures	**Information about and procedure for accessing and inserting:** Excel Help • Key words: Insert a picture or clip art • Select Insert clip art and follow the given procedure (note that you can also select to insert pictures from the web, a file, and so on). **Key features to note, explore, and try out:** • Once a picture or clip art has been inserted into your spreadsheet, you can click on it and a box and handles will appear around it. You can use the handles to alter the size of the picture or you can click, hold, and drag the picture to a new location. • Once the picture is selected, the contextual Picture Tools/Format tab appears. Within the set of tools you can adjust the picture (e.g., contrast, color), add various border styles, crop it, or alter its size.
Word wrap within cells 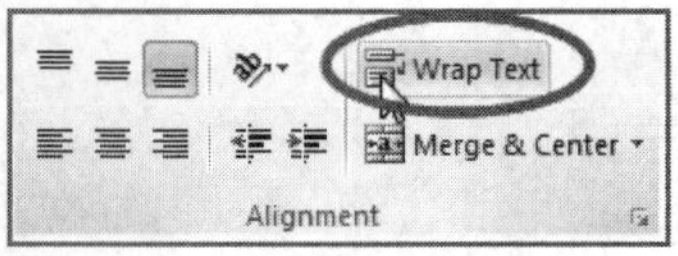 	**Information about and procedure for allowing:** Excel Help • Key words: **Word wrap** (or Text wrap) • Select Wrap text automatically and follow the given procedure **Key features to note, explore, and try out:** • Highlight the cells where you want the text to be wrapped. • Go to **Home** tab >>> **Alignment** group >>> **Word** text button

Freeze panes to lock rows or columns  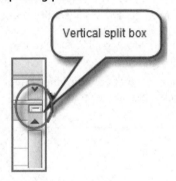	Because spreadsheet can become very long or very wide (thus the name spreadsheet), it often becomes difficult to see and remember specific important information (e.g., column titles) when that info has been scrolled off the screen. At times, it is helpful to freeze an important row (e.g., the row with all of the headers for the columns) so that when scrolling occurs, that specific row (or column) remains in the same position. **Information about and procedure for accomplishing:** **Online help:** www.office.com • Key words: Excel freeze pane • Select the article "Freeze or lock rows and columns" (Excel 2010) and follow the procedures given. **Key features to note, explore, and try out:** • Select a row below or a column to the right of where you want the freeze to occur. • Go to **View** tab >>> **Window** group >>> **Freeze** pane drop-down gallery. • Select the option that you desire. • To unfreeze, return to the Freeze pane drop-down gallery and you will notice that there is now an Unfreeze panes option.
Splitting panes	Similar effect can also be achieved by splitting the pane. This is done by pointing your mouse cursor to the split box located at the top of the vertical scroll bar (used to split the pane horizontally) and to the right of the horizontal scroll bar (used to split the pane vertically). As you go over the split box your pointer will change into a two-headed arrow. Click and drag the split bar down or to the left. When you no longer want the **split pane,** simply double click anywhere on the split bar.
Renaming worksheets	**Information about and procedure for allowing:** Excel Help • Keywords: Sheet tab • Select: Select one or multiple worksheets This will guide you in how to move between various worksheets within the Excel workbook. When you create a workbook, Excel automatically names the worksheets as *Sheet1, Sheet2, Sheet3,* and so on. To be more descriptive, you may want to rename those sheets. This is very easily accomplished: • Double click on the sheet tab of the worksheet you want to rename. See Figure 3.2 and 3.16 in the lower left corner. • Simply type in the new name. 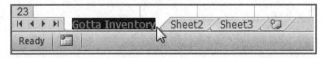

(continued)

Number formats	**Information about and procedure for accomplishing:**
	Excel Help • Key words: Format numbers • Select Quick start: Format numbers in a worksheet and follow the given procedure. **Key features to note, explore, and try out:** • Go to **Home** tab >>> **Number** group and review the different options for how to format the numbers. Don't forget that additional options are given by clicking on the **Number dialog box expander** within that same **Number** group.
Hide or unhide columns and rows	There are times that you may not want some of your rows or columns to be visible. For example, if you want to show grades to a specific student but you don't want to reveal other students' grades within the same spreadsheet, you can hide those other rows or columns of data. **Information about and procedure for accomplishing:** **Online help:** www.office.com • Key words: Excel hide columns • Select the article "Show or hide columns and rows" (Excel 2010) and follow the procedures given. **Key features to note, explore, and try out:** • Select the rows or columns that you want to hide. • Go to **Home** tab >>> **Cells** group >>> **Format** drop-down gallery >>> **Visibility** >>> **Hide&Unhide** >>> **Hide Row (or Hide Columns)**. • You can also use this same procedure to locate and unhide those rows and columns that may have previously been hidden. **Note:** A quick way to accomplish the same thing is to highlight the row or column you wish to hide and then right click on it. This will bring up a shortcut menu that has an option to hide or unhide the selected item.
Move (or copy) columns and rows Paste / Cut / Copy / Format Painter / Clipboard	**Information about and procedure for accomplishing:** Excel Help • Key words: Move columns rows • Select Move or copy rows and columns and follow the given procedure. **Key features to note, explore, and try out:** • Select the row or column that you want to move (or copy). • Go to **Home** tab >>> **Clipboard** group >>> **Cut** (or **Copy**). • Right click on the row below or the column to the right of where you want your respective row or column to be moved. The right click will bring up the shortcut menu. On that menu, select Insert Cut Cells (or Insert Copied Cells). **Note:** A common mistake is to attempt to move or copy a row or column by using the Paste **(Home** tab >>> **Clipboard** group) instead of the Insert Cut (or Copied) Cells. However, if Paste is used, you will find out that you have *replaced* the destination row or column content with that which you wanted to move or copy. Be careful in what you are doing.

Printing	Often when it comes to printing your work, it saves time, paper, and ink if you first preview what will be printed. Through the Print Preview process, you are able to make needed changes prior to the hard copy being produced.
	Information about and procedure for accomplishing:
	Excel Help ❓
	• Key words: Print Preview
	• Select Preview worksheet pages before printing and follow the given procedure.
	• Also select Quick start: Print a worksheet
	Key features to note, explore, and try out:
	• Go to Print Preview by clicking **File** tab >>> **Print**. Print Preview will appear and allow you to review what the worksheet will look like when it is printed.
	• From within Print Preview you can select Page Setup. Page Setup allows you to control these (and other) options for your worksheet.
	• Within this same area, you can adapt the settings, such as:
	○ Control the exact number of pages to be printed
	○ Change the **page orientation** (i.e., Portrait or Landscape orientations).
	○ Set the margins for the printed page(s).
	○ Scale the page (reduce it proportionally) so that it fits to an exact size (this allows you to make sure a worksheet that is a bit too big to be printed on a single page can quickly be resized to fit and print on one page).
	○ Add a header and footer to the printed page(s) (click on the Page Setup button to open the window to allow additional features, including adding headers and footers).

Level 2a Workout: Practice using additional Excel features

Before moving on to your own work, it might be wise to try a few exercises with the Gotta Have It Store.

1. Go to the text's accompanying website and open the unfinished version of Gotta Have It Store.
2. Try to do the following. If you have difficulty, review the procedures given in the step-by-step procedures of the Level 1 scenarios, the suggestions for accessing Help, and the information provided with Scenario 3 and Figure 3.16.
   a. Create additional columns for the different markup retail prices and so on.
   b. Add formulas to calculate the projected markup prices, the subtotals, and grand totals. If easier, try using the Insert Function dialog box to add the needed formulas.
   c. Move the columns or rows from one location to another.
   d. Complete formatting of the worksheet by doing the following:
      • Naming your worksheet
      • Word wrapping the cells that have overly long titles and so forth
      • Adding color to highlight and organize the data
      • Adding relevant pictures, clip art, and so on
   e. Hide and then unhide specific rows or columns.
   f. Freeze panes or split panes to work with the expanded spreadsheet.

PDToolkit
for
*Teaching and Learning with
Microsoft® Office 2010 and
Office 2011 for Mac*

Go to PDToolkit for Teaching and
Learning with Microsoft® Office 2010
and Office 2011 for Mac to locate
Workout Level Two for Chapter Three.

PDToolkit
for
*Teaching and Learning with
Microsoft® Office 2010 and
Office 2011 for Mac*

Go to PDToolkit for Teaching and
Learning with Microsoft® Office 2010
and Office 2011 for Mac to locate
Workout Level Two for Chapter Three.

Note: Each of these key features is demonstrated on the mentoring videos within the website that accompanies this book.

3. Answer the following questions and complete the following tasks:

- What if the markup were 25% or 75%? Create two additional columns in your spreadsheet to reflect these potential changes in markup.
- Create a chart that compares profits for the school given the different retail markup levels (25, 50, 75, and 100%). *Hint:* Use AutoSum to tabulate the total amount of sales and subtract the wholesale cost of the items. This will leave you with the overall profit made by the school at each markup level. Create a chart that highlights these differences.
- How does the use of graphs or visual representations of data aid in the decision-making process for the school store?
- In what ways can the use of a spreadsheet (in particular, the visual representation of data through graphs and charts) assist teachers as they assess students and reflect on classroom strategies and activities?
- How can spreadsheets help with data-driven decision making (using data to justify or confirm choices) in schools?

Now that you have seen a few examples of spreadsheets and how they are constructed and formatted, it is your turn to try your hand at it.

Level 2b Workout: Working with water

Spreadsheets can offer students, teachers, administrators, and school personnel a valuable tool to collect, aggregate, and analyze data. The term *data-driven decision making* is frequently used in educational texts, forums, and agencies to reflect the ability of a school and its stakeholders to pursue change based on evidence rather than a personal preference or whim.

In this Workout, you'll have an opportunity to walk through the basic steps of collecting, aggregating, and analyzing data that has a universal context for all humans: water use. Based on the data you collect and manipulate, you will then be asked to reflect on your findings. Follow these next steps to begin.

Step 1: As a means to demonstrate data collection, aggregation, and analysis, your initial task is to chart your household's water use. Pick a five-day period of time when most members are at home and collect the frequency of the following activities:

- Baths
- Showers
- Teeth brushing
- Hand and face washing
- Face or leg shaving
- Dishwasher
- Dishwashing by hand
- Loads of laundry (machine)
- Toilet flushes
- Glasses of water (for drinking)

There are several ways to tally the frequency of these activities: a household journal in a common location, sticky notes posted throughout the home (next to the kitchen sink, for example) to allow participants to self-report, and so on.

Step 2: Create an Excel spreadsheet to calculate the total use of the household and the number of gallons of water used per person.

- All calculations *must* be done with formulas.
- Be sure to use the following formulas: basic multiplication of cells, division of cells, and SUM.
- *Note:* Showers are the only item that must be multiplied by frequency and length of time.

- Format the cells for visual clarity. Use color and font choice to clearly present your data.
- Use the following data rates to calculate the water use. The rates are *per use:*

Bath: 50 gallons	**Dishwasher:** 20 gallons per load
Shower: 2 gallons per 1 minute	**Dishwashing by hand:** 5 gallons per load
Teeth brushing: 1 gallon	**Clothes washing (machine):** 10 gallons per load
Hands and face washing: 1 gallon	**Toilet flush:** 3 gallons
Face/leg shaving: 1 gallon	**Water to drink:** 8 ounce glass = 0.0625 gallon

Data rates are courtesy of the US Geological Survey (USGS) website at http://ga.water.usgs.gov/edu/sq3.html.

Step 3: Using the data you have collected, create a chart (design of your choice) to represent the water use by the household. Clearly label the components of your chart. Include a descriptive title and legend.

Step 4: Create a MS Word document that includes the chart and incorporates the following discussion components:

- Include a title for the report.
- Compose an introductory paragraph that describes the data-collection process.
- Include the chart in the MS Word document.
- Within the body of the report, address the following questions:
  - Which activity used the most water for your household? Which used the least amount of water?
  - What is the average number of gallons each member of your household used?
  - What other water-using activities occurred in your household that we did not calculate?
- Conclude the report by reflecting on the following questions:
  - The USGS reports that the average US citizen uses 80 to 100 gallons of water per day. Based on this rate, does it seem that your household is above or below the national average of water use? Why do you think that is?
  - Looking at the data you have collected, what steps might members of your household take to further reduce the amount of water used?

Table 3.2 Level 2b Workout and Practice Checklist: Working with water

Spreadsheet Content	___ Content is accurate.
	___ Content is free from spelling and grammatical errors.
	___ Totals for the total water use for the household and the number of gallons of water used per person are calculated and reported.
	___ Proper formulas (e.g., basic multiplication and division of cells, SUM) were used within the spreadsheet.
	___ Proper data rates were used to calculate the water usage.
	___ Proper citation was given for the data rates that were used.
Spreadsheet Format	___ A new worksheet within the spreadsheet program was created.
	___ Column and row headings were inserted, aligned, and formatted appropriately.
	___ Cells were formatted for visual clarity (i.e., gridlines, color, font color, size and style, and so on were used to add clarity and not distract from the data).
	___ Column widths were sized appropriately so that titles and data could be easily read.
	___ A clearly labeled chart was created from the data that represents water use by the household.
Report Content and Format	___ A clearly written, word-processed report that includes a discussion of the data, chart, and overall household water use was completed.
	___ The report is free of grammatical and spelling errors.
	___ The content of the report should include a description of the water use in the household (e.g., which activity uses the least or most water, number of gallons each member used, what additional water-using activities should have been included in the report but were not, better ways to monitor water use).
	___ The report concludes with recommendations of ways to further reduce the amount of water used within a household.

LEVEL 3: INTEGRATION AND APPLICATION IN THE CLASSROOM

What should you be able to do?

Here is where you get to actually use this software to help yourself and your students. This section aims to help you begin to see all of the many applications that are possible when you use a spreadsheet. You should be able to use these examples as a springboard to launch ideas on ways to improve levels of student learning and your personal productivity.

Introduction

For many of us, thinking of spreadsheets generally conjures up thoughts of a fancy grade book. That's fine. However, it's time for you to expand on this a bit—and perhaps to see this as a tool for a wide variety of tasks as well as a tool to help your students learn. Read and reflect on the examples given in this section. Think about ways you can integrate spreadsheets into your life and your curriculum. There will be times when integrating Excel or some similar spreadsheet will enhance the overall learning of the student.

Spreadsheet integration

Creating the enhanced learning experience: A partial lesson plan

TOPIC:

A study of the people, places, and cultures of an African country.

OVERVIEW:

As explained in Chapter 2 ("Word Processing"), Mr. Carpenter is an eighth-grade social studies teacher at Lowell Middle School and he is beginning a unit of study on the African country of Zimbabwe. One of his past students, Jonathon Rogers is a graduate student working on an internship for an international health and education organization located in Zimbabwe. During the next school year, Mr. Carpenter wants his students to gather and exchange information about the Zimbabwean people and country with Jonathon's help. Through Jonathon's work assignment, he will be visiting many schools as well as health facilities. Mr. Carpenter's classes hope they will be able to contact Jonathon through the postal service, e-mail, and voice-over Internet protocol (e.g., Skype) to gather their desired information.

      One goal of the instructional unit is for the students to discover what life is like in another country and culture. Through various discussions, Mr. Carpenter's classes identified several relevant points of interest that they wanted to examine and use to make comparisons.

SPECIFIC LEARNING TASK:

One specific area of interest was of the types and amounts of food eaten by similarly aged students in the two countries. The goal was to gather data from students in both countries on what they commonly eat. Once gathered, cross-country comparisons could be examined as well as comparisons with governmental nutritional guidelines.

SAMPLE LEARNING OBJECTIVES:

Students will be able to do the following:

1. Describe the most common foods eaten by the sample of students from the two different cultures.
2. Identify and describe foods common between the two cultures.
3. Based on the collected data, identify potential discrepancies between US governmental nutritional needs of students in both countries.

PROCEDURE:

1. Subdivide each of Mr. Carpenter's eighth-grade classes into three research groups.

   - *Research Group A:* This group will gather and report data on common food eaten by a sample of students in Mr. Carpenter's class.
   - *Research Group B:* This group will work with Jonathon and gather data on common food eaten by a similar sample of same-aged Zimbabwean students.
   - *Research Group C:* This group will research government-suggested nutritional information on the types and amounts of food that should be eaten by similarly aged students.

2. Create small data journals to collect data on foods eaten. Each journal should have a place to record the type and amount of food eaten during the morning, afternoon, and evening of each day for a fourteen-day time period. Also include instructions for the students to describe foods that individuals from other cultures may not recognize.

3. Randomly select ten students (five girls and five boys) from Mr. Carpenter's class and contact Jonathon to see if he likewise can get ten participants from one of the schools he's working with.

4. Have Jonathon review the data journals and ask for any needed clarification on food types and so on and then e-mail the completed journals to Lowell Middle School. Members of Groups A and B will examine their respective journals and enter the data received.

5. Group C will record the suggested governmental types and amounts of food.

6. Students will compare the data from the two countries and the suggested governmental standards and

   a. Determine most common food eaten within each country

   b. Determine foods commonly eaten by students in both countries

   c. Determine general nutritional value of the common foods eaten by the individual students in both countries

   d. Present a data chart that illustrates the comparisons between countries and the standards

7. Write a short paper about a proposed visit to Zimbabwe and what types of food they could expect to encounter. Use the data chart to identify which foods they would be excited about trying and what foods they probably would try to avoid.

QUESTIONS ABOUT SPREADSHEET INTEGRATION:

This lesson could be completed in a number of ways. One specific method would be to use a spreadsheet, such as Excel, to help gather, analyze, and report the results of the collected data. Use these reflective questions to explore the value of potentially integrating a spreadsheet within such a lesson as outlined by Mr. Carpenter.

- How can spreadsheets be used by the teacher and the students within this lesson plan? Provide at least two examples of use for each.
- What could be added to a spreadsheet to further compare the nutritional value of the food consumed? In other words, what type of a column could be included to provide students with a means to rank the nutritional value of the reported types of food consumption?
- After you have entered such a column (e.g., nutritional value), which features or tools of Excel could be used to manipulate and analyze the data?
- In addition to nutritional value, what other types of data on food consumption could be collected to assist in the cultural comparison?
- Which type of chart would be most helpful in providing a cultural comparison based on food consumption? Would more than one chart be necessary? Explain.
- How could this data (numerical and via charts) be used to aid the students in creating long-term predictions regarding the health of all groups of students?
- How could this data (numerical and via charts) be used to make recommendations for dietary change?

- What types of follow-up activities could accompany this lesson plan? What types of projects (individual or class) could be built on this data collection and analysis? Describe at least two distinct, student-centered learning projects.
- What if a teacher does not have access to a colleague in Zimbabwe? What are some alternative methods or resources for gathering a similar set of comparative data?

Level 3a Workout: Integrating spreadsheets

This is a good time for your practice. First, reflect on the partial lesson plan given previously. Next, think about the use of spreadsheets within applied classroom settings. Finally, work through each of the following steps.

1. Read each of the following situations. Imagine being directly involved in the planning for each of these projects. Select one (or more if you wish) for further consideration.

Favorite Color:

A third-grade teacher at Johnson Elementary asked his students to tell him which color was the most preferred. To investigate, he had his students go out after school for ten consecutive days and identify and record 20 different human-made items that they encountered (e.g., vehicles, houses, clothes). They were to report each item and its main color. From their findings they were to determine which was the most recorded color, the least used color, and if certain items were colored more frequently one color than another.

Holiday Wrap:

For a school project, the seventh-grade students of Mayflower Middle School have decided to open a gift wrapping business at one of the small center shops in the local mall. They need to project their costs for the coming months of September through December. They also need to show how many volunteers should be working at any one time for all of the shifts. Additionally, they need to show the amount of projected money they will earn based on the number of boxes wrapped, size of the box, and time required to wrap. Last, they need to consider if competition from other gift wrapping stores should be considered and what can be done to affect their overall prices.

Utilities Manager:

How much raw sewage is processed each day at the local sewage treatment plant? Which days of the week produce the highest and lowest amounts of sewage? Are there typically high and low months or weeks of the year? Based on charts of processed sewage, identify potential causes of the fluctuations in the amount of sewage that is treated.

Growth Rate:

Is there a way to compare the population growth rate of different countries of the world and then predict which ones may have problems in the future based on rapid, stagnant, or decreasing growth rates? Which areas of the world would you predict would have the greatest amount of worry in the next few decades based on their current level of population growth?

2. Based on your selected project, consider the following questions that concern the integration of word processing. Mark your response to each question.

Integration assessment questionnaire (IAQ)

Will using spreadsheet software as a part of the project:	
Broaden the learners' perspective on potential solution paths and answers?	__Yes __ No __ Maybe
Increase the level of involvement and investment of personal effort by the learners?	__Yes __ No __ Maybe
Increase the level of learner motivation (e.g., increase the relevance of the to-be-learned task, the confidence of dealing with the task, and the overall appeal of the task)?	__Yes __ No __ Maybe
Decrease the time needed to generate potential solutions?	__Yes __ No __ Maybe
Increase the quality and quantity of learner practice working on this and similar projects?	__Yes __ No __ Maybe
Increase the quality and quantity of feedback given to the learner?	__Yes __ No __ Maybe
Enhance the ability of the student to solve novel but similar projects, tasks, and problems in the future?	__Yes __ No __ Maybe

3. If you have responded "yes" to one or more of the IAQ questions, you should consider using a spreadsheet to enhance the student's potential learning experience.
4. Using the example lesson plan, develop a lesson plan based on your selected project. Within the plan, indicate how and when the learner will use a spreadsheet. Additionally, list potential benefits and challenges that may occur when involving this software in the lesson.

Level 3b Workout: Exploring the NETS connection

PART A: Once you have an understanding of the features and applications of general spreadsheet skills, it is important to provide a context for the professional purpose that these skills can have in the classroom. By using the National Educational Technology Standards (NETS) developed by the International Society for Technology in Education (ISTE), the next few tasks will provide a foundation for the importance of integrating this chapter's skill set into any teacher's professional practice. There are two sets of NETS: one designed for the skills needed by teachers (NETS-T), the other for the skills needed by K–12 students (NETS-S). A complete listing of these standards can be found in the Appendix of this book.

PART B: The following chart provides examples of how the use of a spreadsheet application can directly align with the NETS-T and the NETS-S. As you read these strategies, try to consider additional connections that could be made between these standards and this set of skills. Additionally, consider the answer to the focus questions presented for each unique standard.

NETS-T and NETS-S	Example Activities and Focus Questions
NETS-T 1. Facilitate and Inspire Student Learning and Creativity NETS-S 1. Creativity and Innovation	• Use surveys to collect data and feedback regarding an issue at a school. Manipulate the data through the use of a spreadsheet to aid in discussing the issue or streamlining the decision-making process. • Create multiple charts from the same data set to demonstrate how data can be manipulated through its visual representation. • Collect, store, and compare monthly temperature averages for key cities in strategic locations of the world. Compare those averages with the average temperatures of the students' home town. **1.** How could a teacher inspire an artistic student to find creative outlets through a spreadsheet? **2.** Why is it important to teach students to read graphs and charts in a scientific manner?
NETS-T 2. Design and Develop Digital-Age Learning Experiences and Assessments	• Record and chart student performance through the use of an individual grade book. (Of course, the teacher would still maintain the official grade book.) Create charts to showcase the student's areas of strength and weakness.

(continued)

NETS-S 4. Critical Thinking, Problem Solving, and Decision Making	• Conduct role-play scenarios in which students must develop a budget to save for a class field trip, purchase, or donation. Use spreadsheets to keep accurate records, develop a weekly goal, and make predictions about the final outcome. • Have the students compare the amount of soda, juice, and water that is purchased from the school's vending machines during different times of the day, days of the week, or months of the year. They could also calculate the amount of money earned by the school from these machines given the cost of the repair and maintenance. **3.** Consider the aspects of spreadsheets that may enhance the exploration of alternative problem analyses, data comparisons, predictions, and ultimate solutions. How does the what-if? capabilities afforded by spreadsheets allow increased levels of creative problem solving? **4.** Practically speaking, how could a spreadsheet be used to organize data in the classroom for students? **5.** How can a spreadsheet improve how the collection, analysis, and assessment of student work or data are completed? Could this increased information be used to improve the learning environment and experience?
NETS-T 3. Model Digital-Age Work and Learning NETS-S 2. Communication and Collaboration NETS-S 3. Research and Information Fluency	• Use spreadsheets to accurate aggregate data that will be used in a report or persuasive paper. • Complete a class survey and present the findings to peers. Develop corresponding graphics that are visually appealing and demonstrative of the findings. • Have students guess what the most popular color of cars or truck is and then have them count the different colors that pass on a street near the school during a twenty-minute time period. Analyze the data and graph the results. **6.** How could a teacher best demonstrate the ability of spreadsheets to regularly aid in the decision-making process? **7.** How early can a child learn about data-driven decision making? Explain. **8.** In what ways could spreadsheets be used to facilitate the communication and collaboration among teachers, students, parents, and subject matter experts on specific projects that ultimately affect student learning?
NETS-T 4. Promote and Model Digital Citizenship and Responsibility NETS-S 5. Digital Citizenship NETS-S 3. Research and Information Fluency	• Read an article that contains a data set appropriate to the age of your students. Have all students create a chart to illustrate what they felt was the most critical component of the article. Compare and contrast the completed charts along with the selected focus of the data. **9.** Why is it important to teach students to be strong consumers of information? **10.** How could a classroom teacher help to strengthen the analytical skills of parents? Would this benefit the classroom? Why or why not?
NETS-T 5. Engage in Professional Growth and Leadership	• Develop a professional development library of best practices and findings within a spreadsheet. Search for key terms or concepts when needed. • Regularly read articles from the field to maintain currency of content and skills of data analysis. **11.** Why is it important for teachers to continually contribute to the field of education? **12.** How important is it for teachers to be critical consumers of the findings presented in the field? Explain.

Collaborating and coauthoring in Excel 2010

As explained in Chapter 2 ("Word Processing"), collaboration is a key expectation and is highlighted within the NETS. Similar to Word, Excel spreadsheet documents can also be created, evaluated, and adjusted by groups of individuals working on the same document or spreadsheet but at different times and in different locations. In this case, the same process is used (e.g., first obtaining a Windows Live SkyDrive account; available at www.skydrive.live.com). Within this free Internet storage space, you can create synched folders to store your Excel documents. Others who have access to the synched folders can likewise go to their SkyDrive accounts and open the exact same document from their location. As long as they have an Internet connection, they can access your synched file and the documents therein whether they are in the next room, next city, state, country, or continent. This opens up all types of opportunities for individuals to combine efforts and use the power of teams to accomplish tasks. It helps individuals to learn how to work together and it allows individuals to develop skills at evaluating the contributions of others. Think of possible ways that Excel spreadsheets and charts could be co-developed by teams of individuals. For example:

- Students could develop a single data spreadsheet to report the data they are collecting for an experiment. These students could be from different classes at various schools in vastly different locations—all using the same data sheet to report their findings.
- Girl Scouts ordering boxes of Girl Scout cookies could access the unit's common spreadsheet to update the current number of cases of cookies that need to be placed on the next order.
- A budget spreadsheet showing expenditures and incomes for a small organization or even a family could be developed and multiple individuals could access and adjust data as the month progressed.
- In a statewide competition, a spreadsheet used to tally the judges' rankings could be accessible and useable by all competition officials statewide.

Further ideas on using the spreadsheet as a learning tool

Note: These ideas are to help you generate your own thoughts of what can be done. Don't let it bother you if they're not the right content or grade level; use the idea and adapt it to be helpful within your own situation. These are meant to be a stimulus for additional ideas.

Here are a few ideas that may help you see how a spreadsheet might be beneficial:

1. Give or generate a set of data and have students analyze and summarize the data by developing different formulas (e.g., means, standard deviations) to compare the results.
2. Have the students develop a survey, then collect, record, and analyze the data using statistical functions within the spreadsheet. Moreover, use the chart feature to report the data that they collected.
3. Collect, store, and compare monthly temperature averages for key cities in strategic locations of the world. Compare those averages with the average temperatures of the students' home town.
4. Have the students collect data on the growth (e.g., height, loss of teeth) of their classmates during the course of a school year. Compare that data with students in other classes, other grades, other schools, or other countries.
5. Have students develop a personal budget for their current level of living. Also have them budget for when they enter college, the military, or the work force.
6. Have students create a sign-up chart for using specific items within the classroom (e.g., a special learning center, the computer, a special place to sit and read).
7. In a business class, have students monitor the price of specific stocks and note trends that may suggest optimal buying or selling times.
8. In a physical education class, have students create a spreadsheet that collects and analyzes weekly efforts in speed, endurance, strength, and so on.
9. Have students maintain a statistical record of their favorite professional sports star and compare performance levels across several years.
10. Have students design a judge's rating sheet for a club or sport (e.g., gymnastic, dancing, skating, diving).
11. Using the rows and columns of a spreadsheet, have the students design a sign-up sheet for use of the computer lab. This could also be converted to be used as a work assignment sheet for various jobs in the classroom on different days of the week.
12. With the rows and columns as a guide, have students develop crossword puzzles covering key words in a history, geography, science, or other school subject lesson.

Additional ideas for using a spreadsheet as an assistant

1. *Grade book.* Student scores can be recorded, edited, sorted, summarized, and reported with relative ease.
2. *Life organizer.* With all of those columns and rows, a spreadsheet is a good tool for developing a calendar or a daily meeting or work schedule. If you need to develop a set schedule for the lab, the spreadsheet can easily be formatted to display the times in a clear manner. It also works well to create quick and easy seating charts.
3. *Estimator.* Use it to record the current state and progress of students' efforts and then estimate where goals should be set. For example, a teacher in a high school weight-lifting class can record a student's name, current weight, lifting capabilities, and then project what

future goals for lifting should be set. The charting function allows for these goals to be shown in a visual manner. *Note:* This is also a good thing for personal weight management programs (those things we refer to as *diets* and *watching our weight*).

4. ***Personal budgets.*** Create a list of daily, weekly, monthly expenses and income to monitor what can or can't be afforded.

5. ***Calculator.*** Calculate mortgage rates and the monthly cost of owning a home.

6. ***Schedules.*** Develop time sheets for a small business and the work schedules of the employees. This can also be adapted for work schedules for individuals on school projects.

7. ***Money tracker.*** Use it to account for all fundraiser money sales, book order sales, lunch money, and so forth.

MS Excel for Mac 2011

ORIENTATION

This section assumes you have previewed the full Chapter 3 and have a grasp of the general workings of the spreadsheet. This section of the chapter focuses specifically on the use of MS Excel that has been created to work on the Macintosh operating system. In most cases, there is a close similarity to how MS Excel for the PC (Excel 2010) functions, but there are some unique differences that we will highlight within this addendum.

What's the MS Excel for Mac 2011 workspace look like?

Figure 3.17 is an example of MS Excel for Mac 2011.

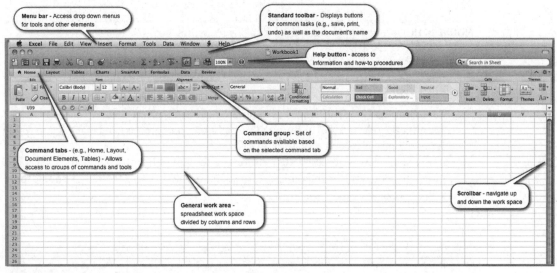

FIGURE 3.17 View of a Microsoft Excel for Mac work area

What commands can be used?

Within the Mac version of MS Office, there are drop-down menu options (see Figure 3.18) and a ribbon of tools that runs across the top of the work screen. So, for example, if you wished to insert a chart into your document, you could accomplish that by going to the **Menu** bar >>> **Insert** drop-down menu >>> **Chart.**

Likewise, you could use the ribbon and click on the **Chart** tab >>> **Insert Chart** command group >>> **Chart** button. To remain consistent with the MS Office 2010 PC version, we will focus most of our comments on using the ribbon to accomplish the tasks within this text. Some basic things to note about the

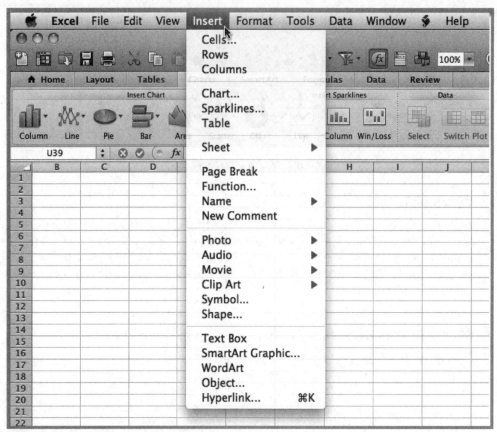

FIGURE 3.18 View of the Menu bar with drop down Insert menu revealed

use of the ribbons:

- The command groups change based on the command tab selected.
- Many of the selected tool buttons within the command groups can be opened to reveal galleries of options related to that tool.
- Contextual tabs with associated contextual command groups appear when a specific object like a chart, formula, picture, graphic, or table is selected in the spreadsheet (see Figure 3.19).

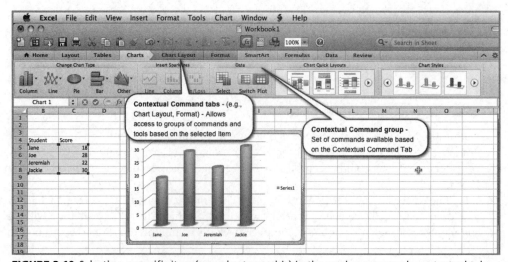

FIGURE 3.19 Selecting a specific item (e.g., chart, graphic) in the workspace reveals contextual tabs and associated contextual commands that can be accessed and used with the selected item

Orientation Workout

Return to the Orientation Workout on page 81 of this text and complete it as it is designed. The main purpose of this Workout is to get you familiar with how to enter data, work with formulas, and so on within the workspace as well as accessing and using the various tools on the menu bar and ribbons.

LEVEL 1: DESIGNING, CREATING, AND PRODUCING A USEFUL DATA-BASED CLASS PROJECT

Scenario 1

To accomplish this Level 1 task, review Scenario 1 (page 82), specifically focusing on Figure 3.7 and the text formatting features highlighted by the callouts within that figure. Using Figure 3.7 as a guide, re-create that document by following these steps:

No.	Feature	Steps to Get It Done
1.	**Create a new worksheet**	1. Launch Excel. If a new worksheet doesn't appear, click on the File menu and select New Workbook. **Note:** When you select the File menu, you can also choose to open various Excel spreadsheet templates (e.g., **New from Template** >>> **Consultant Time Tracker**).
2.	**Insert, align, and format column headings**	1. To insert a column heading, click on the cell where you want the heading to be inserted. For our example, click on cell A1 and then type the word *Class*. Hit the tab key and cell B1 will be highlighted. Type in *Jan*. Hit the tab key and continue until all of the headings have been entered. 2. To align the contents of a cell (column or row), highlight the cell you wish to align and then click on the Home tab and select your preferred alignment from the Alignment group (e.g., left, center, right) as shown in Figure 3.20. 3. To format items in a cell (row or column), select what you wish to format and then click the type of formatting (e.g., font type, size, boldface, italic) that you desire (**Home** tab >>> **Font** group). See Figure 3.20 for examples of the highlighted formatting features.

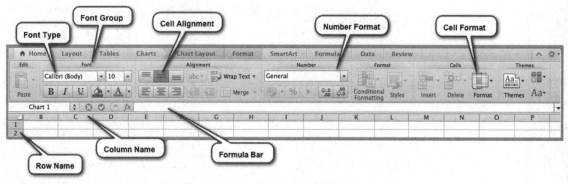

FIGURE 3.20 Home tab with various formatting commands highlighted

3.	**Enter classes and the main data of the spreadsheet**	1. Click on a cell (e.g., A2) and enter in the name of the first class of Mr. Rena. Click on the tab key and enter that class's total cans donated during the month of January, click the tab key and enter the total for the second month of the project, and continue until all classes and their respective data have been entered. Leave the Total per class column empty of all data. Additionally, don't put any data in for the Total by month row. We'll do that in just a minute. 2. If any entry errors are made, click on the cell and go to the Formula bar and make the needed editorial changes.

(continued)

4.	**Adjust column width (or row height)**	1. Directly beneath the Formula bar, each column is labeled with a letter. Click on the letter of the column that you wish to adjust (e.g., A). The whole column will be highlighted. Then move your mouse pointer to the line that divides the target column and the next adjoining column. The pointer will change into a two-headed arrow. 2. With the two-headed arrow showing, click and hold the mouse, and drag it to the right or left. 3. When you have determined the correct size, release the mouse and the column size has been altered. **Note:** This same procedure works for adjusting the height of rows. **Another note:** To be precise, you can set a column width or a row height to an exact measurement (go to **Home** tab >>> **Cells** group >>> **Format** >>> select the option for column width or row height).
5.	**Add gridlines**	1. Select all of the cells, rows, or columns where you want the gridlines or borders to be displayed. 2. Go to the Format Menu and select Cells. 3. Choose the Border tab and select the type of gridline you desire (check out the different line styles, colors, thicknesses, and placements available).
6.	**Formatting cells (and the things in them)**	1. To change the alignment of column headings, cell data, and so on, select the cells you want to format. For example, select all of the headings from cell A1 to G1. Refer to Figure 3.20 and Feature 2 (steps 2 and 3—formatting column headings). 2. Go to **Home** tab >>> **Font** group to see the options you have available to use. For additional options, select the **Format** menu >>> **Cells**. 3. To change font style, click the Font tab and select the type, style, size, color, and any other effects that you desire. Click the OK button and what you selected will be applied to all selected cells. 4. To change the alignment (center, left, right, and so on) or to change the direction of the words within your selected cell(s), click on the Alignment group. **Note:** At times you may wish to have certain cells (e.g., column headings) type the words vertically or at a slant. This Format Cells window is where you make such changes. 5. Other cell formatting functions include choosing borders for the cells, adding patterns to the cells, and protecting the cells in certain ways. All of these functions are completed through this Format Cells window. **Note:** Excel also has predefined styles that can be readily accessed **Home** tab >>> **Themes** group to format cells. 6. Changing the cell format. It is also possible to modify the way in which Excel views the data contained in the cell. Select the cell. From the **Home** tab >>> **Number group** select the drop-down menu to select the type of format you wish to apply.
7.	**Inserting a formula to calculate a total**	1. Click on cell G2. This is the cell where the overall total for the first-hour class (sum of all cans collected over the spring semester by the first-hour class) should be calculated. 2. Instead of manually entering the total here, we'll enter a formula that tells the spreadsheet how to complete the calculations and then to post the result in this cell. 3. On the Formula bar (see Figure 3.20) enter the following equation: =Sum(B2:F2). This translates into Sum up all of the totals found in cells B2 through F2 and put the total in cell G2.

8.	**Use the fill handle**	1. Once one formula has been constructed as in G2, you can use that same one for all of the other totals that need to be calculated in the Total per class column (G2 through G6). Click on cell G2.
		2. A box will be drawn around the total that now appears in that cell. Note that in the lower right-hand corner a small black square (known as a *handle*) appears. Place your cursor over that small handle and it will turn into a thin cross.
		3. Click and hold the mouse and drag it from cell G2 to G6. Release the mouse and the formula you created in G2 has been filled into all of the other cells below it relative to the data in each cell's respective row.
		Note: Another way of completing this fill command is to enter the formula (or whatever you want to fill) into the cell (e.g., G2 in our example), select that cell and all other cells that you want to fill, then go to **Home** tab **>>> Edit** group **>>> Fill** button. 
9.	**More formulas and fills**	1. Click on cell B8 and enter the following formula on the Formula bar: =Average(B2:B6). Hit the Enter key and the average of all classes for number of recycled cans for January is now reported in cell B8.
		2. Click on B8, find the handle, and click, hold, and drag to the right. This should efficiently fill in the averages for all of the rest of the months as well as the total-per-class columns.
		Note: The spreadsheet has lots of built-in formulas. To view these click **Formula** tab **>>> Function** group. The Reference button is a very helpful resource to learn more about the available functions and their purpose. The Formula Builder button will walk a new user through the steps of applying a formula to data.
		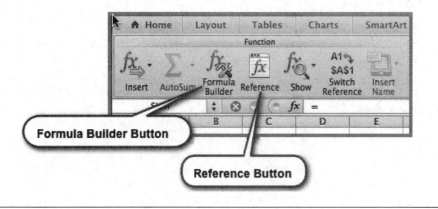

Scenario 2

To accomplish this Level 1 task, review Scenario 2 (page 87), especially focusing on Figure 3.11 and the specific text formatting features highlighted by the callouts within that figure. Using Figure 3.11 as a guide, re-create that document by following these steps. Figure 3.21 identifies different features of the Mac Excel 2011 spreadsheet program that may be accessed and used to complete this task.

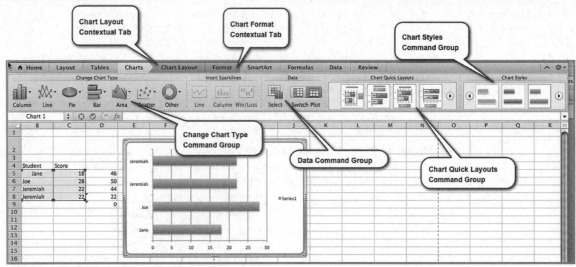

FIGURE 3.21 Charts

No.	Feature	Steps to Get It Done
1.	Insert a new row (or column)	1. To insert a new row, place your cursor in the row (or column) immediately after where you want your new row (or column) to appear. 2. Go to **Home** tab >>> **Cells** group >>> **Insert** >>> select the option for **Insert Rows** (or **Insert Columns**). The new row is inserted into the sheet directly above (or to the left of) where your cursor was placed.
2.	Merge cells	1. Select/highlight all of the cells that you want to merge. **Note:** The cells must be next to each other in the adjoining row(s) or column(s). 2. Go to **Home** tab >>> **Alignment** group >>> **Merge** gallery button. The cells will be automatically merged.
3.	Shade or color specific rows (or cells, columns)	1. Select the row(s), column(s), or cell(s) you wish to shade. 2. **Home** tab >>> **Font** group >>> **Fill Color** button (the **Fill Color** button looks like a paint can). Select the color or pattern that you wish your selection to contain and then click OK.
4.	Create a chart of specific data	1. Select the data you want displayed within the chart. In the first chart of Figure 3.11, we selected cells A2 through G7. Do this by holding down the Command key and clicking and holding the mouse key down while dragging the pointer from cell A2 down to cell G7. Selected data (and headings) in columns A, C, D, E, F, and G will then be highlighted. 2. With the data selected, click on theCharts Command tab. Review the possible charts listed on the embedded chart gallery and select your preference within the Chart group of tools. **Note:** To review other options for chart types, click on the new chart and the Charts contextual tab will appear. Go to the **Chart Layout** tab >>> **Change Chart Type** contextual command group.

5.	Format changes on the chart	Often charts need to be adapted in various ways. Several of these possible adaptations have been highlighted in Figure 3.13. To alter charts after they have been created, consider the following steps:
		1. For simple editing changes to elements (e.g., titles, legends) that already appear on the chart, simply click directly on the element that you want to change. A box and handles will appear around the element. Words within the box can then be selected and edited or the element's location can be changed by clicking and dragging it to the new location.
		2. Use the Chart Layout contextual tab and the Chart Format contextual tab to make changes to the overall design and layout of the chart.
		  a. *Alter titles, legends, data tables, and gridlines.* Select the chart. Click on the Chart Layout contextual tab and select the appropriate button for the changes you need to make. Each button has a drop-down menu of options specific for the item being modified.
		  b. *Alter format or stylistic elements.* Select the chart. Click on the Chart Format contextual tab. . Several command groups will appear including: Chart Element Styles, Text Styles, Arrange, and Size. Select the command group and appropriate button for the changes you need to make.

Level 1a and 1b Workouts

Return to the Level 1a and 1b Workouts found on pages 90 and 91, respectively. Complete the Workouts using Figures 3.7 and 3.11 as guides for your work.

LEVEL 2: TABLES, TEMPLATES, AND OTHER GOOD STUFF

What should you be able to do?

The focus within Level 2 is to help you use Help and other resources to access and use various other features of the MS Excel application.

Similar to Help in Windows, there is also Help in MS Excel and most other sophisticated spreadsheet software. To use Help, click the Help button on the tab bar of the standard toolbar (see Figure 3.17).

As shown in Figure 3.22 you can also access the help function through the Help drop-down menu on the menu bar.

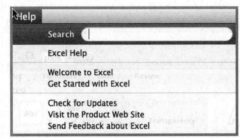

FIGURE 3.22 Accessing Help through the main menu bar in MS Excel for Mac

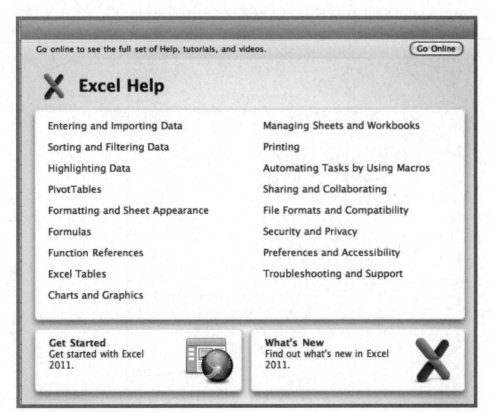

FIGURE 3.23 Excel Help window for Mac

Clicking the Excel Help button opens the Help window (see Figure 3.23). From here you can browse general Help topics, enter key words to search for a specific question that you might have, explore addition online Help topics, review tutorials to help you get started, and so on.

Scenario 3

To expand your capabilities and begin to see how Help can be accessed and used to find additional features, review Scenario 3 on page 92, paying close attention to Figure 3.15 and the callouts of its various features. Using Figure 3.16 as a guide, practice using the highlighted features by accessing and using each of the following word processing features.

Feature	Steps to Get It Done
Using formulas and functions	Within Excel Help • Key words: Formula • Select: Create a simple formula and follow the given procedure. • For more advanced calculations, it may be more efficient to click on the Formula bar button (see Figure 3.20) to produce the Insert Function dialog box and then select from the available functions.
Inserting graphics or pictures	Within Excel Help • Key words: Add picture • Select: Add or replace a picture and follow the given procedure.
Word wrap within cells	Within Excel Help • Key words: Word wrap • Select: Fix data that is cut off in cells and follow the given procedure. • **Home** tab >>> **Alignment** group >>> **Word wrap** button is another way to accomplish this.
Freeze panes to lock rows or columns	Within Excel Help • Key words: Freeze panes • Select: Freeze rows and columns and follow the given procedure.
Renaming worksheets	When you create a workbook, Excel automatically names the worksheets as *Sheet1, Sheet2, Sheet3*, and so on. To be more descriptive, you may want to rename those sheets. This is very easily accomplished: • As shown in Figure 3.24, highlight the sheet tab of the worksheet you want to rename. • Simply type in the new name. 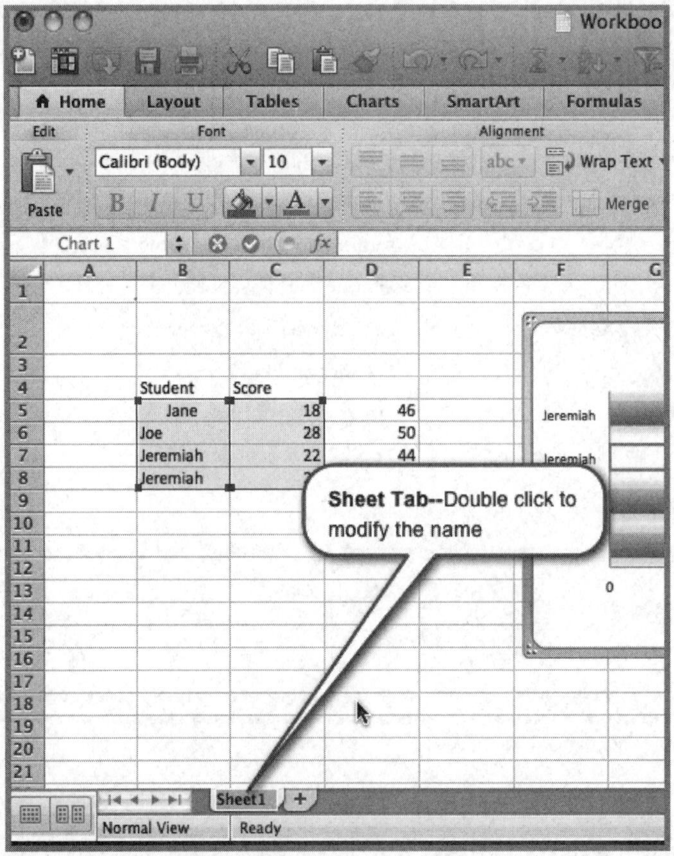

FIGURE 3.24 Renaming a worksheet

Hide or unhide columns and rows	There are times that you may not want some of your rows or columns to be visible and thus you can hide specific rows or columns of data.
	Within Excel Help
	• Key words: Hide columns • Select: Display or hide rows or columns and follow the given procedure. • Go to **Home** tab >>> **Cells** group >>> **Format drop-down gallery** >>> **Hide Row** (or **Hide Columns**).
Move (or copy) columns and rows	Within Excel Help
	• Key words: Move columns rows • Select: Move or copy cells, rows, or columns and follow the given procedure.
Printing	Within Excel Help
	• Key words: Print Preview • Select: Preview pages before printing and follow the given procedure. • Also review Print a sheet or notebook and Print a sheet on just one page.

Level 2 Workout

Return to the Level 2a and 2b Workouts found on pages 97 and 98, respectively. Complete the Workout using Figure 3.16 as a guide.

4 DATA MANAGEMENT

More MS Excel: The Basics of Collecting, Organizing, and Retrieving Loads of Information

INTRODUCTION

What should you be able to know and do?

In a world where we have access to a huge amount of information, having a way to organize, store, and retrieve that information is critical. Databases help you select, compare, and identify information that can lead to more effective learning and decision making. Within this introduction to databases, we want you to discover the following:

- What a **database** is, what it can do, and how it can help in teaching and learning
- How to justify the use of the database as an effective tool—by knowing when and why it should or shouldn't be used

Terms to know			
Boolean searches	field	mail merge	search
database	filter	record	sort

What is a database and what does it do?

Databases are exactly what the name implies—bases for specific data. They are specialized storage bins where one can place information and then later recall it. The trick is knowing how to get the information into the database so that it can later be located and recalled. Databases are incredibly important in a society that needs access to all kinds of information. How that information is organized is very important—or finding it can become a very arduous task.

A familiar example of an old and new database can be found in many libraries. Years ago (although it really hasn't been that long ago), most libraries had a large catalog of 3-by-5-inch cards that contained information about each of the books in the library. To find a book, you first went to the card catalog and looked for a card by the book's title, author, or subject. Once you located an appropriate card, you could get information about the topic to access the book on the proper library shelf. Today, most of those card catalogs have been replaced by a computerized database. Using the same organizational structure, the computer can be used to search the library's database based on a specific book's author, title, or subject.

What are some commonly known databases?

Standard software varieties:

- Microsoft Access
- FileMaker
- Corel WordPerfect Office X5 Paradox
- Sun Microsystems StarOffice Base
- dBASE plus

Web 2.0 varieties:

- Zoho Creator

Can you use something else instead (for example, Excel)?

Yes, many of the basic functions of the database can be accomplished by using a spreadsheet program such as Microsoft's Excel. That is, if you know spreadsheet basics, you may already know most of the needed functions to have it serve to manage your data. For this reason, we are going to concentrate on Excel as a tool that can be used to carry out simple data management functions.

Note: There are times when a commercial database program is needed. If the amount of data you are working with is huge or if you need specialized forms to enter the data or to retrieve it, then you may want to consider learning and using a commercial database program. Our contention is that most teachers and students don't need that kind of power (and the accompanying headaches) for most of the tasks they will use a database for.

Why bother learning how to use a database?

- *Organization is the name of the game.* A database can help you organize vast amounts of information. If you have access to lots of information, organization is important.
- *Sorting with lightning speed.* Databases allow you to **sort** information automatically in a number of different ways. For example, an electronic student database can be sorted to produce an alphabetical list of all students. However, with the right information, you can also sort to list all students in alphabetical order based on their grade, gender, color of eyes, and shoe size if you desire. Multiple sorts can add to the power of the database.
- *Speed searches.* By using the **search** mechanism, you can have the computer find information you seek in a fraction of the time and effort needed to do it manually. Have it find one specific student and his or her associated information. Or have it find all instances of a specific characteristic for a data set (e.g., all students who have birthdays in October).
- **Boolean searches.** These types of searches allow you to search for specific information that contains specific words, letters, numbers, and so forth, but also to ignore other bits of information that you really don't want. For example, search for information on Lincoln, *not* Nebraska.
- *Grasp overwhelming amounts of information.* Using the combined features of search and sort, you can identify specific bits of important information that allow you to see relationships that may not have been readily apparent—for example, noting the elective courses frequently taken by high school students who are successful at gaining entrance into prestigious colleges.
- *Make comparisons.* Wouldn't it also be nice if you could pull out information and have it compare it for you? For example, search the electronic recipe database and have it identify and print all recipes that (1) use chicken, (2) feed up to six people, and (3) can be prepared in twenty minutes or less.
- *Multiple uses.* It isn't too difficult to begin to think about databases teachers might find helpful. Student information, books I own, books students have borrowed, lesson plans, supplies I have on hand versus supplies that are needed, electronic portfolios, quotes, references, pictures—the list goes on. These are all things that could be referenced, stored, searched, sorted, compared, and retrieved—if you have a knowledge of databases and how to use them to your advantage.

How are databases used at school? A brief list of ideas

By the teacher:	By the student:
• Student information	• References for a research paper
• Lesson plans	• Compare information on jobs, cities, businesses, weather
• Mail merge data	• Addresses of friends and relatives
• Articles, books, software, and so on in a personal library	• Compiled record of all work completed
• Electronic student and personal portfolios	• Information on scholarships, grants, loans for college

ORIENTATION

What's the workspace look like?

Figure 4.1 is an example of a database of information on books pertaining to copyright and plagiarism. This database was created in Microsoft Excel and should be familiar from our work in Chapter 3 ("Spreadsheets"). Instead of focusing on using the spreadsheets' capabilities with numbers, here we are using its rows and columns to store specific text information. Similar to the workspace when Excel was used as a spreadsheet, there are command tabs, each containing groups of related commands, as well as ways to adjust the cells, columns, and rows.

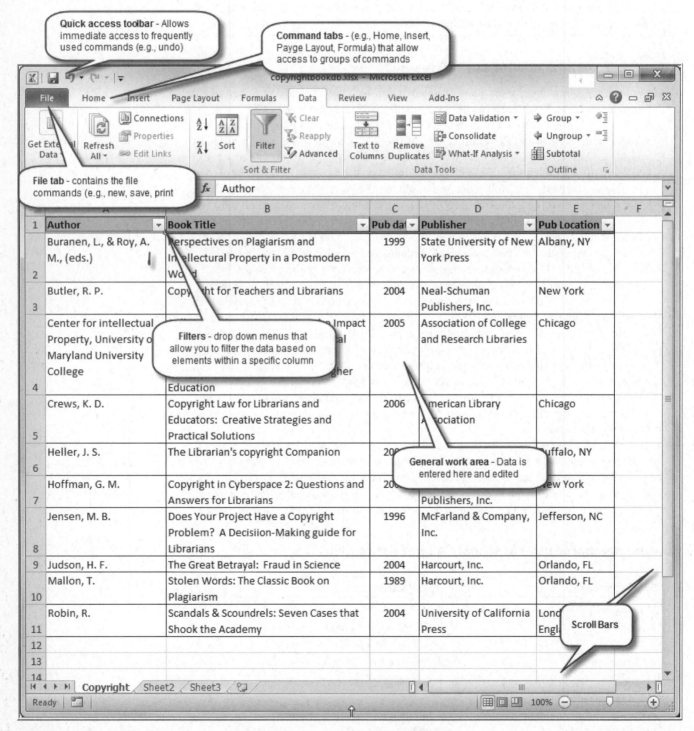

FIGURE 4.1 View of Microsoft Excel work area used to organize and manage textbook data

What commands can be used?

As we pointed out in Chapter 3 for Excel spreadsheets—and the other MS Office applications (e.g., MS PowerPoint, MS Word)—there is a ribbon of tools that runs across the top of the work screen. Within each ribbon various command tabs (e.g., Home, Insert, Page Layout, References) can be selected, which then reveal an associated command set or group. Once a command tab has been selected this specific group remains visible and ready for use. Items within the set may appear as individual items or as a gallery of related items. For example, selecting the Data tab (see Figure 4.2) in Excel reveals a group of commands that deal specifically with sorting and filtering data as well as other things.

For more information about the Excel ribbon and command tabs, please review the Excel Orientation video on the website that accompanies this book.

Databases, records, and fields

Remember the last time you went to a new doctor or dentist? On that initial visit the office administrator had you fill out some forms. The forms asked for your name, address, phone number, as well as your insurance company, policy number, and health history.

Ever wonder what happened to that form after you completed it? In most cases, it was taken back and put into a folder with your name on it. Then it was placed in a filing cabinet with other patient folders. The filing cabinet that holds all of the patients' files is known as a *database* and the individual file or form that you filled out is your **record.** On that record you filled in bits of information (address, medications you currently take, and so forth) and each bit of information is known as a **field.**

Electronic databases are set up exactly the same way. The database holds numerous records and each record has specific fields of information. From our example in Figure 4.1, the database consists of all of the combined books listed. Each row indicates a specific record of one of those books. Each record is made up of several fields of information (e.g., the author, title, publication date of a specific text).

Here is another example: Suppose your high school dance team is raising money by conducting a dance clinic for the area elementary school students. On the registration form you ask the students for their name, address, grade level, gender, T-shirt size, and years of dance experience. As the registrations come in, you develop an electronic record for each student by inputting the individuals' fields of information (e.g., name, address, grade level, and so on) for each student. Your database is the full set of all individuals who have registered. There is an individual record for each participant and you have a set number of fields of information about each participant (e.g., grade level).

What can be in a field?

Plenty. It could hold a letter of the alphabet, a name, a number, a picture, an audio or video clip, or even a whole chapter of a textbook. Some databases allow you a huge amount of space to put whatever you want within the field. In Excel, for example, in one cell (field) you can put as much as 32,000 characters of text. That is similar to about a chapter of text from a usual high school text.

The power of "sort and filter"

The power of the database is that it allows you to quickly sort and **filter** information it holds. For example, you can sort all of the records based on any or all fields contained within the records.

PDToolkit
for
Teaching and Learning with Microsoft® Office 2010 and Office 2011 for Mac

Go to PDToolkit for **Teaching and Learning with Microsoft® Office 2010 and Office 2011 for Mac** to locate the mentoring videos for Chapter Four.

FIGURE 4.2 The ribbon holds the command tabs, command groups and sets, and individual commands

Thus, you can sort each of the records alphabetically based on the name field (or gender field, or address field, or any other field) that is common within all of the records.

Even more powerful is the ability to search for a subset of the records based on a specific field. For example, the database can quickly search all the data for specific information and filter out only that which is desired. So if you want to find out how many participants in your dance clinic are male, you could filter based on the gender field and bring out only those records of male participants.

You begin to see the real power of this information when you think about a doctor who wants to examine the records of all patients aged between fifty and sixty, who have had an office visit in the last five years and have been diagnosed with diabetes. Or perhaps the teacher who desires to search from her database of hundreds of lesson plans to identify and filter out any and all that deal with science experiments involving copper for fourth- and fifth-grade students. Instantaneously, this information could be filtered and delivered.

Orientation Workout: Explore the territory

Turn on the computer and launch MS Excel or a similar program. Once it appears on the screen, try the following:

1. Create a new Excel spreadsheet.
2. Explore the various tabs on the ribbon and examine the different command groups.
3. On the new spreadsheet, practice entering information by clicking on any cell in the workspace.
   - Enter a word or series of words.
   - Highlight some or all of the words you enter.
   - Click on various command tabs, groups, and individuals commands tools. Note how your highlighted words change based on the tool that you have selected to use.
4. Review Chapter 3, Level 1, on how items are formatted within the spreadsheet. The same formatting can be used when Excel is used as a database. Attempt to set up headings, expand the width of the columns, and adjust the word wrap to achieve some sense of how data can be inserted in this tool.
5. Play with it for a short while to get a feeling for what can be done and how easy it is to use.

LEVEL 1: REVISITING THE RECYCLING PROJECT

What should you be able to do?

At this level, your focus is on using various tools and techniques to store data in a database and make the data retrievable in various forms.

What resources are provided?

PDToolkit
for
Teaching and Learning with Microsoft® Office 2010 and Office 2011 for Mac

Go to PDToolkit for **Teaching and Learning with Microsoft® Office 2010 and Office 2011 for Mac** to locate the Workout Level One for Chapter Four.

PDToolkit
for
Teaching and Learning with Microsoft® Office 2010 and Office 2011 for Mac

Go to PDToolkit for **Teaching and Learning with Microsoft® Office 2010 and Office 2011 for Mac** to locate the mentoring videos for Chapter Four.

Basically, Level 1 is divided into a common scenario, selected solutions, and a practice exercise (i.e., Workout). The scenario has been constructed to allow you to examine a common situation and how it could be addressed through the use of this software. To do this, we have provided the following:

1. Draft spreadsheet documents (which you can use to practice and review how the features are used to address the problems presented within each scenario).
2. Quick reference figures (see Figures 4.3 to 4.5), which identify the key features that have been incorporated within the solution presentation. These allow you to rapidly identify the key features and reference exactly how to include such features within your own work.
3. Step-by-step instructions on how to incorporate all highlighted features within your work.
4. Video mentoring support that will guide you through the integration of each of the highlighted features.
5. Workout exercises that allow you to practice identifying and selecting which software features to use, when to use those features, how they should be incorporated, and to what degree they are effective.

How should you proceed?

If you have *little or no experience* with MS Office 2010 and particularly Excel, then we suggest you do the following:

1. Read and review Scenario 1.
2. Examine the quick reference figures (Figures 4.3 to 4.5) and all included features.
3. With the step-by-step directions provided, use the software and practice creating the database and completing a sorting and filtering of the data.
4. If you have any confusion or difficulty with these processes and tools, access the videos and monitor the features as they are demonstrated and discussed within the short video clips.
5. Once you feel comfortable, go to the Workout and work through the problem and exercises it outlines.

If you have *experience* with Excel 2010, you may want to review the scenario and the quick reference examples first. If sorting and filtering are unfamiliar, then you may wish to access and use the step-by-step procedures as well as the mentoring support videos. Once the review has been completed, then move directly to the Workout exercise and create your own database by incorporating similar elements as shown in these figures.

Scenario 1: The recycling project workers

Remember from the Level 1 exercise within Chapter 3 ("Spreadsheets"), John Rena's science classes worked on a spring semester aluminum can recycling project. John found it helpful during that time to have contact information for each of his students involved in the project. Using his spreadsheet program as a database, John created a record for each of his students (e.g., address, phone, parents' names) and put it within the same workbook as the data from the recycling project. The rows and columns on this worksheet and database are not to be calculated; however, they can be manipulated. Note Figure 4.3 is a screen shot of a sample of John's full student database with all of the rows representing individual student records and the columns representing the specific fields of information found within each record. Note also how the data in this fashion can now be manipulated by sorting it in a specific way (Figure 4.4 reveals students based on the class periods when they take science) and by filtering it (Figure 4.5 reveals only those who participated as leaders in the recycling project) in order to get quick, specific information from the overall data.

No.	Feature	Steps to Get It Done
1.	**Create and populate a new database**	1. Launch Excel. If a new worksheet does not appear, click on the File tab and select New. 2. Select the Blank Workbook and click on the Create button. A new, blank worksheet should appear and you can begin entering data. 3. Go to Chapter 3 ("Spreadsheets") and review steps 2 through 6 in Level 1. These steps will guide you in the following: • Insert, align, and format column headings • Enter data • Adjust columns and rows • Add gridlines • Format cells
2.	**Sort the records**	1. Click anywhere within the database. 2. Go to **Data** tab >>> **Sort & Filter** group >>> **Sort** command button. The Sort dialog box (see Figure 4.6) will appear. You can also get this same Sort Window by clicking **Home** tab >>> **Editing** group >>> **Sort & Filter** command button >>> and then select the **Custom Sort** option.

(continued)

	A	B	C	D	E	F	G	H	I	J
1	Last Name	First name	Class period	Leader	Phone	Address	City	State	Zip	Parents
2	Barrymore	Cade	5	no	478-5211	134 South 300 North	Lafayette	IN	47905	Mr. & Mrs. Barrymore
3	DeFore	Alexis	3	yes	472-4578	11439 US Hwy 245	Lafayette	IN	47908	Beverly DeFore
4	Drury	Landon	3	no	447-0999	2393 W. 100 N	Lafayette	IN	47905	John and Dee Drury
5	Jeski	Robert	4	no	472-8356	4839 W. 100 N.	Lafayette	IN	47905	Mr. & Mrs. Jeski
6	Moreno	Elizabeth	2	yes	424-2252	3147 St. Rd. 39	E. Lafayette	IN	47902	Barry and Elana Swartz
7	Packard	Dale	1	no	472-6854	5214 Autumn Ln.	Lafayette	IN	47905	Mr. & Mrs. Packard
8	Polk	Madison	4	yes	472-7531	434 W. Monty St.	Lafayette	IN	47908	Roberta Thomas
9	Primm	Kenny	1	no	421-0990	200 Ferry St.	Lafayette	IN	47905	Jacob and Bernice Pietro
10	Sanchez	Valerie	1	yes	538-7732	2905 Holly Hill Dr.	Lafayette	IN	47905	Louis and Claudia Sanchez
11	Saterwaite	Kimberly	5	yes	424-6587	106 Meridian St.	E. Lafayette	IN	47902	Mr. & Mrs. Tim Saterwaite
12	Scherrer	Mark	2	no	572-8876	3626 Debbie Drive	E. Lafayette	IN	47902	David Scherrer
13	Smith	Fiona	4	no	424-9921	2561 Midline Ct.	E. Lafayette	IN	47902	Andrew Smith
14	Trager	Carlie	5	no	472-7753	2340 yeager Rd.	E. Lafayette	IN	47902	Bonita and Charles Welcher
15	Washington	Violet	2	yes	478-3321	300 Main St.	Lafayette	IN	47905	Suzy and Dave Washington
16	Weingram	Ralph	3	yes	443-9090	452 Rockhill Dr.	Lafayette	IN	47905	Terra and Bill Weingram

Can data   **Student Info**

FIGURE 4.3 A sample of Mr. Rena's database of student information

	A	B	C	D	E	F	G	H	I	J
1	Last Name	First name	Class period	Leader	Phone	Address	City	State	Zip	Parents
2	Packard	Dale	1	no	472-6854	5214 Autumn Ln.	Lafayette	IN	47905	Mr. & Mrs. Packard
3	Primm	Kenny	1	no	421-0990	200 Ferry St.	Lafayette	IN	47905	Jacob and Bernice Pietro
4	Sanchez	Valerie	1	yes	538-7732	2905 Holly Hill Dr.	Lafayette	IN	47905	Louis and Claudia Sanchez
5	Moreno	Elizabeth	2	yes	424-2252	3147 St. Rd. 39	E. Lafayette	IN	47902	Barry and Elana Swartz
6	Scherrer	Mark	2	no	572-8876	3626 Debbie Drive	E. Lafayette	IN	47902	David Scherrer
7	Washington	Violet	2	yes	478-3321	300 Main St.	Lafayette	IN	47905	Suzy and Dave Washington
8	DeFore	Alexis	3	yes	472-4578	11439 US Hwy 245	Lafayette	IN	47908	Beverly DeFore
9	Drury	Landon	3	no	447-0999	2393 W. 100 N	Lafayette	IN	47905	John and Dee Drury
10	Weingram	Ralph	3	yes	443-9090	452 Rockhill Dr.	Lafayette	IN	47905	Terra and Bill Weingram
11	Jeski	Robert	4	no	472-8356	4839 W. 100 N.	Lafayette	IN	47905	Mr. & Mrs. Jeski
12	Polk	Madison	4	yes	472-7531	434 W. Monty St.	Lafayette	IN	47908	Roberta Thomas
13	Smith	Fiona	4	no	424-9921	2561 Midline Ct.	E. Lafayette	IN	47902	Andrew Smith
14	Barrymore	Cade	5	no	478-5211	134 South 300 North	Lafayette	IN	47905	Mr. & Mrs. Barrymore
15	Saterwaite	Kimberly	5	yes	424-6587	106 Meridian St.	E. Lafayette	IN	47902	Mr. & Mrs. Tim Saterwaite
16	Trager	Carlie	5	no	472-7753	2340 yeager Rd.	E. Lafayette	IN	47902	Bonita and Charles Welcher

Can data   **Student Info**

FIGURE 4.4 Mr. Rena's sample database *sorted* based on his student's class period

	A	B	C	D	E	F	G	H	I	J
1	Last Name	First name	Class period	Leader	Phone	Address	City	State	Zip	Parents
4	Sanchez	Valerie	1	yes	538-7732	2905 Holly Hill Dr.	Lafayette	IN	47905	Louis and Claudia Sanchez
5	Moreno	Elizabeth	2	yes	424-2252	3147 St. Rd. 39	E. Lafayette	IN	47902	Barry and Elana Swartz
7	Washington	Violet	2	yes	478-3321	300 Main St.	Lafayette	IN	47905	Suzy and Dave Washington
8	DeFore	Alexis	3	yes	472-4578	11439 US Hwy 245	Lafayette	IN	47908	Beverly DeFore
10	Weingram	Ralph	3	yes	443-9090	452 Rockhill Dr.	Lafayette	IN	47905	Terra and Bill Weingram
12	Polk	Madison	4	yes	472-7531	434 W. Monty St.	Lafayette	IN	47908	Roberta Thomas
15	Saterwaite	Kimberly	5	yes	424-6587	106 Meridian St.	E. Lafayette	IN	47902	Mr. & Mrs. Tim Saterwaite

Can data   **Student Info**

FIGURE 4.5 Mr. Rena's database *filtered* to show only those students who performed the role of leaders on the recycling project

		3. Within the Sort dialog box, click the down arrow in the Sort by section (if you don't see a Sort by section, click on the Add Level button and the Sort by section will appear). A list of the column headings will appear. Select the field you want to base the sort on (e.g., Mr. Rena selected Class period as the column [field]). **4.** Click OK and the sort will be completed. **5.** To really get a hang of this, try sorting a number of different ways and use descending as well as ascending orders.

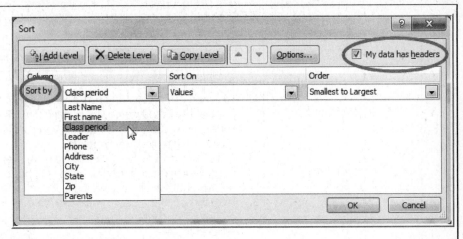

FIGURE 4.6 Sort window

Note: In the Sort dialog box you can also select whether you have a header row on your database. This tells the database or spreadsheet to consider the first row as a listing of headings or as a record of data. In this case, we have a header and thus it needs to be marked as such.

3.	**Create a comprehensive sort**	There may be times when you want to complete a sort of several different kinds of data at once. For example, in the database of students for the recycling project, you may find it helpful to see the database of students grouped by the city in which they live and then, within those cities, grouped by whether they were a leader in the recycling project. Such comprehensive sorts are completed in the following manner.

1. Click anywhere within the database and get the Sort window to appear (**Data** tab >>> **Sort & Filter** group >>> **Sort**).
2. In the Sort by section, click on the drop-down arrow and click on the field (column header) on which you want the first or primary sort to be based.
3. Click on the Add Level button and a new sort selection row (Then by) will appear.
4. In the Then by section, click on the drop-down arrow and click on the field (column header) on which you want the second sort to be based (see Figure 4.7).
5. Continue to add levels as needed for the comprehensive sort.
6. Once you have selected all of the levels and sort columns, then click OK and the sort will be completed.

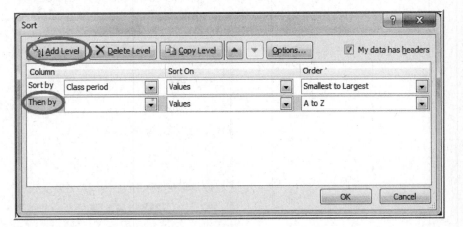

FIGURE 4.7 Sort window with an added level

Note: Within the Sort dialog box it is also possible to select what values to Sort On and to select the Order of the sort. By changing the order, for example, you can alter the usual a to z alphabetical listing.

4.	**Filter the records**	1. Select your full database, including the column headings.
		2. Go to **Data** tab >>> **Sort & Filter** group >>> **Filter** command button.

3. Note that little down arrows have now been posted by each of the column headings (see Figure 4.5). Here's an example:

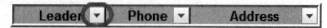

4. To filter the information, simply select the field title (column heading) you want to use as a filter, click its down arrow, and select the criterion on which the filter is to be based. For example, if you only wanted to select students who participated as group leaders in the recycling project, you would go to the leader column, click on the down arrow, and make sure only the "yes" alternative is checked from the list of possibilities given. Once your criterion is selected, click on the OK button and the database reveals only those records of the students designated as leaders in the project.
5. To restore all of the data, simply click on the Clear button (**Data** tab >>> **Sort & Filter** group). A filter doesn't lose the extra data—it just allows you to see only what you have selected to see.
6. Try a number of these simple filters to learn how they work.

Note: If you only have a small number of items in your database (e.g., only ten students), sorting and filtering may not seem all that important. However, as the database increases in size (to potentially thousands), then the ability to sort and filter increases in value.

| 5. | **More advanced and custom filters** | 1. Begin the filtering process in the same way that the records were filtered in the previous steps (**Data** tab >>> **Sort & Filter** group >>> **Filter**). |

1. Begin the filtering process in the same way that the records were filtered in the previous steps (**Data** tab >>> **Sort & Filter** group >>> **Filter**).
2. Once the down arrows are positioned by each of the field headings, select the key criterion that you desire by selecting the appropriate column.
3. Click the down arrow for the selected column and select Text Filter and then Custom Filters . . . . A Custom AutoFilter dialog box will appear (see Figure 4.8).

Note: If your selected column has only numbers in it (e.g., the *Class Period*, or the *Zip* columns from our example), then clicking on the down arrow will give you the option for Number Filter and then Custom Filters . . . . In both cases, you end up with the same Custom AutoFilter dialog box appearing.

4. In the Custom AutoFilter dialog box, use the down arrow button to select the comparison operator you wish to use (e.g., equals, contains, and so on). In the box next to the comparison operator, enter the criterion you wish to compare. For example, to find just those students whose phone numbers begin with the prefix 472, select the comparison operator of Begins with and type in *472* in the box to the right.
5. Click OK and note how the filter has worked.

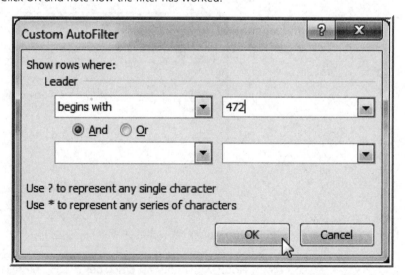

FIGURE 4.8 Custom AutoFilter dialog box that is used to access specific information within the database

Note: The Custom AutoFilter dialog box also allows you to add other filters with the words *and* or *or*. So you could filter for zip codes that equal 47905 or 47908. This would retrieve all records with either of those two zip codes and not return any others (e.g., 47902).

6.	Combining for even more advanced filtering and sorting	What happens when you want to find very specific records? Using a combination of advanced filters and sorts, you can use the database software to identify, locate, and retrieve very specific elements of information. For example:
		1. Begin with the full database set of records.
		2. Use the AutoFilter to select only those students who performed the role of leaders in the project.
		3. Use a Custom AutoFilter to select only those leaders who live in either the 47902 or the 47908 zip code areas.
		4. Sort the remaining list in descending alphabetical order based on first name.
		Note: As suggested here, it is possible to run a number of different individual filters to select very specific records.
		Now imagine you have your own personal book library of five hundred or more books in a database. Similar to Figure 4.3, you might have included the author, title, publication date, and so forth. In addition, however, you might also have included specific key words (e.g., topics or themes, age-appropriate level) that are relevant to each book. With such a database it would be possible for you to quickly identify all books that are by a specific author or about a specific topic that could be read by a certain audience—and it could be done in a matter of a fraction of a second.

Level 1a Workout: Practice using the basic database features

For you to feel comfortable using a database, you really need to practice developing and playing with a set of data in this format. With this first Workout, we want you to review all that was presented in the step-by-step procedures. However, there are many other things that were not touched on within this chapter, so as you work on this exercise, please explore and try some of the new aspects you encounter. In addition, you may need to refer to Chapter 3 ("Spreadsheets") to recall and use some of the basic Excel features.

Go to PDToolkit for **Teaching and Learning with Microsoft® Office 2010 and Office 2011 for Mac** to locate the Workout Level One for Chapter Four.

Here is a basic outline of what you need to do:

1. Review Figures 4.3 to 4.5.
2. Either open the existing version of student database on the website that accompanies this book or if you like, you can open a new worksheet and enter the information yourself. Once opened (or once you have typed it in), your worksheet should look something like Figure 4.3.
3. Using that database, complete the following:
   a. Add an additional field of information (e.g., favorite subject in school, sports he or she plays, total cans contributed) by inserting a new column heading and filling in an estimate of the data for each of the students.
   b. Add records for several other students to the list and fill in all of the relevant fields of information.
   c. Save the newly revised spreadsheet or database to your hard drive, flash drive, and so on. Use a specific name that you can remember and access at a later time.
   d. Select a field of information and sort the data based on that field.
   e. Select one of the cities listed and filter the data so that only those students living in that specific city are listed.
   f. Complete an advanced filter by having the database reveal only those students who live in the city of Lafayette with a last name that begins with either a *W* or a *B*.

Note: Refer to specific feature numbers and the given step-by-step procedures as needed. Additionally, use the mentoring videos to help guide you through any specific procedure that needs additional clarification.

Level 1b Workout: Creating your own database

We all work and interact with databases. In this Workout, identify something in your life that you can develop into a simple database. It might include a list of the music you own (a compilation of all of your CDs and MP3 files), electronic games that you have mastered, collections you have assembled (e.g., stamps, coins, Beanie Babies), family medical records, or articles assembled for a literature review.

For the Level 1b Workout, create a database that includes your own data. Your database should include a minimum of ten records with a minimum of five fields of information for each record.

Table 4.1 Level 1 Workout and Practice Checklist: Creating, sorting, and filtering a database of information

Database Content	___ Records were organized in a clear, logical manner.
	___ Relevant fields of data were included.
	___ The full database was sorted based on a selected field of information.
	___ A comprehensive sort was completed using a minimum of two levels of information fields.
Database Sort	___ A specific subset of data was generated through a simple filtering of the data based on a selected field of information.
	___ An additional subset of data was identified through the use of a custom filter that employed a minimum of one comparison operator.
	___ A final subset of data was created that included data that was sorted and filtered.

As you can see, there is a variety of the type of data that can be collected. After you have determined what data you will use, do the following:

1. Open your spreadsheet program and create a draft worksheet that includes your columns and rows of your data. Include column titles.
2. Review Scenario 1 and all of the sorting and filtering features demonstrated within Figures 4.3 to 4.5.
3. Print a copy of the full database as you have completed it.
4. Complete a sort of the full database and print a copy of the newly sorted data.
5. Filter the database in some relevant manner and print a copy of the filtered data.
6. On the full database, complete an advanced filter with an additional sort and print the results.
7. Compare all of the printouts and note the potential value of each of the sorted and filtered data.

Use Table 4.1 as a checklist to guide your efforts.

LEVEL 2: MAIL MERGE AND OTHER GOOD STUFF

What should you be able to do?

A real time saver comes with being able to use the data stored within a database. One of the best examples of such a use is **mail merge.** In this section, we want you to develop a database file of information and merge it with a form letter. This will require you to effectively use the Help feature of Excel.

Getting some Help

As shown in Chapter 3, Help is an important element of the Excel and similar software programs. To use it, click the Help button on the tab bar of the main ribbon.

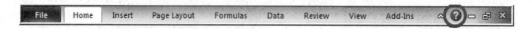

Clicking the Help button ❓ opens the Help window. From here you can browse general Help topics, bring up a general table of contents of all Help topics, complete a search for a specific question that you might have, and so on (see Figure 4.9).

By typing in key words or even a full question, Help will respond with a variety of potential answers for you to investigate. Help generally does not have all of the answers but it will have a lot of them. Make sure you get a sense for how it works and how often it can be of assistance.

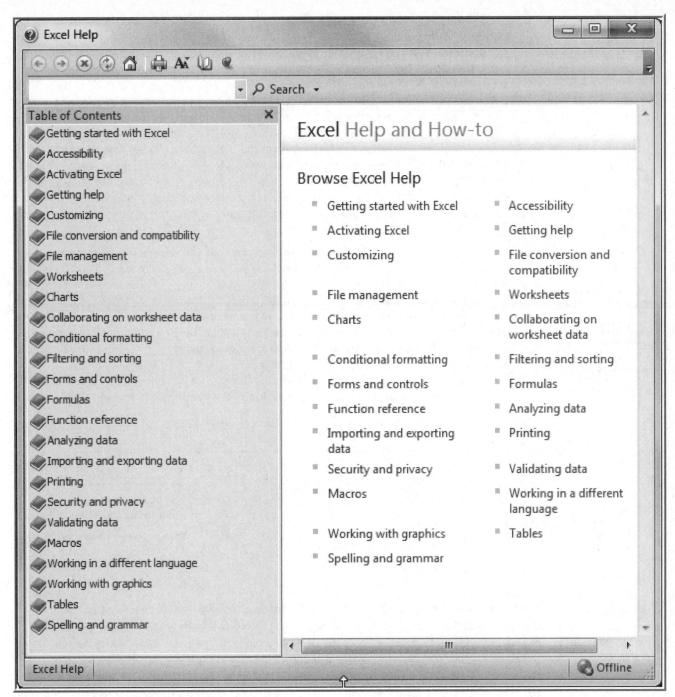

FIGURE 4.9 Excel Help window

Scenario 2: "Thanking those who helped"

Let's imagine that John Rena is still using his spreadsheet database for his recycling project. Now that the recycling program has come to a successful conclusion at the end of the school year, he feels it necessary to send out some thank-you notes to his students and their parents for all of the time and effort they put into making the project work. To do this, he is going to use the database of information that he has on all of his students. With that information, he can access names, addresses, parents' names, and even the names of those who served in leadership roles within the project.

With so many students involved, it could take quite a bit of time to handwrite all the needed notes. As we learned from Chapter 2, a word processor could help by writing a single letter and then entering different names and addresses for each of the students and printing each individual letter—but that also would take a lot of time for all of his students. With the data from the project collected within his spreadsheet and all of his student information data within his database, it is now possible for John to create one letter that grabs the needed information from the database to automatically personalize each letter. So even though he writes just one letter, this process will create a letter for each student that is addressed to each individual and that contains data relevant to that individual (e.g., personal address, data from his or her specific class period, parents' names). (Note: This is the same process used for the "personalized" junk mail you receive.) By allowing the computer to merge information from the database with a letter composed on a word processing program, John will save a lot of time. Letters, forms, mailing labels, and so on can be created to use data interactively from a selected database. The end result is the best of both worlds: a single document is created that magically pulls specific information from the database so that it appears written specifically for each student. This is known as a mail merge.

Within Level 2 of this software application, we want you to explore how to create a form letter or mail merge document, and then have you create one for your own use. Take a close look at the word-processed letter (see Figure 4.10). We have left _____ spaces where the merged information is to go. (See Figure 4.11 with the merged fields inserted.) Once the information is merged with this form letter, then output such as Figure 4.12 can be created with very little additional effort. Note that only a single word document has been created, but when printing the documents, as many as needed can be produced, each with the _____ filled in with personally relevant information drawn from the database.

If you need any of these features and procedures to be demonstrated, access the website that accompanies this book and view the mentoring videos for support.

for
Teaching and Learning with
Microsoft® Office 2010 and
Office 2011 for Mac

Go to PDToolkit for **Teaching and Learning with Microsoft® Office 2010 and Office 2011 for Mac** to locate the Workout Level Two for Chapter Four.

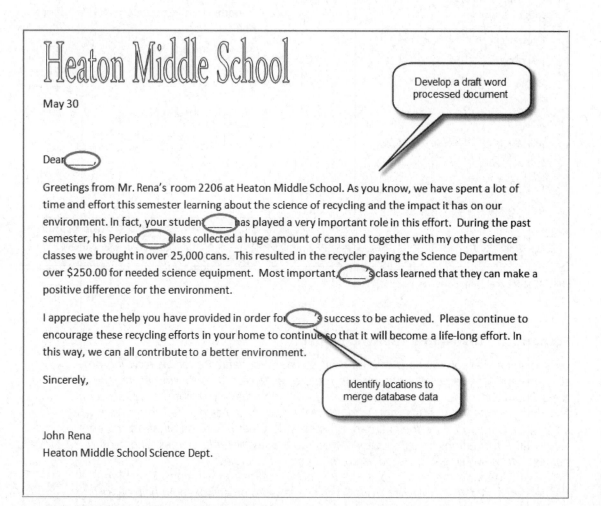

FIGURE 4.10 Sample letter that indicates where merging will occur

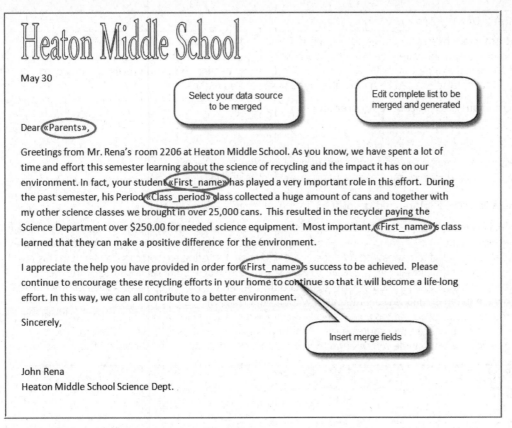

FIGURE 4.11 An example letter with merged fields inserted

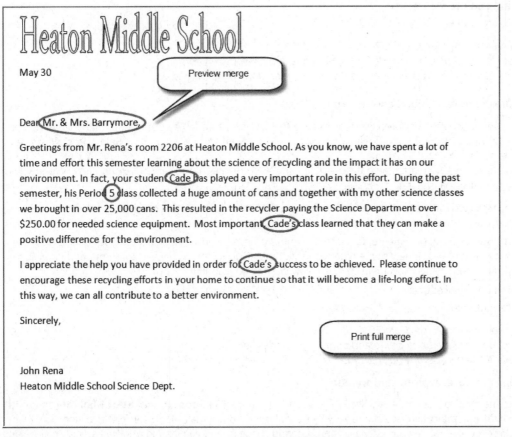

FIGURE 4.12 An example mail merge letter with actual student data inserted

Feature	Steps to Get It Done
Develop a draft word-processed document with placeholders for data to be merged	**Important note:** In most cases, you'll find it easier to complete the mail merge from within MS Word or similar word processing software. Likewise, the best Help to guide you through the merging process is found within MS Word. A major part of that mail merge, however, is connecting the word-processed document to a data source. That data source can be the database you have created within Excel. **Information about and procedure for creating:** www.office.com Help • Key words: Mail Merge Word 2010 • Select *Use mail merge to create and print letters and other documents.* • Select *Set up the main document and follow the given procedure.* **Key features to note, explore, and try out:** • To begin the mail merge, within MS Word go to **Mailings** tab >>> **Start Mail Merge** group >>> **Start Mail Merge** (see Figure 4.13). From the drop-down gallery, select Letters. If you already have a document prepared, you can select to navigate to that document and open it. In addition, you can also select at this point to use the step-by-step Mail Merge Wizard to walk you through each of the various steps of the merge. • Similar to what is shown in Figure 4.10, create a draft word-processed document. As you create it, think of how the database data will be integrated within the document. • You may find it convenient at this point to leave placeholders or spaces in locations where data will be merged. • Review the step-by-step procedures given within Scenarios 1 and 2 of Chapter 2 ("Word Processing"). Those procedures will guide you through the process of setting up and formatting a draft document. **FIGURE 4.13** Mailings tab with mail merge command groups
Select your data source to be merged	**Information and procedure:** www.office.com Help • Key words: Mail Merge Word 2010 • Select *Use mail merge to create and print letters and other documents.* • Select *Connect the document to a data source and follow the given procedure.* **Key features to note, explore, and try out:** • Once your document has been created, it's time to connect it with the source of data that will be merged into it. Within MS Word, go to **Mailings** tab >>> **Start Mail Merge** group >>> **Select Recipients** (see Figure 4.13). • If you have already created the database, you can select the alternative for *Use existing list . . .* and navigate to that spreadsheet or database. **Note:** If your selected database or spreadsheet has multiple worksheets, you will need to select which worksheet contains the data you wish to merge. **Important note:** You can only merge data into a document from one data worksheet. If your data is on more than one worksheet, create a new single data worksheet that includes all the needed to-be-merged data, then connect your word-processed document to that newly created data source.
Edit the list to be merged	**Information and procedure:** www.office.com Help • Key words: Mail Merge Word 2010. • Select *Use mail merge to create and print letters and other documents.* • Select *Refine the list of recipients or items and follow the given procedure.* **Key features to note, explore, and try out:** • Once the data source has been selected, you can click on the **Mailings** tab >>> **Start Mail Merge** group >>> **Edit Recipient List** (see Figure 4.13). This will bring up the Mail Merge Recipients dialog box. From this box you can refine your list via sorting, filtering, finding, and eliminating duplicates, and so on. You can also go directly to your data source (e.g., dbase1.xls) and edit the data.

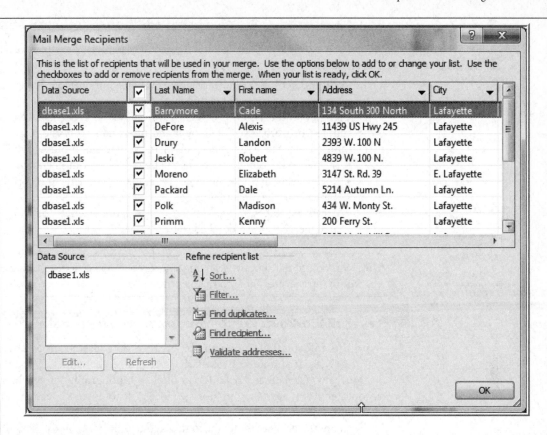

Insert merge fields	**Information and procedure:**

www.office.com Help

- Key words: Mail Merge Word 2010
- Select *Use mail merge to create and print letters and other documents.*
- Select *Add placeholders, called mail merge fields, to the document* and follow the given procedure.

Key features to note, explore, and try out:

- In your word-processed document, place your cursor where you want the data to be inserted.
- Go to the **Mailings** tab >>> **Write & Insert Fields** group >>> **Insert Merge Field** (see Figure 4.13).
- A drop-down gallery of the potential fields of information that can be inserted will appear (these are the column heads from your source database or spreadsheet). Select the category you wish to merge at that point in your document.
- A placeholder (e.g., <<Parents>>) with the title of the merged category will be inserted in your document where your cursor was located.
- Repeat this procedure and insert placeholders for all needed merges within your document.

Preview and print results	**Information and procedure:**

www.office.com Help

- Key words: Mail Merge Word 2010
- Select *Use mail merge to create and print letters and other documents.*
- Select *Preview and complete the merge and follow the given procedure.*

Key features to note, explore, and try out:

- Go to the **Mailings** tab >>> **Preview Results** group >>> **Preview Results** (see Figure 4.13).
- Check to see that the document now has the correctly inserted merged data for your first recipient. Also check and make sure your inserted merged information is formatted correctly (e.g., no added or missing spaces).
- You can click through the entire database and see each of the merged documents.
- Once you are satisfied with your results, click on the **Mailings** tab >>> **Finish** group >>> **Finish & Merge** (see Figure 4.13).
- From the drop-down gallery of options, select print. A small dialog box will appear that will allow you to select which of the documents you wish to send to the printer.

Level 2a Workout: Practice using additional database features

Before moving on to your own work, it might be wise to try a couple of exercises with Mr. Rena's class's database.

1. Go to the website that accompanies this book and open Mr. Rena's database that includes information on some of his students.
2. Using the information provided within the Level 2, Scenario 2, of this chapter, create a simple word-processed document and insert data from the recycle students' database of information. Make sure when you merge you do a minimum of the following:
   - Include at least four or five merged fields within your document.
   - Review, edit, and select four or more final documents to be printed with different data merged on each document.
   - Create envelopes or mailing labels for each of the letters that you created using the same mail merge process and data source.

Note: For additional support, each of these key features is demonstrated on the mentoring videos within the website that accompanies this book.

Level 2b Workout: Create your way to manage data

With this information and example, create a database (from Microsoft's Excel) that you can use. Keep it simple at first. Perhaps it can be for your CD collection, your book collection, your Christmas card address book, a bibliography of special articles, inventory of school items you have in your storage place at school, your special medications—something pertinent to your life.

Adapt the database so that it contains something you can use. Practice sorting and looking at different views of the database through the use of various filters. Finally, save your database, close it, and then open MS Word. Complete a mail merge using a new document you create and the data from the records within your database. Examine each of the merged documents and begin to imagine all of the ways that this tool might be able to help you with various bits of data that you have laying around.

Use Table 4.2 as a checklist to make sure you have included a number of key features that have been highlighted within Scenarios 1 and 2 of this chapter (see Figures 4.3 to 4.5 and 4.10 to 4.12).

Note: Invoke Rule 2—Save your work!

Table 4.2 Level 2 Workout and Practice Checklist: Completing a mail merge

Data Source	___ A database of relevant information was created.
	___ All data fields are clearly labeled and organized.
	___ A new word-processed document was created.
	___ The document has been clearly written with no spelling or grammatical errors.
Original Document Content	___ The document has been formatted for efficient and effective reading and comprehension.
	___ Placeholders for the to-be-merged data have been inserted.
	___ A final subset of data was created that included data that was sorted and filtered.
Merged Document	___ Data from data source was properly merged into new merged document.
	___ Copies of the merged document, with different data within each copy, were produced.

LEVEL 3: INTEGRATION AND APPLICATION

What should you be able to do?

It's important for you to picture how the use of a database can be relevant to you and your students. This section aims to help you see all of the many applications possible when you use a database. You can use these examples as a springboard to launch ideas on ways to improve levels of student learning and your personal productivity.

Introduction

Within Levels 1 and 2 of this chapter, we focused on database management from the perspective of your learning to use it. But to extend its use, you need to think about data management as a means to enhance the learning experience of students. There are times when integrating databases within a learning situation may actually improve the learning opportunities and possibilities of the learners. However, there are other times when such integration would be more of a hassle than the potential benefits warrant. Learning to tell the difference can help you be successful in what you develop and use in your classroom.

Database management integration

Creating the enhanced learning experience: A partial lesson plan

TOPIC:

A study of the people, places, and culture of an African country.

OVERVIEW:

Mr. Carpenter (as explained in Chapters 2 and 3) is a middle school social studies teacher determined to help his students expand their understanding of various countries of the world. For this school year, his classes have the opportunity to work with Jonathon Rogers, a university graduate student who is on an internship working for an international health and education organization in the African country of Zimbabwe. With Jonathon's help, Mr. Carpenter's eighth-graders are able to obtain firsthand information about the country, people, and culture of Zimbabwe.

Through research, the students have learned that Zimbabwe is a country with many exotic animals. In fact, much of its total economy is based on the tourist industry. People from all over the world travel to this African country to see elephants, tigers, and giraffe in their natural habitats.

SPECIFIC LEARNING TASK:

Zimbabwe is a country of national parks that have been set aside to protect the animals and habitats found there. Each of the parks is noted for unique animals and plants. Members of the class are to research the parks and obtain information about the location and size of the park, the types of animals and plants that reside there, and the major problems inherent with protecting, operating, and maintaining each park.

SAMPLE LEARNING OBJECTIVES:

Students will be able to do the following:

1. List and describe (e.g., animal and plant life, geographical features) several national parks within Zimbabwe.
2. Plan a safari through Zimbabwe to photograph and videotape exotic animals in their natural habitats.
3. Describe the problems and challenges that administrators and governmental officials face as they attempt to preserve the wildlife and habitats of the national parks of Zimbabwe.

PROCEDURE:

1. Examine the following list of National Parks within Zimbabwe: Chimanimani National Park, Chizarira National Park, Kazuma Pan National Park, Mana Pools National Park, Zambezi National Park.
2. Divide the class into groups and have each group complete Internet and library research on their selected national park.
3. Have each group answer the following questions about their national park:
   a. Where is their park located (i.e., in what part of Zimbabwe)?
   b. What is the size of the park?
   c. What types of animals and plants are found within the park?
   d. What are some unique characteristics of the park? That is, if you were to visit this park, what are some key things you should really do and see?
   e. What are the chief problems or challenges facing the park in today's world?
4. Contact Jonathon to see if he can obtain any further information about the parks (e.g., has he visited one? Has he any stories? Can he suggest anyone to contact to get further information? Does he have any pictures?).
5. Have the students compile a report or presentation on their selected park.
6. Following the presentations, facilitate a discussion focused on the challenges facing the parks today. Potential lead questions could be as follows: Should a poor country such as Zimbabwe be investing money in the parks at this time when the level of poverty of the people is so high? Should outside (richer) countries help to take care of the parks and wildlife found within Zimbabwe?

QUESTION OF DATABASE INTEGRATION:

This activity could be completed with or without the use of database software. Use these reflective questions to explore the value of potentially integrating database software within such an activity as outlined by Mr. Carpenter.

- What benefit would there be to compiling the information on the national parks in a database? How could such a database be used in a classroom setting?
- How could such a database be used to compare and contrast various elements of the individual parks?
- Could a database be used to organize resources for a research project?
- How could a national parks database aid in teaching students about identifying issues that face the parks and suggesting potential solutions for these issues?
- How could a lesson (from a future teaching area or grade level) that uses databases to promote critical thinking be described briefly?

Level 3a Workout: Integrating database management

Using the example lesson plan as a guide, follow the steps in this Workout as you think about the potential use of databases within various applied settings.

1. Read each of the following situations. Imagine being directly involved in the planning for each of these projects. Select one (or more if you wish) for further consideration.

Bird Watchers:

A fourth-grade teacher wants her students to learn how to categorize. On a field trip to the local zoo, she has her students record all of the different types of birds that they see and that are identified within the zoo. Once back into the classroom, the students begin to list the different characteristics of the birds (types of food they eat, country of origin, feather colors and markings, distances and speed of flight, color and size of eggs, and so on). Once the list has been gathered, students are given novel examples and are asked to group the birds with those from the list that are most similar based on various critical characteristics.

Internet Websites:

Do the types of favorite Internet sites visited frequently by individuals differ based on gender, age, or racial background? This was a question posed by a high school psychology teacher. To measure the potential differences, a survey was created for all elementary, middle, and secondary students in the school district. Responses asked for students to indicate what were their top three favorite Internet sites, what were the top three most useful, and how much time they spent weekly on the Internet.

Theme Park Comparisons

Which are the best theme or amusement parks in the world? Mr. Ramollo wants his fifth-grade students to compare various theme or amusement parks around the world to see which ones would be rated the very best. Students needed to develop a list of key characteristics for the theme parks and then use the Internet to investigate which theme parks achieved the highest ranking for each of the categories.

Internet Cafés:

An investor wants to know where would be the best place to make an investment in an Internet café. Such cafés are used throughout the world as places individuals can visit to rent time on a computer to use e-mail and surf the Internet. The cafés seem to have their greatest success in those countries that have high populations, relatively low income, and poor postal systems. How can this investor determine some locations throughout the world that may be prime areas for such an investment?

2. Based on your selected project, consider the following questions that concern the integration of database management software. Mark your response to each question.

Integration assessment questionnaire (IAQ)

Will using database management software as a part of the project:			
Broaden the learners' perspective on potential solution paths and answers?	___ Yes	___ No	___ Maybe
Increase the level of involvement and investment of personal effort by the learners?	___ Yes	___ No	___ Maybe
Increase the level of learner motivation (e.g., increase the relevance of the to-be-learned task, the confidence of dealing with the task, and the overall appeal of the task)?	___ Yes	___ No	___ Maybe
Decrease the time needed to generate potential solutions?	___ Yes	___ No	___ Maybe
Increase the quality and quantity of learner practice working on this and similar projects?	___ Yes	___ No	___ Maybe
Increase the quality and quantity of feedback given to the learner?	___ Yes	___ No	___ Maybe
Enhance the ability of the student to solve novel but similar projects, tasks, and problems in the future?	___ Yes	___ No	___ Maybe

3. If you have responded "yes" to one or more of the IAQ questions, you should consider using database management software to enhance the student's potential learning experience.
4. Using the sample lesson plan, develop a lesson plan based on this project. Within the plan, indicate how and when the learner will use a database. Additionally, list potential benefits and challenges that may occur when involving this software in the lesson.

Level 3b Workout: Exploring the NETS connection

PART A: Once you have an understanding of the features and applications of general spreadsheet skills, a deeper understanding of the analytical power of data analysis can be focused on. By using the National Educational Technology Standards (NETS) developed by the International Society for Technology in Education (ISTE), the next few tasks will provide a foundation for the importance of integrating this chapter's skill set into any teacher's professional practice. There are two sets of NETS: one designed for the skills needed by teachers (NETS-T), the other for the skills needed by K–12 students (NETS-S). A complete listing of these standards can be found in the Appendix of this book.

PART B: The following chart provides examples of how the use of a spreadsheet application (with an emphasis on data analysis) can directly align with the NETS-T and the NETS-S. As you read these strategies, try to consider additional connections that could be made between these standards and this set of skills. Additionally, consider the answer to the focus questions presented for each unique standard.

NETS-T and NETS-S	Example Activities and Focus Questions
NETS-T 1. Facilitate and Inspire Student Learning and Creativity NETS-S 1. Creativity and Innovation	• Have the students identify different symptoms of various ailments or conditions. Also have them include the name of the ailment and potential prescriptions to overcome the problem. Give the students specific scenarios that require them to filter their database based on symptoms and determine possible prescriptions for solutions. • Give the students a table for them to investigate and fill out. The table might include comparative fields of information about countries, people, places, and so forth. Help the students see trends in the data by sorting or filtering based on specific criteria. For example, have them collect data on weather patterns for various geographic regions around the world. Based on a comparison of average temperatures, encourage the students to make predictions about the region's agriculture, architecture, and cultural trends such as clothing, food, and transportation. 1. How can the manipulation of data (through a spreadsheet) aid in the process of prediction? 2. Given these scenarios, brainstorm an activity that would promote the use of the data and the incorporation of a student's imagination. One example is designing a clothing line based on the climate and terrain of the area.
NETS-T 2. Design and Develop Digital-Age Learning Experiences and Assessments NETS-S 4. Critical Thinking, Problem Solving, and Decision Making	• Have the students collect data within a specific experiment. For example, using different degrees of acid-based water for plants, measure the growth rate of different types of plants. With the database compare various acid levels and predict what the impact of acid rain would be on plant life given certain concentrations of acid within the rain. • Have the students develop a database about their favorite animal (or state, or national park, or relative). Have them list all of the salient features of their animal (name, what it looks like, color) and then have them all combine their efforts into a single database of information. Have the students then search and sort based on specific characteristics and note the common elements of the different selected animals. 3. In what ways could the use of database management software facilitate the higher-order skills of comparison, synthesis, and evaluation between large sets of information? 4. Drawing comparisons between objects (or people, animals, places, etc.) that are not seemingly similar can be a very powerful tool to reinforce critical thinking skills. How could a comparative analysis of data be used in a lesson in each of the following subject areas: math, science, social studies, art, literature, music? Provide at least one example (brief) for each.
NETS-T 3. Model Digital-Age Work and Learning NETS-S 2. Communication and Collaboration NETS-S 3. Research and Information Fluency NETS-T 5. Engage in Professional Growth and Leadership	• Have the students create a reference database of research articles (including author, title, full publication information, key words, and short annotated bibliography) and then merge the information into the reference section of a research paper you have assigned. • Using this reference list database, have students cooperatively create a database of articles about a specific topic (e.g., cyber ethics) and combine their efforts together into a single large database for students to use on a related research project. 5. In this scenario, how does the use of a spreadsheet aid in the collaboration of the students? 6. Do students need to be taught how to analyze data or is it something that they learn intuitively? Explain your thoughts.

NETS-T 4. Promote and Model Digital Citizenship and Responsibility NETS-S 5. Digital Citizenship	7. Describe how teachers might use a similar database for the development of their professional knowledge. • Develop databases about different types of governments from countries of the world. Include information about population, average income, religious affiliations, and so forth. Filter to compare information about the country's population, such as religious affiliations. 8. Consider the previous example. How do tasks that require a critical analysis of data relating to world events or positions relate to the digital age? How does this relate to students? 9. How could the use of a spreadsheet database be beneficial to promoting critical thinking in learners with differing abilities? 10. How could the use of a spreadsheet database aid a teacher in creating a differentiated learning environment?
NETS-T3. Model Digital-Age Work and Learning	Due to the practical nature of spreadsheet databases, there are many ways that a teacher can promote their use by incorporating them into classroom procedures and production: 1. *Organizer.* For the classroom teacher, databases are frequently used to help organize information. For example, if you have a personal book collection, it would be wise to have a database that lists all of the relevant information about the books, their locations, and so on. You can even get fancy and indicate which of the books has been borrowed and by whom. This is a great way to avoid buying multiple copies of the same book and to know where they are all located. 2. *Label maker.* Create all kinds of folder labels. In your filing cabinets you have all kinds of folders with different lesson plans, activities, and so forth. A database of these titles with the ability to mail merge labels allows you to quickly print off labels for those folders. 3. *Label maker II.* On the first day of class (or when you are going on a field trip, dividing kids into special activity groups, for example), create name tags via a label mail merge with your student info database. 4. *Mailing lists.* Create info sheets of all of your students, parents, and possible others. You can keep specific information about each of your students and use that to sort, filter, or merge within personalized letters. 5. *Lesson plans.* List all of your lesson plans based, for instance, on content, type of learner, instructional methods, and media. 6. *Electronic portfolios.* Create a database that allows you to know what is in each of your students' portfolios, assessment information, location of the pieces, and so forth. With electronic means you can even save and duplicate versions of the students' work when needed. 7. *Examples.* Use a database to list all of your examples of your past students' work, what lesson plan the project relates to, key words about it, and where it is located so that you can find it again to show other students.

Collaborating and coauthoring in Excel 2010

As explained in the previous two chapters, collaboration is a key expectation and is a skill that is highlighted within the NETS. Refer to Chapter 3 ("Spreadsheets"), page 76, to review how documents created specifically in Excel (such as the simple databases created in this chapter) can be developed by groups of individuals working on the same document even when they are in various locations throughout the world.

Further ideas on using data management as a learning tool

Note: These ideas are to help you generate your own. Don't let it bother you if they aren't the right content or grade level—use one and adapt it to be helpful within your own situation. These are meant to be stimuli for additional ideas.

Here are a few ideas that may help you see how a database might be beneficial:

1. Give the students a table for them to investigate and fill out. The table might include comparative fields of information about countries, people, places, and so forth. Help the students see trends in the data by sorting or filtering based on specific criteria. For example, have them collect data on weather patterns for various geographic regions around the

world. Based on a comparison of average temperatures, what could the students predict about the type of agriculture that can be produced in that region?

2. Have the students collect data within a specific experiment. For example, using different degrees of acid-based water for plants, measure the growth rate of different types of plants. With the database compare various acid levels and predict what the impact of acid rain would be on plant life given certain concentrations of acid within the rain.

3. Have the students create a database of the world's most recognized scientists during the seventeenth, eighteenth, nineteenth, and twentieth centuries. Have them categorize the type discoveries made and the country of origin. Have the students examine, sort, and filter the data to see from which parts of the world the most notable discoveries came and if there are specific trends based on location, century, and so on.

4. Have the students identify different symptoms of various ailments or conditions. Also have them include the name of the ailment and potential prescriptions to overcome the problem. Give the students specific scenarios that require them to filter their database based on symptoms and determine possible prescriptions for solutions.

MS Excel for Mac 2011: Excel as a database

ORIENTATION

This addendum assumes you have previewed the full Chapter 4 and have a grasp of the general workings of the spreadsheet. The full version of Chapter 4 contains the complete discussion of data management and the terms associated with it. Those terms and basic concepts will not be repeated in this section.

This section of the chapter focuses specifically on the use of MS Excel 2011 (for the Mac) as a data management tool. In most cases, there is a close similarity to how MS Excel for the PC (Excel 2010) functions, but there are some unique differences that we will highlight within this addendum. It is highly encouraged that you have an understanding of the basics of MS Excel 2011 (or read Chapter 3) prior to working through this chapter.

What's the MS Excel for Mac 2011 workspace look like?

Figure 4.14 is an example of MS Excel for Mac 2011.

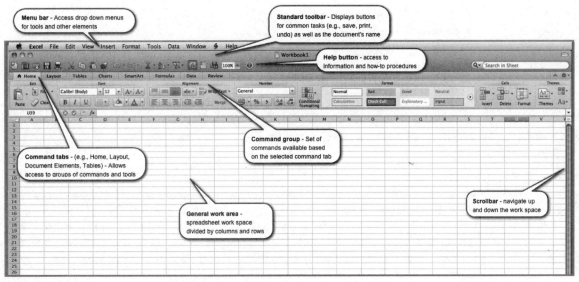

FIGURE 4.14 View of a Microsoft Excel for Mac work area

What commands can be used?

Within the Mac version of MS Office, there are drop-down menu options (see Figure 4.15) and a ribbon of tools that runs across the top of the work screen. So, for example, if you wished to insert a chart into your document, you could accomplish that by going to the **Menu bar** >>> **Insert** drop-down menu >>> **Chart**.

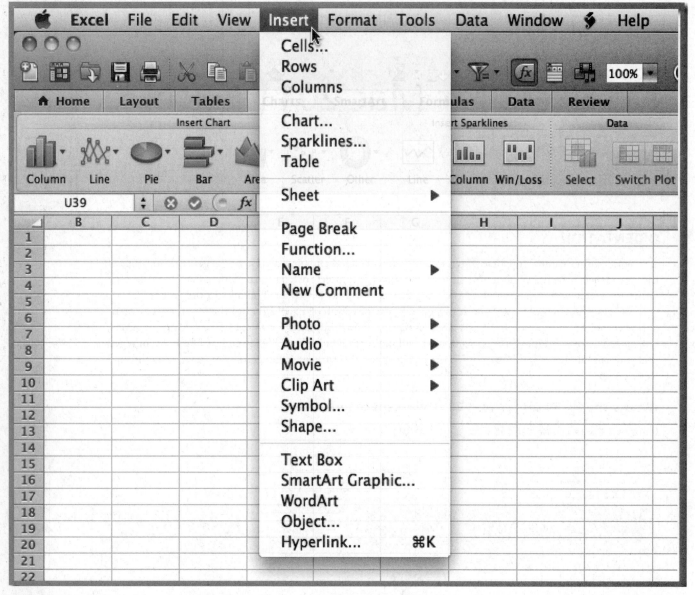

FIGURE 4.15 View of the Menu bar with drop down Insert menu revealed

Note: The menu bar provides quick access to a variety of relevant dialog boxes. For example, when you choose to insert a function via the menu bar, a dialog box will appear that will give you a number of options of what type of formula you would like to use. As shown in Figure 4.15 you can explore these menu bar options to see all of the different dialog boxes (e.g., Page Break, Function, Table, Chart) that can be accessed.

Likewise, you could use the ribbon and click **Chart** tab >>> **Insert Chart** command group >>> **Chart** button. To remain consistent with the MS Office 2010 PC version, we will focus most of our comments on using the ribbon to accomplish the tasks within this text. Some basic things to note about the use of the ribbons:

- The command groups change based on the command tab selected.
- Many of the selected tool buttons within the command groups can be opened to reveal galleries of options related to that tool.
- Contextual tabs with associated contextual command groups appear when a specific object like a chart, formula, picture, graphic, or table is selected in the spreadsheet (see Figure 4.16).

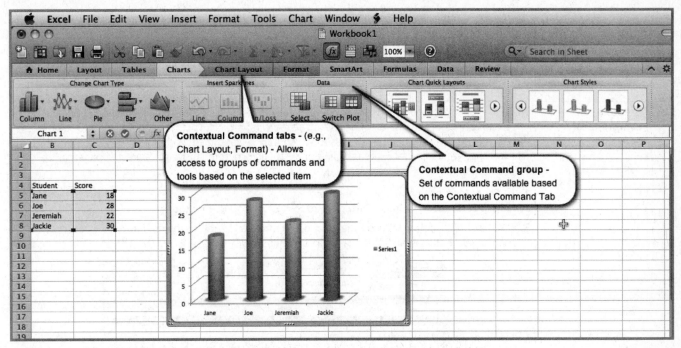

FIGURE 4.16 Selecting a specific item (e.g., chart, graphic) in the workspace reveals contextual tabs and associated contextual commands that can be accessed and used with the selected item

Orientation Workout

Return to the Orientation Workout on page 120 of this text and complete it as it is designed. The main purpose of this Workout is to get you familiar with how to enter data, work with formulas, and so on within the workspace as well as accessing and using the various tools on the menu bar and ribbons.

LEVEL 1: REVISITING THE RECYCLING PROJECT

Scenario 1

To accomplish this Level 1 task, review Scenario 1 (page 121), specifically focusing on Figures 4.3, 4.4, and 4.5. Using these figures as guides, re-create those documents by following these steps.

No.	Feature	Steps to Get It Done
1.	**Create and populate a new database**	1. Launch Excel. If a new worksheet does not appear, click on the File menu and select New Workbook from the list. 2. A new, blank worksheet should appear and you can begin entering data. 3. Go to Chapter 3 ("Spreadsheets") and review steps 2 through 6 in Level 1. These steps will guide you in the following: insert, align, and format column headings; enter data; adjust columns and rows; add gridlines; and format cells.
2.	**Sort the records**	1. Click within at least one cell within a range. 2. Go to **Data** tab >>> **Sort & Filter** group >>> **Sort** drop-down button.

		3. Select from the drop-down list to sort the data. The standard options are to sort in ascending or descending manner. To customize the sort further (or to sort by a specific field) select Custom Sort . . . . **4.** A list of the column headings will appear. Use the Field Selection list to choose the field you want to base the sort on (e.g., Mr. Rena selected Class period as the column [field]). Click OK and the sort will be completed. To really get a hang of this, try sorting a number of different ways and use descending as well as ascending orders.
3.	**Create a comprehensive sort**	There may be times when you want to complete a sort of several different kinds of data at once. For example, in the database of students for the recycling project, you may find it helpful to see the database of students grouped by the city in which they live and then, within those cities, grouped by whether they were a leader in the recycling project. Such comprehensive sorts are completed in the following manner. **1.** Click at least one cell within a range. **2.** Go to **Data** tab >>> **Sort & Filter** group >>> **Sort** drop-down button. **3.** In the Sort by section, click on the drop-down arrow and click on the field (column header) on which you want the first or primary sort to be based. 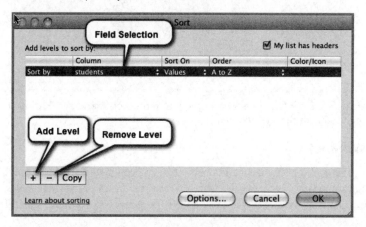 **4.** Click on the + which is the Add Level button and a new sort selection row (Then by) will appear. **5.** In the Then by section, click on the drop-down arrow and click on the field (column header) on which you want the second sort to be based. **6.** Continue to add levels as needed for the comprehensive sort. **7.** Once you have selected all of the levels and sort columns, click OK and the sort will be completed. **Note:** Within the Sort dialog box it is also possible to select what values to Sort On and to select the Order of the sort. **Another note:** In the Sort dialog box you can also select whether or not you have a header row on your database. This tells the database or spreadsheet to consider the first row as a listing of headings or as a record of data. In this case, we have a header and thus it needs to be marked as such.
4.	**Filter the records**	Select your full database, including the column headings. Go to **Data** tab >>> **Sort & Filter** group >>> **Filter** drop-down button and select the filter you'd like to apply (By Cell Value, By Cell Color, etc.). 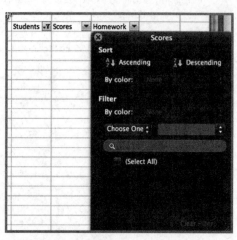

		Note that little down arrows have now been posted by each of the column headings. To filter the information, simply select the field title (column heading) you want to use as a filter and click its down arrow. A window will appear that allows you to select the criterion on which the filter is to be based. For example, if you only wanted to select students who participated as group leaders in the recycling project, you would go to the leader column, click on the down arrow and make sure only the "yes" alternative is checked from the list of possibilities given. Once your criterion is selected, click on the OK button and the database only reveals those records of the students designated as leaders in the project. To restore all of the data, go to **Data** tab >>> **Sort & Filter** group >>> **Filter** drop-down button and select clear filter. A filter doesn't lose the extra data—it just allows you to see only what you have selected to see. Try a number of these simple filters to learn how they work.
5.	More advanced and custom filters	1. Using the same process described in step 4, use the down arrows to open the Filter window. 2. Choose the Custom Filter drop-down button to select the criterion you would like to use to develop your filter (contains, equals, does not contain, etc.). 3. Use the down arrow button to select the comparison operator you wish to use (e.g., equals, contains, and so on). In the box next to the comparison operator, enter the criterion you wish to compare. For example, to find just those students whose phone numbers begin with the prefix 472, select the comparison operator of Begins with and type in the 472 in the box to the right. Explore the options in this window. There are many ways that you can filter your data.
6.	Combining for even more advanced filtering and sorting	1. Begin with the full database set of records. 2. Use the AutoFilter to select only those students who performed the role of leaders in the project. 3. Use a Custom AutoFilter to select only those leaders who live in either the 47902 or the 47908 zip code areas. 4. Sort the remaining list in descending alphabetical order based on first name. **Note:** As suggested here, it is possible to run a number of different individual filters to select very specific records.

Level 1a and 1b Workouts

Return to the Level 1a and 1b Workouts found on page 125. Complete the Workouts using Figures 4.3, 4.4, and 4.5 as guides for your work.

LEVEL 2: MAIL MERGE AND OTHER GOOD STUFF

What should you be able to do?

The focus within Level 2 is to help you use Help and other resources to access and use various other features of the MS Excel application.

Similar to Help in Windows, there is also Help in MS Excel and most other sophisticated spreadsheet software. To use Help, click the Help button on the tab bar of the standard toolbar (see Figure 4.14).

As shown in Figure 4.17 you can also access the help function through the Help drop-down menu on the menu bar.

Help

Search

Excel Help

Welcome to Excel
Get Started with Excel

Check for Updates
Visit the Product Web Site
Send Feedback about Excel

FIGURE 4.17 Accessing Help through the main menu bar in MS Excel for Mac

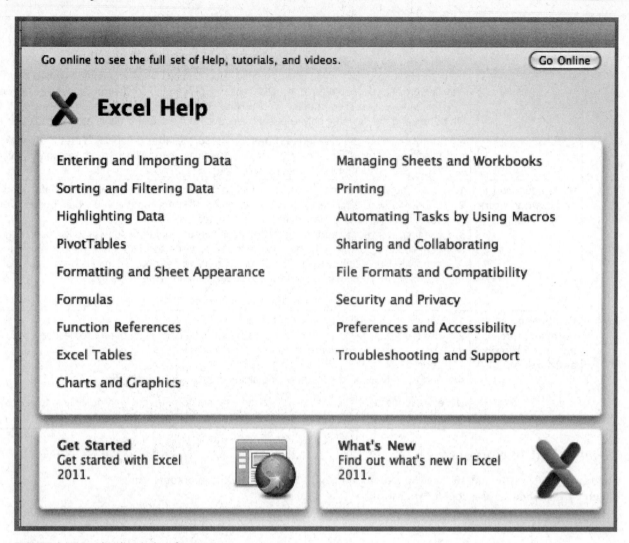

Go online to see the full set of Help, tutorials, and videos.   (Go Online)

X Excel Help

Entering and Importing Data	Managing Sheets and Workbooks
Sorting and Filtering Data	Printing
Highlighting Data	Automating Tasks by Using Macros
PivotTables	Sharing and Collaborating
Formatting and Sheet Appearance	File Formats and Compatibility
Formulas	Security and Privacy
Function References	Preferences and Accessibility
Excel Tables	Troubleshooting and Support
Charts and Graphics	

Get Started
Get started with Excel 2011.

What's New
Find out what's new in Excel 2011.

FIGURE 4.18 Excel Help window for Mac

Clicking the Excel Help button opens the Help window (see Figure 4.18). From here you can browse general Help topics, enter key words to search for a specific question that you might have, explore additional online Help topics, review tutorials to help you get started, and so on.

Scenario 2

To expand your capabilities and begin to see how Help can be accessed and used to find additional features, review Scenario 2 on page 127, paying close attention to Figures 4.10, 4.11, and 4.12 and their respective callouts. Using these figures as guides, practice using the highlighted features by accessing and using each of the following word processing features.

Feature	Steps to Get It Done
Develop a draft word-processed document with placeholders for data to be merged	**Important note:** In most cases, you'll find it easier to complete the mail merge from within MS Word or similar word processing software. Likewise, the best Help to guide you through the merging process is found within Word. Information about and procedure for creating: http://www.microsoft.com/mac/how-to Help • Key words: Mail Merge Word 2010 • Select: Use mail merge to create and print letters and other documents. • Select: Set up the main document and follow the given procedure.

Key features to note, explore, and try out:

1. To begin the mail merge, within MS Word click on the Tools menu found at the top of the screen. Select Mail Merge Manager.
2. The Mail Merge Manager window appears (see Figure 4.19). There are six steps to creating a mail merge document. Each step is numbered. Click on the drop-down menu for each in chronological order. Answer the basic prompts to create a product specific for your needs.
3. Similar to what is shown in Figure 4.12, create a draft word-processed document. As you create it, think of how the database data will be integrated within the document.
4. You may find it convenient at this point to leave placeholders or spaces in locations where data will be merged.
5. Review the step-by-step procedures given within Scenarios 1 and 2 of Chapter 2 ("Word Processing"). Those procedures will guide you through the process of setting up and formatting a draft document.

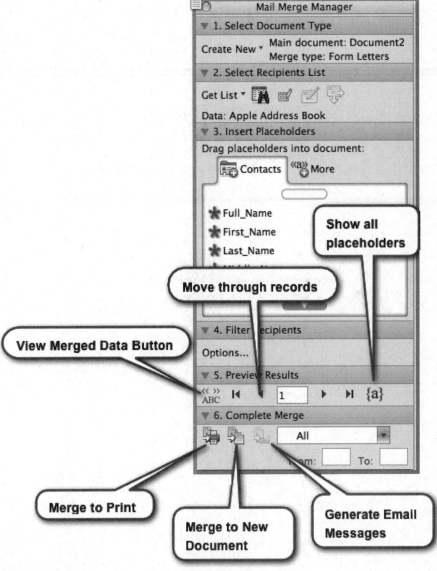

FIGURE 4.19 Commands for completing a mail merge

Mail Merge Step 1: Select Document Type	In the Mail Merge Manager: 1. Click the drop-down button for step 1. Choose Create New and select the type of item you'd like to create (label, letter, envelope, etc.).
Mail Merge Step 2: Select recipients list	In the Mail Merge Manager: 1. Click on the Get List drop-down button and locate the source for the data you will be using. 2. It is recommended that this data set is developed in MS Excel prior to starting the document but there are options available to allow for an as-needed development.

(continued)

Mail Merge Step 3: Insert Placeholders	In the Mail Merge Manager: 1. In the letter (or other product) be sure to leave spaces for the merged fields to be applied. Return to the Mail Merge Manager window and click the third step. 2. Drag the appropriate data types to their selected location in your document. **Note:** At this point, just the placeholder will appear in your document. See step 5 for details on viewing the merged data.
Mail Merge Step 4: Filter Recipients	In the Mail Merge Manager: 1. Determine which recipients from your data source will be included in the final merging. 2. Click Options and Query Options window appears. 3. Select the groups you want to include and click OK.
Mail Merge Step 5: Preview Results	In the Mail Merge Manager: 1. Preview the letter (or other product) and click the View Merged Data button to see the populated document. 2. Use the arrows to move through the records.
Mail Merge Step 6: Complete the Merge	In the Mail Merge Manager: 1. Click on the drop-down menu for step 6 Completing the Merge. 2. Select the option that best meets your needs. Options include Merge to Print, Merge to New Document, Generate Email Messages.

Level 2 Workout

Return to the Level 2 Workouts found on page 132. Complete these workouts using Figures 4.10, 4.11, and 4.12 as guides.

5 PRESENTATION SOFTWARE
MS PowerPoint: The Basics of Creating Presentations, Handouts, and Much, Much More

INTRODUCTION

What should you know about presentation software?

Presentation software (e.g., Microsoft's PowerPoint) is designed to help you get your message across to others and look good in the process. This software can become one of the most interesting, enjoyable, and fruitful for students and teachers to learn. Within this introduction, we want you to discover the following:

- What a presentation program is, what it can do, and how it can help in teaching and learning
- How to justify the use of the presentation program as an effective tool—by knowing when and why it should or shouldn't be used

Terms to know			
action buttons	master slide	slide layout	transitions
animations	Microsoft PowerPoint	slide reading view	video clips
audio clips	normal view	slide show view	WebQuest
custom animation	Notes page	slide sorter view	website
design templates	presentation software	SmartArt	
Handout page	slide	templates	

What is presentation software and what does it do?

Presentation software is a computer application that allows you to do just what the name implies—create and deliver presentations. For teachers and students a great deal of learning focuses on presentations of some kind—thus this application is one that should become a regular in your learning arsenal.

Review Figure 5.1 and note the three slides that have been created as part of a presentation about computer hardware. With relative ease, you can build individual slides and then sequence them together into a full **slide** show. On each slide you can put text, pictures, Internet links, **audio clips, animations**, **video clips**—the list goes on. Plus you can instruct this program to create handouts and run itself automatically if you want the no-hands approach.

With all of these benefits, it's also a great tool to have students use as they design and create their own presentations.

What are some commonly used presentation-type software?

Standard software varieties:

- **Microsoft PowerPoint**
- Apple Keynote
- Corel WordPerfect Presentations

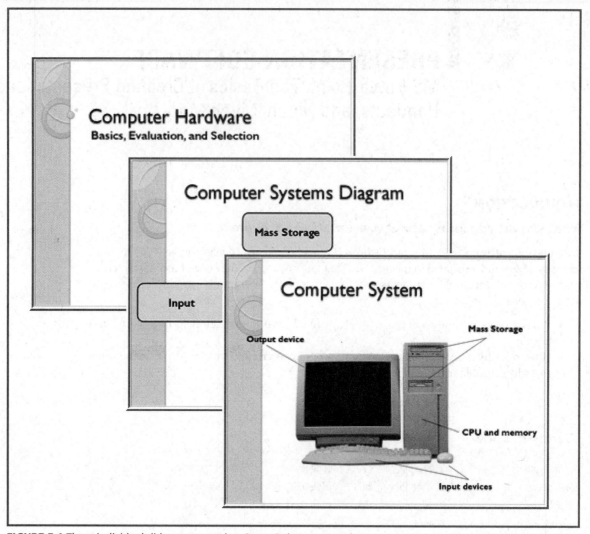

FIGURE 5.1 Three individual slides or screens in a PowerPoint presentation

- Lotus Freelance Graphics
- Sun Microsystems StarOffice/OpenOffice Impress

Web 2.0 varieties:

- Google Docs (Presentations)
- Zoho Show

Note: We focus on MS PowerPoint (PPT). However, *all of what we present can be done in most of these other presentation programs listed.* So if you don't have access to MS PPT, don't be alarmed—you can still complete the projects and learn the basic skills.

Why bother learning how to use PPT or other forms of presentation software?

- *Quality shows.* PPT allows you to create presentations that will pleasantly surprise you. Suddenly your work can look better and your message will be cleaner and clearer for your audience.
- *It's fast.* Because many of the processes within this program are automated, you can learn to develop presentations in very quick order. You can brainstorm using an outlining function within the program and immediately turn the outline into a basic set of presentation slides. This helps when time is important (and when is time *not* important?).

- *It's easy to adapt.* Once you have the basics of a presentation completed, you can easily adapt and change it to fit a new audience. It also works well with other programs. If you have a graph in Excel and want it included—PPT can do that. Or if you have a poem in a word-processed file, a simple cut and paste and it's now in your presentation.
- *Ease of adding multimedia.* Sometimes a picture can say a thousand words—so here's the chance to use visuals, audio, video clips, additional **websites,** and so forth to enhance your presentation. All can be added with relative ease and speed.
- *Two (or three) things at once.* Guess what? As you are working to develop your presentation slides, PPT automatically creates handouts you can print, copy, and have ready to distribute. Likewise, as you finish your presentation, if you want to put it on the web it is ready to go. Such features allow you to look like you put in more effort than actually needed.
- *Helps with learning.* Often we hear, "The teacher actually learns the most." You can use this to the benefit of your students by having them develop presentations.
- *It's not just for oral presentations any more.* PPT can be a very effective and efficient way to create individualized instruction. For example, PPT can be used to set up learning centers that allow learners to select the sequence of information, give responses, and receive feedback on their efforts.
- *Creates its own backup system.* Suppose you go to a convention to deliver your presentation and they don't have the computer setup that you need. You can simply print your presentation and copy it as a transparency to be used on a usual overhead machine or create handouts that can be used if the bulb in the overhead is having problems.

How are presentation programs used at school? A brief list of ideas

By the teacher:	By the student:
• *Lectures and presentations*	• *Student-made presentations*
• *Individual tutorials*	• *Oral reports*
• *Parent-teacher nights*	• *Electronic portfolios*
• *Classroom handouts*	• *Group projects*
• *Staff development*	• *Science experiments*

ORIENTATION

What's the workspace look like?

Figure 5.2 shows the workspace of a common presentation program (MS PowerPoint). This figure depicts an example of a presentation currently being developed. Note the use of the outline area to add content quickly and the note area used to add notes for the speaker. To view this example presentation, go to the website that accompanies this book.

What commands can be used?

As in all MS Office applications (e.g., MS Word, MS Excel) there is a ribbon of tools that runs across the top of the work screen. Within each ribbon the actual tools that can be used to develop presentations are grouped together under the various command tabs (e.g., Home, Insert, Design, Animation). Selecting a specific tab reveals an associated command set or group. Once a command tab has been selected, this specific group remains visible and ready for use. Items within the set may appear as individual items or as a gallery of related items. For example, selecting the Design tab (see Figure 5.3) in PPT reveals a group of commands that deals specifically with the orientation of the slides, selecting or creating themes for the slide backgrounds, and how items can be arranged and grouped within the presentation.

It should be noted that there are additional commands that will occasionally be needed. These contextual commands appear when a specific object like a picture, graphic, table, or chart is selected.

For more information about the PPT ribbon and command tabs, please review the mentor videos on the website that accompanies this book.

PDToolkit
for
Teaching and Learning with Microsoft® Office 2010 and Office 2011 for Mac

Go to PDToolkit for **Teaching and Learning with Microsoft® Office 2010 and Office 2011 for Mac** to locate Workout Level Two for Chapter Five.

PDToolkit
for
Teaching and Learning with Microsoft® Office 2010 and Office 2011 for Mac

Go to PDToolkit for **Teaching and Learning with Microsoft® Office 2010 and Office 2011 for Mac** to locate the mentoring videos for Chapter Five.

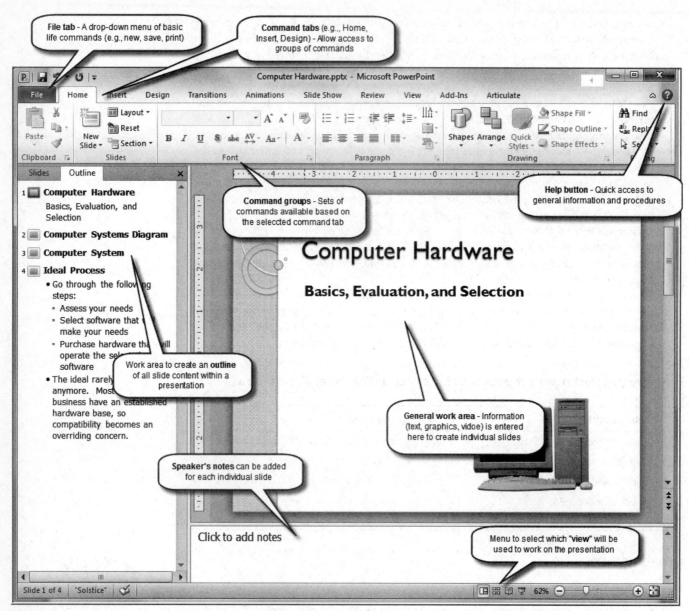

FIGURE 5.2 Normal view of the workspace used to create PPT presentations

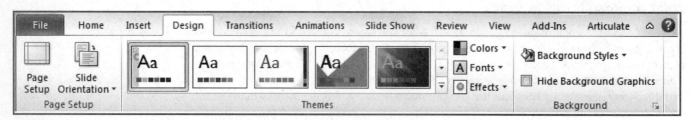

FIGURE 5.3 The ribbon holds the command tabs, groups, and individual commands

Orientation Workout 1: Explore the territory

Turn on your computer and attempt the following:

1. Launch the PPT software.
2. Create a new PPT presentation with a blank first slide.
3. Explore the various tabs on the ribbon and the different command groups.
4. Create three or four new slides.
5. On the various practice slides
   - Add text
   - Change the text's format (e.g., size, style)
   - Change the **slide layout**
   - Adjust the **design templates**
   - Add text to the speaker's notes
   - Switch between different views of the slides (e.g., normal versus slide sorter versus presentation)

Go to PDToolkit for **Teaching and Learning with Microsoft® Office 2010 and Office 2011 for Mac** to locate Workout Level Two for Chapter Five.

Key features

VIEWS. To work effectively within PPT, there are different ways that you can view your workspace (see Figures 5.4 to 5.7). To select one of these views, click on the PPT ribbon's View tab and select from one of the views in the Presentation View command group. In addition, there's a View bar generally located on the lower right portion of the workspace in PPT that looks like

. Clicking on these will also change the workspace view.

Normal View . Note that you can view and work in the outline on the left, the slide itself (main work section), and enter in any speaker notes directly below the slide in **normal view.** This is generally the view used to complete most work (see Figure 5.4).

Note: When you are creating a number of slides and entering a large amount of text or even when you are brainstorming a potential presentation, click on the Outline tab and work in that view. You can expand this view to a majority of the workspace; it's very similar to working in MS Word outline. This can facilitate the development of your presentation.

Slide Sorter View . When you have a number of slides created, it often becomes difficult to change their order, to quickly see where a new slide needs to be inserted, or to delete a slide no longer needed. This is where the **slide sorter view** comes to the rescue (see Figure 5.5). This view allows you to see all of your slides in a smaller version that can easily be grabbed and moved, deleted, added, and sequenced to your specifications. You will also find that this is a good view to use if you are adding **transitions** between slides.

Reading View . **Slide reading view** has been designed to facilitate reviewing an entire slide presentation by a single individual, instead of a full group presentation (see Figure 5.6). Simple control buttons allow for easy control and navigation of the slide show.

Slide Show View . **Slide show view** is the view that you use to present your slide program (see Figure 5.7). Within this view, the slide takes up the full screen and no toolbars or other features are displayed. You should also note that within this view all of the animations and action buttons (more on those later) will be executed when selected to do so.

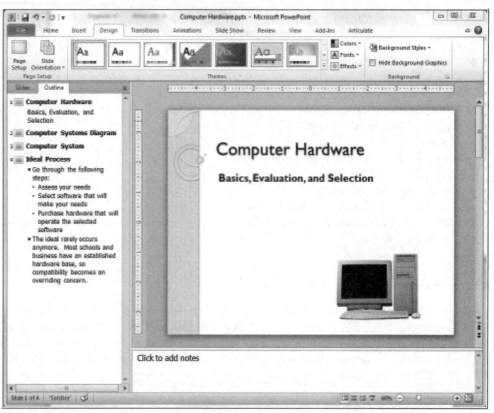

FIGURE 5.4 Normal view of a PowerPoint presentation

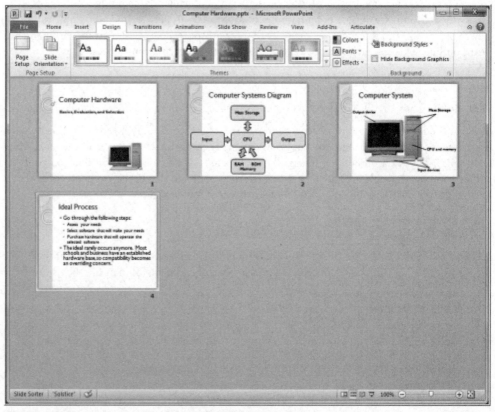

FIGURE 5.5 Slide sorter view of a PowerPoint presentation

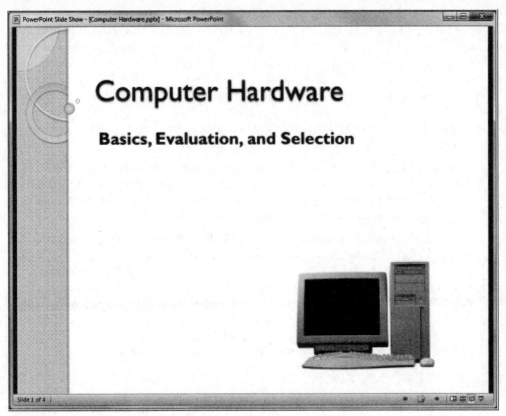

FIGURE 5.6 Reading view of a PowerPoint presentation

FIGURE 5.7 Slide show view of a PowerPoint presentation

SLIDE LAYOUTS.   PPT has a number of different premade layouts that may match what you need for the slide you are about to create. Each layout already has inserted placeholders that may contain pictures, tables, titles, bulleted lists, and so forth. If one of these premade layouts matches your needs, it can be quickly selected and then information can be automatically formatted to meet the specifications of your slide. You point and click and let the PPT layout do the work instead of taking the time to create the layout yourself. This can be a real time saver!

If you don't like the way it looks once you have used a layout, you can adapt it directly or select a different auto layout and have it reformat automatically for you.

How do you access the slide layouts?   Either create a new slide or go to the slide where you want to change the layout. Click the Home tab and then select the Layout button within the Slides group (**Home** tab >>> **Slides** group >>> **Layout**). Once the Layout button has been clicked, the slide layout gallery will appear (see Figure 5.8).

How does the slide layout work?   First, you select the layout of your choice (scroll through the Layout Gallery and click on your selection). The new slide will immediately be adapted to the type of layout you have selected (instructions to Click to . . . within dashed line boxes will indicate the placeholder). As you insert content or pictures, in your slide you simply click in the area where you want to work. All spacing, fonts, and formatting have been done for you. Figure 5.9 is an example of a new slide with a slide layout that has been set up to allow for a title, text, and other elements such as tables, charts, pictures, video, to be quickly inserted. Again, a great way to speed the process along.

Themes

What is a theme?   Themes are already completed design settings that can be selected and applied to your presentation to give it a specific, consistent look. PPT comes with a large variety of professionally designed themes.

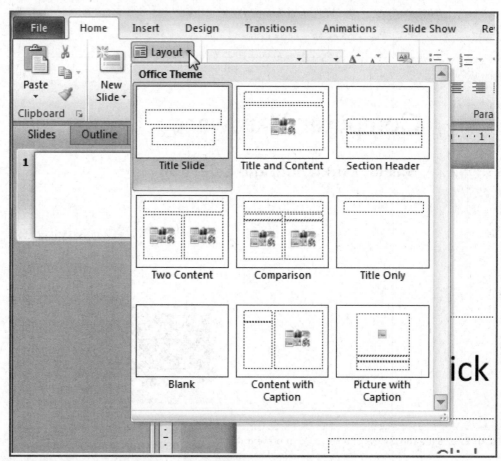

FIGURE 5.8 New slide with Slide Layout Gallery exposed

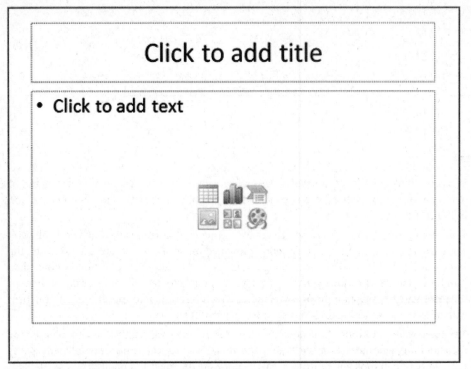

FIGURE 5.9 New slide with a selected slide layout

Why use themes? These **templates** were developed by professionals who have considered the color combinations, font styles, and background graphics to give a presentation an overall polished look. By merely selecting and choosing one of the themes, that look can be incorporated within your presentation without any further effort on your part. This allows you to concentrate on your content for the presentation and not worry about making it look perfect.

How do you select and apply a theme? Simply click the Design tab and review the various themes shown within the theme gallery of the Theme group (**Design** tab >>> **Themes** group >>> **Theme**) (see Figure 5.10). Note that there are extra themes that can be selected using the up and down selection arrows found within the Theme group section.

Other interesting notes about themes:

1. *Preview.* You can preview how a specific theme will look by simply moving your mouse cursor over a targeted theme. The preview lets you see what your slide will look like without actually making the formal change.
2. *Adapting themes.* If you like a specific theme format but prefer to adapt the color scheme, the font styles, or even the special effects, you can do this easily by selecting from the color, font, and effects galleries (**Design** tab >>> **Theme** group >>> **Colors** (or **Fonts** or **Effects**).
3. *Changing a theme.* If you ever desire to change a theme, repeat the process and select a new theme. Once applied, it will automatically replace the previously selected theme.
4. *Applying themes for different slides.* A theme can be applied to a single slide or an entire presentation of slides. To make this selection, right click on any selected theme and make your selection of how it should be applied from the menu options presented.
5. *Additional theme options.* If you would like additional options for various types of themes, go to the Microsoft Office PowerPoint Help and type the key word Theme. A website will be accessed that will allow you to download from various theme options.

FIGURE 5.10 Slide themes found within the Design tab of the ribbon

FIGURE 5.11 Accessing the master slide

Masters

What is a master slide? A **master slide** is a background that repeats on all slides, notes, or handouts of a presentation. It can contain text, graphics, automatic slide numbers, action buttons, and so on.

Why use masters? Masters are real time savers. There are situations in which you will want some element of a slide to be consistently presented on all slides of a presentation (e.g., the same colored background, the school logo, your name, the date, a set of action buttons, slide numbers). The master allows you to create it once and it automatically appears on all slides in the presentation (except for the ones you indicate you don't want it to appear on). This can help with keeping the slides looking consistent (see Figure 5.11).

Are there different kinds of masters? Yes, besides the Slide Master, there is also a master for the **Handout page** and one for the **Notes page.** In this way you can control how all of the pages for your handouts look and how the speaker's notes are designed and published.

How do you access the masters? Simple. On the PPT ribbon, go to **View** tab >>> **Presentation Views** group >>> **Slide Master** (or **Handout Master** or **Notes Master).**

How do you use the masters? Review Figure 5.12. This is a Slide Master that has some suggested elements already set up for you. In the left-hand column, there are different master slide layouts from which to select. Once a layout has been selected, simply click on any of the different elements within the workspace (e.g., title). You can adjust and add to this master just as you would to any other PPT slide. With the Slide Master tab selected, you can adjust what is already there (e.g., change the style, size, font of the heading) and this will automatically be applied to

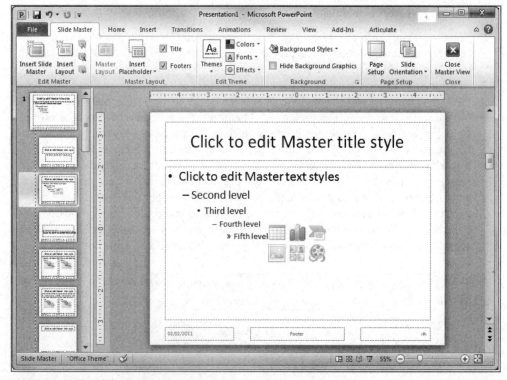

FIGURE 5.12 The Slide Master

all slides currently in your presentation or that will later be added to your presentation. If you don't like your changes, you can always change it back—nothing is permanent. When you are finished working with the Slide Master, click on the Close Master View button and you will return to the usual slides of your presentation.

For a guided tour of these key features, please review the *Orientation* set of mentoring videos on the website that accompanies this book.

Orientation Workout 2: Explore the key features

While in PPT:

1. Open the Computer Hardware PPT slide show. You can find it on the website that accompanies this book.
2. Add a new slide to the end of that presentation (**Home** tab >>> **Slides** group >>> **New Slide**).
3. Select a layout for the new slide (**Home** tab >>> **Slides** group >>> **Layout**). Fill in the placeholders with information relevant to the elements of the layout. Apply the theme to all slides in your Computer Hardware presentation.
4. Change the theme for this slide show (**Design** tab >>> **Theme** group >>> **Theme**). Preview various themes, then select and apply the one that you desire. Once you have applied the theme, alter the color or font scheme.
5. Open the Slide Master (**View** tab >>> **Presentation Views** group >>> **Slide Master**) and alter some feature on the Slide Master (e.g., add your name to the bottom of the Slide Master).
6. Return to your slides and switch to the slide sorter view. Rearrange the order of the slides by clicking and dragging one or more of the slides.
7. Change to the slide presentation view and examine all slides as if it were an actual presentation.

To view a demonstration of how to complete this Workout, review the *Orientation* mentor videos on the website that accompanies this book.

LEVEL 1: CREATING PRESENTATIONS TO TEACH

What should you be able to do?

Given specific guidelines and step-by-step procedures, you will be able to use various tools, techniques, and features of an electronic presentation program (specifically PPT) to design, create, and deliver a presentation.

What resources are provided?

Basically, Level 1 is divided into common teaching scenarios, selected solutions, and practice exercises (i.e., Workouts). The scenarios have been constructed to allow you to examine common problems and how they can be addressed through the use of this software. To do this we have provided the following:

1. Completed PPT presentations that you can review, compare, and learn how the features are used to address the problems presented within each scenario.
2. Quick reference figures that identify (via visual callouts) all of the key features that have been incorporated within the solution presentation. These allow you to rapidly identify the key features and reference exactly how to include such features within your own work.
3. Step-by-step instructions on how to incorporate all highlighted features within your work.
4. Video mentoring support that will support and guide you through the integration of each of the highlighted features.
5. Workout exercises that allow you to practice identifying and selecting which software features to use, when to use those features, how they should be incorporated, and to what degree they are effective.

How should you proceed?

If you have *little or no experience* with MS Office 2010 and particularly PPT, then we suggest you do the following:

1. Read and review Scenario 1.
2. Review the finished PPT presentation for that scenario.
3. Examine the quick reference figures (Figures 5.14, 5.15, and 5.16) and all of the highlights,
4. With the step-by-step directions given for each highlighted feature, use the software and practice using each of the features.
5. Access the videos that explain each of the features and how they are accomplished within the software.
6. Once you feel comfortable with these features, go to Scenario 2 and repeat these same steps with the new features introduced for that scenario in the actual presentation and the quick reference Figure 5.20.
7. After both scenarios have been reviewed, go to the Workout and work through the problems and exercises it outlines.

If you have *experience* with PPT 2010, you may want to review the scenarios and the quick reference figures first. If any of the features are unfamiliar, then use the step-by-step procedures as well as the mentoring support videos. Once the review has been completed, then move directly to the Workout exercise and create your own PPT presentation by incorporating many of the highlighted features.

PDToolkit
for
Teaching and Learning with Microsoft® Office 2010 and Office 2011 for Mac

Go to PDToolkit for **Teaching and Learning with Microsoft® Office 2010 and Office 2011 for Mac** to locate the mentoring videos for Chapter Five.

Scenario 1: How students differ

Janice, another eighth-grade teacher and one who is viewed as the computer "expert" in the school, comes to you with a request. She has been asked by your principal to give a series of short in-service lessons on integrating technology in the classroom. This week's is designed to focus on how technology can address individual student differences. She explains that she needs your help in reviewing the common differences of students faced by teachers and then she will follow with what can be done with technology to address those issues.

Even though you feel this is one more thing to add to your to-do list, you quickly remember all the times Janice has rescued you in the computer lab with her suggestions and practical help. So you smile and hear yourself enthusiastically reply, "Sure, I'd be happy to."

After a day or two of thinking about it (and a little research), you develop the following short outline and send an e-mail to Janice to get her thoughts and approval:

  I. Introduction: How students differ
    a. Begin with a story about how two students differ in the way they approach a problem.

  II. Highlight how students differ
    a. Developmental level
    b. Intelligence
    c. Learning style
    d. Gender
    e. Culture
    f. Socioeconomic status
    g. Special needs
    h. Motivation
    i. Existing knowledge and skills

  III. Define differentiated instruction
    a. Being sensitive to the needs of your students and finding ways to help students make the necessary connections for learning to occur in the best possible way.
    b. Source: Teach-nology Tutorial: http://www.teach-nology.com/tutorials/teaching/differentiate/

Later that day, she sends you back an e-mail with three attached PPT slides (see Figure 5.13). These are the slides she has created based on your outline.

By focusing on each of these individual slides (see Figures 5.14 to 5.16), we are able to highlight all of the key features that were completed in order to create those slides.

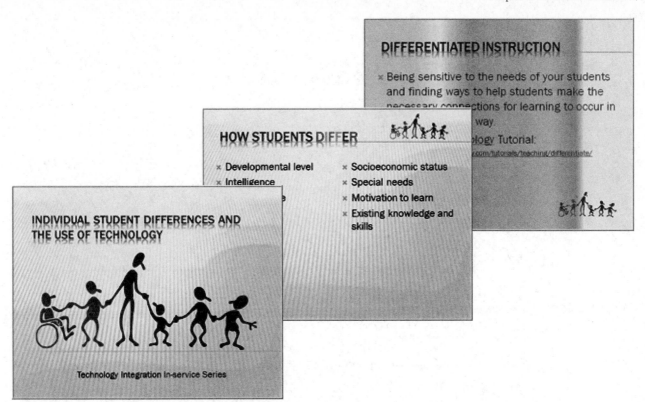

FIGURE 5.13 Beginning slides to an in-service lesson

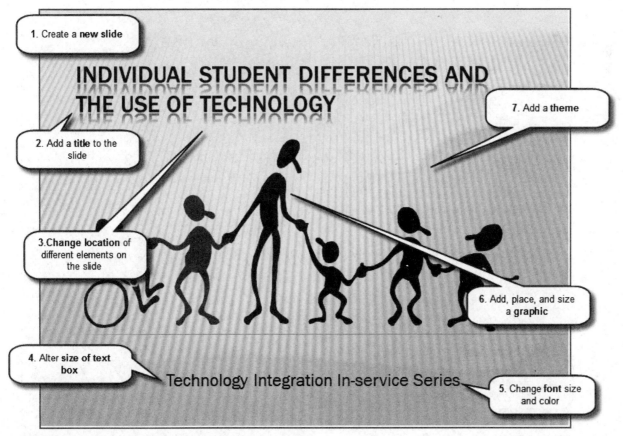

FIGURE 5.14 First slide of the "Student Differences" presentation

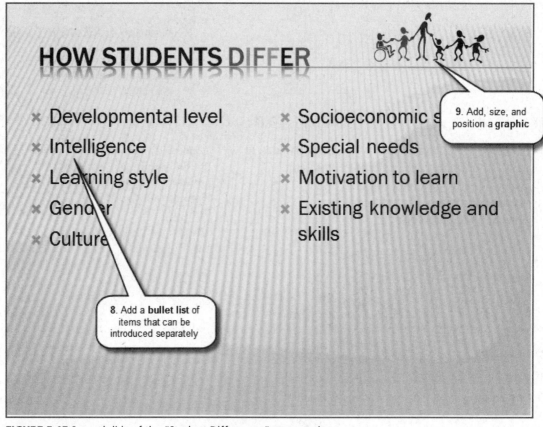

FIGURE 5.15 Second slide of the "Student Differences" presentation

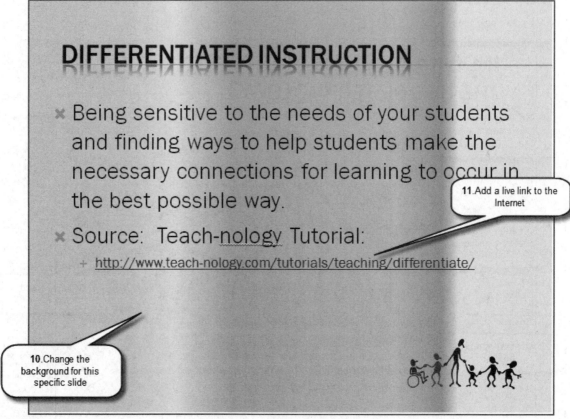

FIGURE 5.16 Third slide of the "Student Differences" presentation

These are common features frequently used within PPT presentations. You may be familiar with many of them if you have used such programs before. In addition, other application software (e.g., word processing) programs may also use similar features (e.g., changing font size and color). Use these figures to identify areas that may be new or that you may need some practice with to renew your skills.

To fully appreciate and understand all the features within this short presentation, open the actual program on the website that accompanies this book and view it as a slide show. Use Figures 5.14 to 5.16 to highlight all the key features that have been implemented within the show.

If you find some of the features new or that you need additional experience using, create a new slide in PPT and follow the step-by-step procedure for that specific feature. If you need additional guidance on how it can be completed, go to the website that accompanies this book and access the mentor video for that feature. The video will walk you through exactly how to use the feature.

Go to PDToolkit for **Teaching and Learning with Microsoft® Office 2010 and Office 2011 for Mac** to locate Workout Level One for Chapter Five.

Go to PDToolkit for **Teaching and Learning with Microsoft® Office 2010 and Office 2011 for Mac** to locate the mentoring videos for Chapter Five.

No.	Feature	Steps to Get It Done
1.	**Create a new slide**	1. Start PPT and create a new PPT presentation (**File** tab >>> **New**). 2. When the New Presentation window appears, click on the Blank Presentation icon and then the Create button (**Blank Presentation** >>> **Create**). 3. A new presentation should be opened with one slide. The slide will have a layout similar to a title slide. **Note:** As you click to create a new presentation, note all of the possible templates that you can also select and use. These have been developed by professional designers to give you a template for your work if you so desire. Take the time to explore and see what they have to offer.
2.	**Add a title to the slide**	When you open a new blank presentation, the slide layout for the first slide will be a Title slide layout—each slide thereafter will be the Title and content layout slide. 1. Click on the area in the new slide designated for the title. Type in the title of this slide (e.g., *Individual Differences . . .*). 2. Click on the subtitle area of the slide and type in the subtitle (e.g., *Technology Integration . . .*). Note how the slide auto layout controls the location, font type, and size.
3.	**Change the location of different elements of the slide**	1. To move any element on a slide, click once on the item you want to move and handles (little boxes) with a line around the item will appear. 2. Move your cursor directly over the line and it will turn into a four-way arrow. 3. Click, hold, and drag the item to the new location on the slide and then release the button. Individual Difference and the Use of Technology
4.	**Alter the text box size**	1. Click once on the text box and the handles will appear. 2. Move the cursor over one of the handles and it will change into a two-way arrow. 3. Click, hold, and drag. The size of the box will change in the direction you are dragging. Play with the different handles and see their different effects on the size of the box. Technology Integration In-Service Series

(continued)

5.	**Change font size, color, and the like.**	1. Select (highlight) the words you would like to change. 2. On the main ribbon, select the Home tab and review all of the selections within the font group. 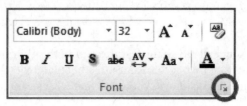 3. Select the type, size, color, and special effects that you desire. 4. To see additional options, click the icon in the lower right portion of this group and the font dialog box will appear.

6.	**Add, size, and place a graphic**

		1. *Get the graphic* (e.g., picture, clip art).
		  a. On the main ribbon, click **Insert** tab >>> **Illustrations** group >>> **Clipart . . . .** The Clip Art task pane will appear.
		  b. In the Clip Art task pane, enter a key word that describes the type of clip art you are searching for (e.g., sports) and then click on the Go button. Various small versions of the clip art should appear in the task pane.
		  c. Scroll through the different alternatives presented in the task pane. Use the Find more at Office.com to expand your search if needed.
		  d. Click on your selected clip art and the picture will automatically be inserted within your document.
		2. *Size the graphic.* If your inserted clip art is the perfect size for your document—great, leave it as it is. However, in many cases, the size will not be perfect. Point your mouse at the picture and left click once. You should note that a box is drawn around the picture and handles are placed at each of the corners and in the middle of each of the sides. You can grab a handle by putting your mouse pointer on the handle (note that your pointer changes into a double-headed arrow), left click, and hold it. Dragging a handle will cause the picture to be altered. Try different handles and see what happens to the shape and size of the picture.
		3. *Place the graphic.* Once your picture is inserted and sized appropriately, you can move it to a different location on the slide by putting the mouse on top of the graphic and clicking, holding, and then dragging it to the new location.
		4. *Adapt or adjust the quality of the graphic.* You should also note that once you have selected your picture (the picture has the box around it with the handles) a special set of Picture Tools becomes available (look for the Picture Tools tab immediately above the Format tab on the main ribbon) (see Figure 5.17). You can use these tools for the following:
		
		  • Adjust the picture (brightness, contrast, color).
		  • Change the picture style (border, shape, special effects).
		  • Arrange the picture in relation to other items (bring to the front, send to the back).
		  • Size the picture (crop, alter height and width).
		
		Note: Working with clip art and other graphic files may take a bit of practice. You'll find that some don't look very good when their size is changed to a drastic degree—others work great. You'll also find that access to the Internet gives you an endless supply of various clip art, pictures, and other graphics that you may want to use and insert within your documents. Always remember that there are copyright rules and regulations that apply to using any tangible item from texts, videos, pictures, as well as what is located on the Internet.

		FIGURE 5.17 Picture Tools

7.	**Add a theme**	1. On the main ribbon, click on the Design tab and review all of the themes within the Theme group. By moving your mouse over the different themes, you can preview how they would look once they have been applied. Click on the theme you want applied to your presentation. If you need to change the theme, just make a different selection, click, and the new theme is applied. 2. Once a theme has been applied, you can use other commands within the Theme group to alter the color, font, and the effect within your selected theme. In this way, you can personalize each of these professionally designed themes.

8.	**Add a list of items that can be introduced (animated) one at a time: Animation**	1. Insert a new slide (**Home** tab >>> **Slide** group >>> **New Slide**). 2. Select a layout for the new slide that will allow for a list of items to be entered. Here is an example that could be selected from the list within the layout gallery. Select one that you think will work well.  3. Click in the placeholder for the title and enter your title for the slide. 4. Click in one of the columns and add your content for each of the bullets (e.g., Developmental level, Intelligence). 5. Go to the main ribbon and select the Animation tab. You can add animation (i.e., how your items in your list will appear or be emphasized during your slide show) by selecting one of the options within the Animation group (see Figure 5.18). Additional options for how items will be entered, be emphasized, and how they will exit the slide can also be selected by clicking on **Animation** tab >>> **Animation** group >>> **Add Animation** button >>> and making a selection in the Animation Gallery. 6. Once an animation has been inserted, you can use the same Animation tab to preview the animation, alter the animation effects (Effect options), and control when and how long the item will be shown on the slide (Timing group). 7. To remove an effect, simply select the individual item or list and click the None button within the Animation group. The animation effect is then removed . This is a fun feature to work with. Spend some time trying different effects and different ways to time those effects. **Note:** Not only can you do these **custom animation** effects with bulleted or numbered lists of items, but you can also do the same for any element (e.g., clip art, words, word art) that you select on the slide. By selecting the elements, you can also determine the sequence and the timing for the animation.  **FIGURE 5.18** The Animations tab allows for control of how items are displayed and removed during a slide presentation
9.	**Add, size, and position a graphic**	This is basically a repeat of what we learned in step 6. Notice how you can use a graphic in a smaller version as a logo or theme within other PPT slides.
10.	**Change the background of a specific slide**	1. In some cases you may want one (or more) of your slides to vary from your selected theme in the presentation. To alter the background of one slide, make sure you begin by going to that slide in the presentation. 2. On the main ribbon, click on the **Design** tab >>> **Background** group >>> **Background Styles**. The Background Styles gallery will appear and you can preview how the slide's background can be changed. 3. If you desire a change different from that offered in the gallery, click on the Format Background button and a dialog box will appear with more choices.
11.	**Insert a hyperlink to the Internet**	1. Type the text you would like to serve as the link. If you choose to use the web address as the text that appears, simply type in the address and press the space bar. The link is automatically created for you and the font and style changes to indicate its link to the web. 2. If you would prefer to use customized text for the link, insert the text and select it.

(continued)

3. Click the **Insert** tab >>> **Links** group >>> **Hyperlink** button. The Insert Hyperlink window will appear (see Figure 5.19).

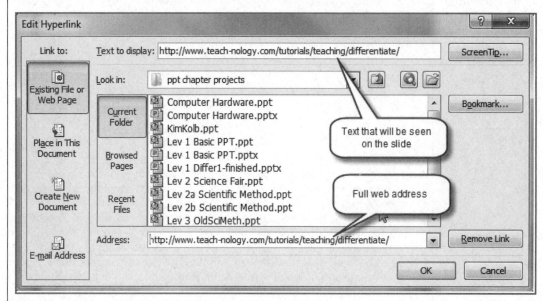

FIGURE 5.19 Using the Insert Hyperlink dialog box to create a hyperlink within the PPT slide presentation

4. In the address section of the window, type in the web address of the website you want linked.
5. In this same window, you may also modify the text you have chosen to display.

Note: This is one case where spelling counts! In either method of creating a hyperlink, be sure to type in the web address accurately and completely (don't forget the http://)!

Another note: With the use of this window, you can also link to more than just websites (e.g., specific documents, an e-mail address).

Scenario 2: The scientific method

Getting ready for the school science fair offers a number of challenges. One of the biggest is persuading parents to buy into the project. For Roberta Andrews, educating her students' parents about the different elements of the project hasn't always been consistent and hasn't produced reliable results in the past. One key element that had often led to confusion—but critical to the projects—is following the scientific method.

This year, Roberta decided to do something different. Early within the school year— in fact, during her school's Meet the Teacher Night—she decided to introduce the topic to the parents. To do this effectively, she thought of using a PPT presentation. This would allow her to present the material in a professional manner and efficiently create handouts that the parents could take home and discuss with their kids. Later, she might actually reuse the presentation as an introduction to the science fair projects for her students and give them the handouts to take home to remind the parents of what they had heard during her presentation.

Go to the text's website and review Roberta's presentation. As you go through it, note how it was constructed and the different elements presented. Several will be similar to those reviewed within Scenario 1. Review the quick reference Figure 5.20, the coordinated step-by-step procedures, and the video mentoring guides to learn how to use each of the features.

PDToolkit
for
Teaching and Learning with Microsoft® Office 2010 and Office 2011 for Mac

Go to PDToolkit for **Teaching and Learning with Microsoft® Office 2010 and Office 2011 for Mac** to locate Workout Level One for Chapter Five.

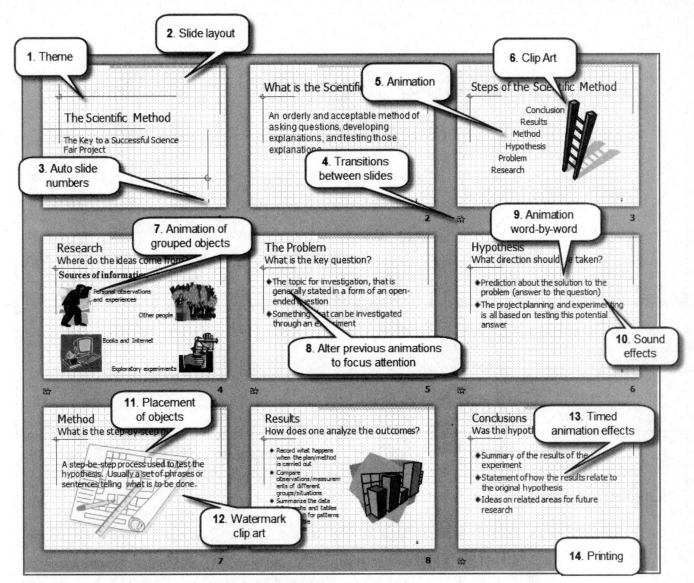

FIGURE 5.20 The "Scientific Method" PowerPoint Slide presentation

No.	Feature	Steps to Get It Done
1.	**Select the theme for the presentation**	1. Different themes for a presentation can be readily accessed (**Design** tab >>> **Theme** group). 2. Review the theme section within the Orientation of this chapter (page 154) for a discussion of the value of themes, their application, how to preview, and so forth. 3. Also review Feature 7 of Scenario 1 for the steps to take to incorporate a theme.
2.	**Select a slide layout**	1. Selecting and altering a slide layout can be quickly accomplished (**Home** tab >>> **Slides** group >>> **Layout** gallery). 2. From the gallery, select the layout that will work best with the content that you want in the slide. There are layouts that can be used for text lists, charts, tables, clip art, movies, and so on. 3. Review page 154 for a discussion of the value of slide layouts, their application, how to use them, and so forth.
3.	**Auto page numbers**	1. Click **Insert** tab >>> **Text** group >>> **Slide Number** or **Header & Footer**. 2. In the pop-up window, select the options you would like to use. To add slide numbers, place a check in front of the Slide number option. Then click Apply to All.

(continued)

Note: Following these same steps you can place page numbers (as well as other header and footer information) on slides, note pages, and handout pages.

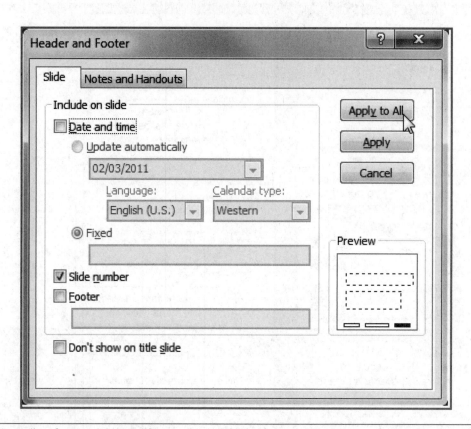

4.	**Transitions between slides**	Transitions allow for one slide to professionally evolve into the next slide during a presentation. For example, as the first slide fades, the next slide emerges from the center of the screen. 1. Go to the slide where you want the transition to occur. 2. Review all of the possible transitions from the transitions gallery (**Transitions** tab >>> **Transitions to This Slide** group). Don't forget to use the up and down arrows to see additional gallery options (see Figure 5.21). 3. Preview the transitions by clicking on a selected transition. 4. Click on the effect you desire. 5. In this same group of commands, you can also select the speed of the transition (see **Timing** group >>> **Duration**), whether to add a sound effect (see **Timing** group >>> **Sound**), and how to advance the slide (e.g., on the click of the mouse or by some predetermined amount of time). **Note:** These steps show you how to create transitions one at a time for each slide (this can become quite burdensome if you have a lot of slides). Notice on the Transition tab there is a button to Apply to All. This will apply your selected transition and timing to all slides in the presentation. You can also select a specific set of slides within the slide sorter view and apply a specific transition to your set. A much more efficient method! 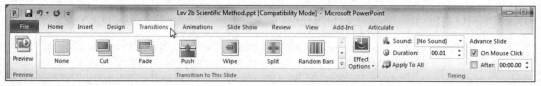 **FIGURE 5.21** Integrating transitions between slides within a presentation
5.	**Custom animation**	Refer to Feature 8 of Scenario 1 (page 163).
6.	**Clip art**	Refer to Feature 6 of Scenario 1 (page 162).

| 7. | **Animation of grouped objects** | At times, you may want to animate a group of objects simultaneously. Depending on how you set up the animation, it will be possible for you to begin a series of animations with simply a click of the mouse. A simple way is to first group the items you want to animate at the same time and then complete a simple custom animation as shown in Feature 8 of Scenario 1.
1. Highlight all the objects you would like to group together within the animation.
2. Once one group is highlighted, click on the group button (**Home** tab >>> **Drawing** group >>> **Arrange** button >>> select from the **Group Objects** menu). All selected items will now be grouped together as a single item (see Figure 5.22). You can also use this same procedure to ungroup a set of previously grouped items.

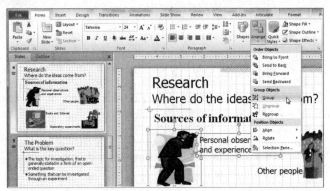

FIGURE 5.22 Grouping multiple objects on a single slide
3. Once all of the different groups of items have been formed, click on the Animation tab.
4. Select the grouped item that you want to appear first and then click on your selected animation effect from the Animation group. Select the type of entrance you desire for the grouped item to be animated as well as the direction and the speed that it should enter (**Animation** tab >>> **Animation** group >>> **Effect Options**). If you want the grouped items to be emphasized in some way or to exit the slide when needed, review the gallery of options (**Advanced Animation** group >>> **Add Animation**).
5. Repeat this process for each of the grouped items that you wish to animate.
6. Click the Preview button to review what you have created. |
| 8, 9, and 10. | **Alter previous animations, animate word by word, and add sounds** | You can alter an animation in a number of ways. This is often done to add emphasis or to draw attention to specific parts of the presentation. Use the following steps to alter previous animations, animate word by word, and add sounds.
1. After applying an animation, make sure the Animation pane is showing (**Animations** tab >>> **Advanced Animations** group >>> **Animation** pane).
2. From the list of animated objects in the Animation pane select the animation you would like to modify. (You can select more than one by clicking and holding down the shift key on your keyboard.)
3. Right mouse click on your selection and then select Effect Options . . . .

4. The Effect Options window will appear. Click on the Effect tab and then you can do any or all of the following under the Enhancements section:
  a. *After animation:* Select how the text that has already appeared will look once a new animation enters the slide (e.g., change color, fade).
  b. *Animate text:* Select how the text should initially enter the slide (e.g., all at once, by word, by letter).
  c. *Sound:* Select sounds that could be included as the text enters the slide (e.g., typewriter, chime, click).
5. Select the enhancements you would like to apply and click OK.
6. Click the Play button to review your modification.

Note: Be careful what you do at this point. Adding too many animations, too many sounds, and especially having animations enter word by word or letter by letter can become extremely annoying for those watching the presentation. Use these effects very sparingly. |

(continued)

11.	Placement of objects	1. Select the object you would like to move by clicking on the outer edge. 2. Click the object (the cursor should change into a four-headed arrow) and hold and drag the object to the location you desire. **Movement Tips** (These work in all MS Office applications!): • *Nudging an object:* To move an item at very small intervals. Select the object. Press the CTRL key on your keyboard while pressing a directional arrow. • *Modify the order of objects* (e.g., bring to front, send to back, and so forth): Select the object and then select the order (**Home** tab >>> **Drawing** group >>> **Arrange** button >>> **Order objects** menu). • *Rotate or flip an object:* Select the object and then select how you want it rotated or flipped (**Home** tab >>> **Drawing** group >>> **Arrange** button >>> **Position objects** menu >>> **Rotate**).
12.	Watermark backgrounds	Watermarks (also known as *washouts*) are images (e.g., pictures, clip art) that are semitransparent and often used in the background. 1. Add an image from Clip Art. (For more detail, see Feature 6 of Scenario 1, page 162.) 2. Select the image. Right mouse click and select Format Picture. 3. When the Format Picture window opens, click on the Picture Corrections button. 4. Modify the images appearance by adjusting the brightness or contrast scales. 5. Position the watermark (see Feature 11). 6. Send the image to the back of the slide (**Home** tab >>> **Drawing** group >>> **Arrange** button >>> **Order objects** menu >>> **Send to Back** button).
13.	Timed animation effects	There are times when you will want your animations to enter based on time and not on the manual mouse click. 1. After applying an animation, make sure the Animation pane is showing (**Animations** tab >>> **Advanced Animation** group >>> **Animation** pane button). 2. From the list of animated objects in the custom animation task pane, select the animation you would like to modify. 3. Right mouse click on your selection and then select Effect Options. 4. The Effect Options window will appear. Click on the Timing tab. Select the options for when to start, how long the delay should be between animations, and the overall speed of the animation. 5. Click the OK button when your timing decisions have been made.
14.	Printing	1. Click **File** tab >>> **Print**. 2. In the Print window, the right side will be a page preview. You can examine how your printed version would look from this preview. 3. On the left side of the Print window you can make selections of how your presentation should be printed. Options for number of copies, printer location, collating choices, and which pages or slides to print. Unique to PowerPoint is the ability to print a variety of formats of your presentation. Use the Full Page Slides drop-down list to select the option that meets your needs. 4. If you choose to print handouts, you will have an additional series of choices within the Handout section (e.g., how many slides to print per page).

Level 1 Workout: Practice using the basic PPT features

Now you get to actually practice using the features of PPT. You need to create a new presentation and begin to select and integrate the different features within your own work. Here's a basic outline of what you need to do.

Determine what content your program should include. To do this efficiently, go to the website that accompanies this book and review the outlines of content that we have already developed for you. You can select the outline that interests you the most and then copy it within the outline view of PPT. Of course, if you have a presentation looming in the near future, you may want to insert your own content and by finishing this Workout you may actually have that task nearly completed.

1. Review the previous two scenarios and their step-by-step procedures for each of the displayed features.
2. Develop a set of slides that includes the basic content.
3. Go through the slides and begin to add the needed features to accentuate the relevant elements of the presentation. Use the Level 1 Workout checklist (see Table 5.1), as well as Figures 5.14 to 5.16, and Figure 5.20 to help you identify all of the features that could be included.

Remember this is a practice Workout—*practice integrating as many features as possible.*

Note: Refer to specific feature numbers and the given step-by-step procedures as needed. Additionally, use the mentoring videos to help guide you through any specific procedure that needs additional clarification.

PDToolkit
for
Teaching and Learning with Microsoft® Office 2010 and Office 2011 for Mac

Go to PDToolkit for **Teaching and Learning with Microsoft® Office 2010 and Office 2011 for Mac** to locate Workout Level One for Chapter Five.

Table 5.1 Level 1 Workout and Practice Checklist: Designing a presentation

Project Content	___ Content is accurate and current.
	___ Content is relevant and cohesive throughout the program.
	___ Content achieves the proper level for the intended audience.
Presentation Format	___ A new presentation was created.
	___ A theme was used to add cohesiveness and consistency throughout the program.
	___ Slides were numbered consistently throughout the presentation.
	___ Transitions between slides were incorporated.
	___ Various slide layouts, consistent with the needs of the content, were used.
Individual Slide Elements	___ Font size, style, type, and location were adapted as needed within the different slides.
	___ Appropriate graphics (e.g., clip art, pictures, images) were properly selected, sized, and placed on slides.
	___ A watermark was created and placed appropriately in the background of a specific slide.
	___ Animation effects (e.g., various manual and timed entrances and exits, fading of past points, sound effects) for individual and grouped objects were incorporated.
	___ Hyperlinks to specific Internet sites, documents, or other slides were created within the presentation.

LEVEL 2: CREATING PRESENTATIONS TO LEARN

What should you be able to do?

In this section we want you to create, edit, and format several original presentations and sets of individualized instructional materials using advanced PPT features. In addition, you should learn to effectively use the Help feature of the software.

Getting some Help

Similar to Help in Windows, there is also Help in MS PPT and most other sophisticated presentation software. To use Help, click the Help button on the tab bar of the main ribbon.

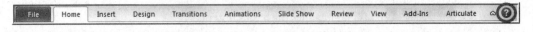

Clicking the Help button 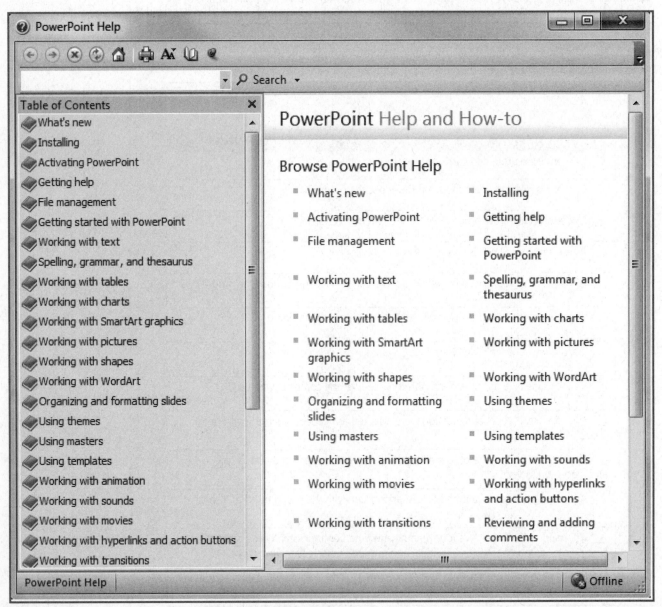 brings up the Help window. From here you can browse general Help topics, bring up a general table of contents of all Help topics, review common commands, and complete a search for a specific question you might have (see Figure 5.23).

FIGURE 5.23 PPT Help window

By typing in key words or even a full question, Help will respond with a variety of potential answers for you to investigate. Help generally does not have all of the answers but it will have a lot of them. Make sure you become familiar with how it works and how often it can be of assistance.

Scenario 3: "The scientific method" repurposed as individualized instruction

After successfully using "The Scientific Method" presentation at Meet the Teacher Night, Roberta Andrews now has other ideas. Using this presentation for the basic content, she quickly adapts it into a self-instructional program that can be used to prepare her students for the development of their science fair projects. Review the program on the website that accompanies this book.

In this case, she wants the program to be used by individual students who can control which portions of the presentation they see and be quizzed on what they have read.

Note how the **action buttons** are used to navigate throughout the program and how they can be used to set up review questions, encourage student interaction, and supply specific feedback.

Here are three slides (Figures 5.24, 5.25, and 5.26) that highlight the key features that have been added within the SciMeth2 version of the "Scientific Method" presentation. Make sure you examine it first on the text's website and then you can examine how these features actually work within a slide presentation.

Once you have reviewed these figures and the actual presentation, review how to find the key information on how to actually develop these features within your projects. In addition, mentoring videos have been created on the website that accompanies this book that will guide you through the use of each of these features.

PDToolkit
for
Teaching and Learning with Microsoft® Office 2010 and Office 2011 for Mac

Go to PDToolkit for **Teaching and Learning with Microsoft® Office 2010 and Office 2011 for Mac** to locate Workout Level Two for Chapter Five.

PDToolkit
for
Teaching and Learning with Microsoft® Office 2010 and Office 2011 for Mac

Go to PDToolkit for **Teaching and Learning with Microsoft® Office 2010 and Office 2011 for Mac** to locate the mentoring videos for Chapter Five.

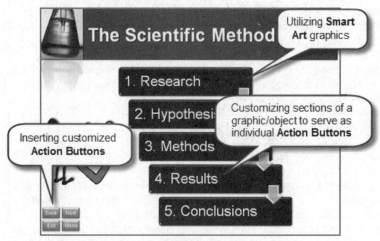

FIGURE 5.24 SmartArt and Action buttons

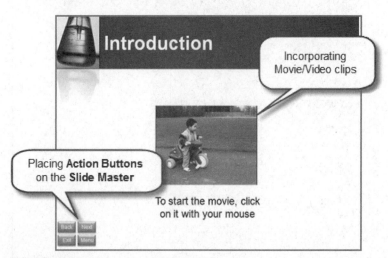

FIGURE 5.25 Incorporating movie and video clips

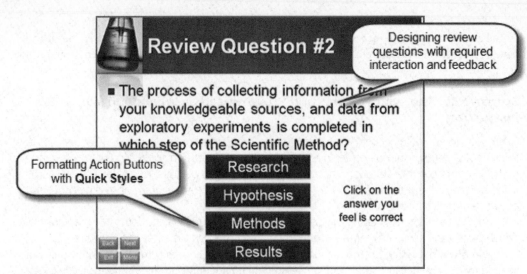

FIGURE 5.26 Formatting action buttons with Quick Styles

Feature	Steps to Get It Done
Inserting customized action buttons	**Procedure for creating and inserting:** PPT Help • Look in Help's Table of Contents for the title: Working with hyperlinks and action buttons **Key features to note, explore, and try out:** • An action button is a premade hyperlink button that can be used to link from a location in your presentation to another slide, a different presentation, a website, document, movie, or sound clip. • A quick way to arrive at the action buttons is **Insert** tab >>> **Illustrations** group >>> **Shapes** >>> **Action Buttons**. • There are several types of action buttons—some that are preformatted with specific looks and hyperlinks and some that you can design yourself. In all cases, you can alter the action to which a button is linked. **Action Buttons** • The size and placement of the action buttons can be altered in a way similar to that used with graphics (see Scenario 1, Feature 6, page 162). • Labels, color, and appearance of action buttons can be altered (e.g., **Home** tab >>> **Quick Styles**). Make sure you have already created the button and that it is highlighted (i.e., handles are showing). • Linking the button to the correct action is completed through the Action Setting dialog box. • Selecting an action button will automatically open the Action Setting dialog box. It can also be opened by selecting the action button then clicking on the Action button (**Insert** tab >>> **Links** group >>> **Action**).

Using SmartArt graphics	**Procedure for creating and inserting:** PPT Help • Key word: **SmartArt** • Select Create a SmartArt graphic and follow the given procedure. • See also Animate your SmartArt graphic. **Key features to note, explore, and try out:** • A quick way to get to the SmartArt graphics is **Insert** tab >>> **Illustrations** group >>> **SmartArt**. • Once a SmartArt design has been selected, you can add text, pictures, graphics, alter color scheme, and so on. (i.e., highlight the selected SmartArt graphic, then select the SmartArt tools above the Design tab). • The size and placement of the graphics can be altered in a similar way as that used with graphics (see Scenario 1, Feature 6, page 162).
Customizing sections of a graphic or object to serve as individual action buttons	To do this, you create an action button that is totally transparent, then you lay it over the top of the target graphic or object (e.g., a picture, graphic, word, SmartArt, and so forth.). Even though you can't see the button, it (and its associated action) will still be present. Clicking on the graphic or object with the transparent button overlay will produce the associated button action (that is, the button will work). • To create 100 percent transparency, select your action button, then click on the **Format** tab/**Drawing Tools** >>> **Shape Styles** group >>> **Shape Fill** >>> **More Fill Colors**. Set the Transparency to 100 percent. Repeat this procedure for the Shape Outline. **Note:** Transparent buttons are especially helpful if you have a large graphic that you would like to embed multiple action buttons. (A great example of this would be a concept map.) Create transparent action buttons and place them on top of the specific components of the graphic.
Placing action buttons on the Slide Master	Action buttons that you want to appear on all of your slides (e.g., buttons to link to the next slide) can be created once and put on the Slide Master. These buttons will then appear on all slides within the presentation. **General information on the Slide Master:** PPT Help • Key words: Slide Master • Select What is a slide master? • Select Create or customize a Slide Master • Also see the Slide Master explanation in the Orientation section of this chapter. **Key features to note, explore, and try out:** • A quick way to get to the Slide Master: **View** tab >>> **Presentation Views** group >>> **Slide Master**. • Action buttons can be added anywhere on the Slide Master and they will appear in that position on all slides. Therefore, place them in a location that will be free of other items on all slides.
Incorporating movie or video clips	**Procedure for incorporating movies or video clips:** PPT Help • In the Help Table of Contents, review the chapter on "Working with movies." • Select Embed or link to a video from your presentation. **Key features to note, explore, and try out:** • A quick way to get to add a movie is **Insert** tab >>> **Movie clips** group >>> **Movie**.

(continued)

Formatting action buttons with Quick Styles	Quick Styles allow you to add high-quality formatting to various shapes, SmartArt, or action buttons in a very efficient manner. Accessing the Quick Styles gallery allows you to preview how the shape will look before the formatting is actually applied. **Procedure for using Quick Styles:** PPT Help • Key words: Quick Styles • Select the What is a theme? And then click on the What are Quick Styles? section. **Key features to note, explore, and try out:** • A quick way to access Quick Styles is to select the shape or action button then **Format** tab >>> **Drawing tools** >>> **Drawing** group >>> **Quick Styles**. • Quick Styles can add shadows, gradients, line styles, edges, and even 3D perspectives to your shapes. • Before or after Quick Style application, you can size and move your shape. This is similar to moving a graphic as explained in Scenario 1, Feature 6 (page 162).
Designing review questions with required interaction and feedback	With the use of action buttons, it is possible to present the learner with a question and several possible alternative responses on a slide. Having each of the possible responses as an action button allows you to have specific feedback slides linked to each alternative. In addition, the feedback may include information about why the response being made was correct or incorrect and additional information to help the student understand why his or her response was correct or not.

PDToolkit
for
Teaching and Learning with Microsoft® Office 2010 and Office 2011 for Mac

Go to PDToolkit for **Teaching and Learning with Microsoft® Office 2010 and Office 2011 for Mac** to locate the mentoring videos for Chapter Five.

Note: Each of these key features is demonstrated on the mentoring videos.

Level 2 Workout: Practice using additional PPT features

Now you try it.

1. Select the content for the presentation. You may use any or all of the following:
   a. Open, adapt, and expand the presentation you created for the Level 1 Workout.
   b. Go to the Level 1 sample outlines and develop your own basic presentation using one of the content outlines that have been provided.

   Note: You will have to gather and add more information to these outlines.

PDToolkit
for
Teaching and Learning with Microsoft® Office 2010 and Office 2011 for Mac

Go to PDToolkit for **Teaching and Learning with Microsoft® Office 2010 and Office 2011 for Mac** to locate Workout Level Two for Chapter Five.

   c. A partially prepared presentation has been developed and can be accessed on the website that accompanies this book. It is a presentation that has been created about using blogs in the classroom setting. You can begin with this basic presentation and practice incorporating the advanced features within it.
   d. Review your calendar, school lesson plans, and so on to see when your next presentation will be. Select one that is coming up in the near future. It can be anything (e.g., class discussion on worm segments, proper swimming strokes, visit to the local art museum). Develop a simple outline of content based on that need.
2. Start PPT and create some slides that cover the key concepts that should be within your presentation.
3. Review the features demonstrated within Scenario 3 of Level 2 (e.g., action buttons, movie clips, SmartArt).
4. Similar to the SciMeth2 presentation create a presentation about your selected content that allows the user the control to navigate through the information (e.g., use of action buttons).
5. Use Table 5.2 as a checklist to make sure you have included a number of key features that have been highlighted within Scenarios 1, 2, and 3 of this chapter.

Table 5.2 Level 2 Workout and Practice Checklist: Designing a learner-centered presentation

Project Content	___ Content is accurate and current.
	___ Content is relevant and cohesive throughout the program.
	___ Content achieves the proper level for the intended audience.
	___ Appropriate directions were incorporated to help the user understand how to navigate within the program.
	___ Review slides with linked feedback slides were incorporated within the presentation.
Presentation Format	___ A theme was used to add cohesiveness and consistency throughout the program.
	___ Slides were numbered consistently throughout the presentation.
	___ Transitions between slides were incorporated.
	___ Various slide layouts, consistent with the needs of the content, were used.
	___ Slide Master was used to retain common elements throughout all slides.
Individual Slide Elements	___ Font size, style, type, and location were adapted as needed within the different slides.
	___ Appropriate graphics (e.g., clip art, pictures, images) were properly selected, sized, and placed on slides.
	___ SmartArt graphics were incorporated.
	___ Animation effects (e.g., various manual and timed entrances and exits, fading of past points, sound effects) for individual and grouped objects were incorporated.
	___ Hyperlinks to specific Internet sites, documents, or other slides were created within the presentation.
	___ Appropriate action buttons were created and used to allow individualized navigation by the user.
	___ Quick Styles were used to modify some of the action buttons.
	___ Movie or audio clips were incorporated within the presentation.

LEVEL 3: INTEGRATION AND APPLICATION

What should you be able to do?

Here's where you get to actually use this software to help yourself and your students. This section helps you see the many applications possible using PPT (or similar software). You can use these examples as a springboard to launch ideas on how to improve levels of student learning and your personal productivity.

Introduction

The examples given in Levels 1 and 2 coupled with your own development efforts should put you in a good position to begin to see the possibilities for this type of presentation program.

Now we want you to expand your use of this program and think of what you can show and demonstrate to others. Here we give you a number of different ideas, some that you may or may not find helpful, but we hope they are ideas that you can expand on to make them relevant to your work and those with whom you work.

Presentation software integration

Creating the enhanced learning experience: A partial lesson plan

TOPIC:

A study of the people, places, and culture of an African country.

OVERVIEW:

Mr. Carpenter, an eighth-grade social studies teacher at Lowell Middle School, is continuing to search for ways for his students to explore Zimbabwe and learn about this African country and its people. Moreover, he wants his students to discover that much can be learned about the people of today by exploring their history and ancestors. With the help of one of his former students, Jonathon Rogers (who now is a university graduate student in Zimbabwe on an internship with an international health and education organization), Mr. Carpenter's hopes to guide his students as they discover the past of this fascinating country.

Through the use of e-mail, regular mail, digital photography, and audio recordings, Jonathon should be able to explore several historically significant sites within the borders of Zimbabwe and then share those with the Lowell social studies classes of Mr. Carpenter.

SPECIFIC LEARNING TASK:

To explore the history of the people of Zimbabwe, the students in Mr. Carpenter's social studies classes were to investigate the ancient city known as the *Great Zimbabwe.* Each class was divided into smaller cooperative groups that would be asked to address one of the following sets of questions:

- What was the Great Zimbabwe? Who were the people that built it? What did the city look like when it was populated? What caused it to decline and decay?
- If one lived in the Great Zimbabwe, what was life like? What did people do, what did they wear, what did they eat, how did they travel from place to place, what did they believe in, and how did they communicate and conduct business? What were some interesting things about living in this city?
- How were the ruins of the Great Zimbabwe discovered? Who made those discoveries? What was done to the ruins after they were discovered? What is the role of the archeologist in uncovering and understanding a people who no longer are alive? What does the Great Zimbabwe look like today?

SAMPLE LEARNING OBJECTIVES:

Students will be able to do the following:

1. Identify and describe important elements and events about life during the time of the Great Zimbabwe and how people lived within that society.
2. Examine and explain potential reasons for the rise and fall of great societies such as those who lived within the Great Zimbabwe.
3. Explain the role of archeologists in the discovery of places and people of the past.

PROCEDURE:

1. Break into the groups, examine the assigned questions for study, and brainstorm methods to investigate.
2. Examine websites and other reference materials for information about the Great Zimbabwe. For example:

- Wikipedia: http://en.wikipedia.org/wiki/Great_Zimbabwe
- Riddle of the Great Zimbabwe: http://www.archaeology.org/9807/abstracts /africa.html
- Mystery of the Great Zimbabwe: http://www.pbs.org/wgbh/nova/israel/zimbabwe.html

3. Contact Jonathon to see if he has visited this archeological site or if he has heard anything about it. Ask for further information if he can find it from individuals who live in the country. If he does visit, have him write his impressions of what it was like and send pictures of what he found.

4. Using the assigned questions as a starting point, create a group presentation about the Great Zimbabwe.

5. Create a follow-up activity that involves the development of learner-focused individualized instruction. Using PPT, create an instructional learning module that individual students can access, navigate, gain information and experience with the content, and be assessed about the information they have experienced.

QUESTIONS ABOUT THE INTEGRATION OF PRESENTATION SOFTWARE:

This lesson could be completed in a number of ways, including simple oral reports, reenactments or role-plays, or video or live presentations by subject matter experts such as archeologists. In addition, the use of presentation software such as PPT can be completed to create overhead slides and handouts to accompany an oral presentation. Use the following reflective questions to explore the potential value integrating PPT or another form of presentation software within such a lesson as outlined by Mr. Carpenter:

- How will the small research groups cooperatively brainstorm and plan the presentation? Can presentation software be used to facilitate the planning process?
- Can the development of specific sets of information (e.g., tables or lists of information, charts, and maps) increase the level of understanding for the individual group members?
- Will the presentation involve the use of audio, visual graphics, and video clips of some kind? Will these items need to be presented in a way that a large (more than ten people) group of people can see and hear?
- During and following the presentation, can learning be enhanced by the production and distribution of a handout of the presented information? Would such a handout facilitate a group discussion on the topic?
- Will there be a need for the presentation to be stored for later use by other classes, individual students, interested parents, faculty, and so on?

Level 3a Workout: Integrating PPT into the real world of learning

1. Read each of the following situations. Imagine being directly involved in the planning for each of these projects. Select one (or more if you wish) for further consideration.

School Days:

The lives of children throughout the world vary based on many different factors. One common element for most is that they go to some form of formal school. But how similar are the experiences that the students have? How does a typical school day in various places of the world compare? What kinds of subjects are studied, how much time is spent on each subject, how much variety is there in how the different subjects are taught? How do kids get to school, how long do they stay there, how much homework do they have? How is the learning of the students assessed? After examining all of these different ways of doing school, what would be an appropriate way to examine and evaluate the similarities and differences among school systems? If asked to suggest a plan for the "best" school system, how would the proposal be created and presented?

Pet Care:

Third-grade students were learning about pets. In separate groups they focused on different common family pets. They studied the types of food needed, the care needed, the living space, and even the amount of play and exercise that the animal needed. Together they decided to make a program that would help other students learn about the care of family pets. They wanted to assemble all of their information and produce a resource for other students to use when they had a question about a pet they might own or might be thinking about owning.

Invention Evolution:

Over time, good ideas have a tendency to evolve. Transportation, for example, has evolved from riding animals to riding in spaceships. As inventions have been used and evaluated, changes naturally occur. In what ways have some of our common tools (the dishwasher, vacuum cleaner, computer, light bulb, television) evolved over time?

Marketing a Business:

A new start-up company has come to your company and asked you to make a presentation about marketing one of its new products. The product is a new form of software that companies use to monitor and report all web activity by their employees. It helps companies make sure employees are properly using the Internet during office hours. How can the new company be convinced that you have the knowledge and capabilities to market their new software?

2. Based on your selected project, consider the following questions that concern the integration of presentation software such as PPT. Mark your response to each question.

Integration assessment questionnaire (IAQ)

Will using presentation software as a part of the project:	
Broaden the learners' perspective on potential solution paths and answers?	___ Yes ___ No ___ Maybe
Increase the level of involvement and investment of personal effort by the learners?	___ Yes ___ No ___ Maybe
Increase the level of learner motivation (e.g., increase the relevance of the to-be-learned task, the confidence of dealing with the task, and the overall appeal of the task)?	___ Yes ___ No ___ Maybe
Decrease the time needed to generate potential solutions?	___ Yes ___ No ___ Maybe
Increase the quality and quantity of learner practice working on this and similar projects?	___ Yes ___ No ___ Maybe
Increase the quality and quantity of feedback given to the learner?	___ Yes ___ No ___ Maybe
Enhance the ability of the student to solve novel but similar projects, tasks, and problems in the future?	___ Yes ___ No ___ Maybe

3. If you have responded "yes" to one or more of the questions, you should consider the use of PPT to enhance the student's potential learning experience.
4. Develop a lesson plan based on this project. Within the plan, indicate how and when the learner will use PPT. Additionally, list potential benefits and challenges that may occur when involving this software within the lesson.

Level 3b Workout: Exploring the NETS connection

Part A: Once you have an understanding of the features and applications of presentation software skills, it is important to provide a context for the professional purpose that these skills can have in the classroom. By using the National Educational Technology Standards (NETS) developed by the International Society for Technology in Education (ISTE), the next few tasks will provide a foundation for the importance of integrating this chapter's skill set into any teacher's professional practice. There are two sets of NETS: one designed for the skills needed by teachers (NETS-T), the other for the skills needed by K–12 students (NETS-S). A complete listing of these standards can be found in the Appendix of this book.

Part B: The following chart provides examples of how the use of a spreadsheet application (with an emphasis on data analysis) can directly align with the NETS-T and the NETS-S. As you read these strategies, try to consider additional connections that could be made between these standards and this set of skills. Additionally, consider the answer to the focus questions presented for each unique standard.

NETS-T and NETS-S	Example Activities and Focus Questions
NETS-T 1. Facilitate and Inspire Student Learning and Creativity NETS-S 1. Creativity and Innovation	• After gathering research online or in print materials, have students develop an outline on a topic focusing first on the content. Once the content has been developed move to the incorporation of graphics, animations, and multimedia components. • Instead of developing traditional presentations, encourage the students to create products that incorporate action buttons as a means to add in nonlinear movement. These products could result in a game, review mechanism, or simply a presentation that allows the user and viewer to choose the next focus or slide. 1. Why is it important to begin even highly creative projects by focusing on the content? 2. How do the interactive features of presentation software applications aid in the promotion of creative expression? 3. What benefit is there in using presentation software over nondigital materials?
NETS-T 2. Design and Develop Digital-Age Learning Experiences and Assessments NETS-S 4. Critical Thinking, Problem Solving, and Decision Making	• Develop reviews using the action button feature to provide enrichment or remediation on a concept taught in class. Use these reviews for whole class participation, an individual practice time, or burn to a CD to be checked out to study at home. Customize these reviews with engaging themes (graphics, audio, video) that the students will enjoy. Students can also be assigned to develop such review tools as well. • Have the students work in groups to develop presentations that feature multimedia components. Assign different tasks and roles to each group member. Encourage students to work independently and collaboratively to develop a well-researched project. Present the result to the class incorporating the voices of all group members. 4. When designing a presentation, how can the use of the outlining feature within PPT (and similar presentation programs) be used to increase collaborative planning between groups of individuals during the planning process? 5. In what ways could the use of linked graphics as well as video and audio clips be integrated to increase levels of learning for diverse audiences?
NETS-T 3. Model Digital-Age Work and Learning NETS-S 2. Communication and Collaboration NETS-S 3. Research and Information Fluency NETS-T 5. Engage in Professional Growth and Leadership	• On a regular basis, use the presentation software as a means to develop in-the-moment discussion responses (small group quick response). For these very brief slideshows, the students (working in a small group) will be given a very short amount of time to answer a prompt or question and display their response via one or two slides. The group then presents their response in a brief presentation to the class (two to four minutes). • Use the students to aid in the development of a slideshow to be used for a parent-teacher-night setting. Provide an opportunity for each student to add pictures, music, or a slide of text that relates to the focus of the classroom. Use the self-pacing features of the software to allow the slideshow to play throughout the event. 6. What advantage is there in using the very fast-paced small group quick response approach on a regular basis? What disadvantages might this present? 7. Presentation software was created to help disseminate information. How could the use of such software improve the communication skills developed by teachers and students? 8. What advantage is there in engaging the students in the development process for products that will be used outside of the classroom (e.g., for parent-teacher night)?

(continued)

NETS-T 4. Promote and Model Digital Citizenship and Responsibility NETS-S 5. Digital Citizenship	• Discuss the use of copyright-protected images, music, and video in relation to the principles of fair use as a natural part of project development. Highlight the need for all to responsibly use the work of others and to always adhere to proper citation. • Develop a digital journal using the presentation software to chart the interest of a student over the course of an academic year. The students could add a new component to their journal following each unit to highlight the new concepts they have learned and to document areas of interest for future exploration.
	9. Why is the topic of copyright considered by many to be difficult to teach? **10.** How could the development of a presentation aid in the promotion of lifelong learning? **11.** In what ways might the digital journal (described previously) aid in the learning process? Explain.

Collaborating and coauthoring in PowerPoint 2010

As explained in Chapter 2 ("Word Processing"), collaboration is a key expectation and is highlighted within the NETS. Similar to Word, PowerPoint projects can also be created, evaluated, and adjusted by groups of individuals working on the same projects but at different times and in different locations. In this case, the same process is used (e.g., first obtaining a Windows Live SkyDrive account; available at www.skydrive.live.com). Within this free Internet storage space, you can create synched folders to store your PowerPoint projects. Others who have access to the synched folders can likewise go to their SkyDrive accounts and open the exact same project from their location. As long as they have an Internet connection, they can access your synched file and the projects therein whether they are in the next room, next city, state, country, or continent. This opens up all types of opportunities for individuals to combine efforts and use the power of teams to accomplish tasks. It helps individuals to learn how to work together and it allows individuals to develop skills at evaluating the contributions of others.

Think of possible ways that PowerPoint projects could be co-developed by teams of individuals. For example:

- After studying a science unit on clouds, a group of students create a PowerPoint presentation to describe different types of cloud formations. Each member of the group works on a different type of cloud and they combine their work together into a single project. Much of the work is completed outside of class when the students are not together.
- A small group of e-learning designers have been hired to create a unit of instruction about a new surgical procedure that has just being introduced and needs to be put in the curriculum at all major medical schools. Members of the team are on two different continents but work together to create one project that is based on PowerPoint.
- Four evening course students have a presentation to deliver next week to their economics class. All four work full time and several travel during a major part of the week. Nonetheless, they are able to create, examine, evaluate, and update their PowerPoint presentation even though they never could find time to meet face-to-face outside of the usual class time.

Further ideas on using PPT as a learning tool

When using presentation software such as PPT, people often think immediately about how to use it merely for verbal presentations. The first few examples are ideas based on such presentations but then look beyond to see other possibilities for this software and how individuals can adapt and use it to learn.

Note: These ideas are to help you generate your own ideas of what could be done. Don't let it bother you if they aren't the right content or grade level—use the idea and adapt it to be helpful within your own situation. These are meant to be a stimulus for additional ideas.

---

1. With the use of scanned pictures, imported videos, sound, and other media, you can readily demonstrate concepts, procedures, and so on to a group of individuals.
2. Have students create their own reports and practice verbal skills by making presentations to the class (e.g., book reports).

3. Have the students create and deliver a group project in which the presentation is the central product they create. For example, have groups of students create science fair oral presentations about their group projects.

4. Develop a debate between two or more groups of students. Each side could develop its own key points and present them to a panel of judges via presentation software.

5. Use the outlining feature within PPT to have groups of students brainstorm certain concepts and how they could be presented for logical explanations.

6. Using action buttons, have the students create interactive presentations that link with the Internet and specific websites for additional information, media, and activities.

7. Create a preview or review quiz or test for students that allows them to make a selection and receive feedback on their performances.

8. Create an interactive calendar that allows students to click on the day and receive information on what will occur, homework assignments, links to various activities, student jobs, and so forth.

9. Create an interactive book club in which students can click on any book (active button) listed and find out something about the book, read student critiques about the book, and perhaps even send questions via e-mail to the author.

10. Create a map of the city (or of the world, or of the human body, and so on) and have transparent action buttons that allow students to click on certain sections to pull up further information about that section.

11. Create a flier for advertising some product or announcement—for example, simple fliers using graphics to promote a school dance, someone's birthday, or a special award.

12. Develop a comparison table that lists the pros and cons to a specific issue (e.g., building a new power plant in a nearby location). Each cell could be hyperlinked to other slides explaining the issues in more detail.

13. Create an interactive timeline based on some period in history. Along the timeline have action buttons that will activate relevant graphics, videos, text, or audio media revealing important elements of that point in history.

14. Have students create a presentation on a proposal for a major course project. Perhaps this can be a presentation about a future science fair project; a major English, history, and math integrated project; and so forth. Have them create handouts of their work and defend their ideas and overall proposal.

15. Create a **WebQuest** (see http://webquest.sdsu.edu/webquest.html) using PPT and hyperlinks as the software instead of a web development editor.

16. Have students create a self-instructional, automatic presentation. Have the program play music in the background as it demonstrates and explains the steps involved in some type of procedure (e.g., how a paleontologist outlines and evaluates a potential dig site, how a farmer tills the ground, the processes used to refine petroleum, how potatoes are processed into potato chips).

17. For a geography, social studies, or history lesson, have each student in a class create a slide about a specific place, people, or time period. Put all of the slides together to form one slide show. Each of the students can then discuss his or her contribution.

Additional ideas on using PPT as an assistant

1. *Handouts.*   Several of the key slides can be quickly printed as handouts for the students. These can then be used while the presentation is being made so that students can concentrate on what is being said versus trying to write down key concepts of the presentation. These also serve as very good advance organizers and as reviews following the presentation.

2. *Notes pages.*   Often presentations are given on several occasions or for different classes. With the notes page, it is possible to create a version of the presentation that also has your notes of what you should say and explain for each of the slides presented. These notes can also be helpful to students who missed the presentation or who may not have caught everything said at the time of the presentation.

3. *Templates.*   Many individuals find that a good presentation can be readily repurposed and adapted for another audience. By using the saved presentation as a template, a few changes can quickly be made and a new presentation is created.

4. *Storage places.*   This is a little different, but individuals have been known to use certain presentations on specific topics as a good place to hold important websites, pictures, ideas, and so on. For example, within a specific science presentation, an individual may find it convenient to create a resource page or slide of other related websites addresses that can readily be found and used if a later need on this topic is discovered or when an update of the presentation is needed. This same idea may hold for specific pictures, graphics, ideas, or sound clips.

5. *Graphics.*   Use the draw function in this program to create all kinds of charts, procedures, and other learning aids that students can see and follow. A seating chart or even an organizational chart, for example, can be quickly created. A job aid (simple procedure to follow) could be created in a matter of seconds (e.g., fire drill procedures, steps to follow to check out a book in the library, steps to completing a proper serve in tennis).

6. *Awards.*   Create certificates for extra effort and merit.

MS PowerPoint for Mac 2011

ORIENTATION

This addendum assumes you have previewed the full Chapter 5 and have a grasp of the general workings of the spreadsheet. This section of the chapter focuses specifically on the use of MS PowerPoint that has been created to work on the Macintosh operating system. In most cases, there is a close similarity to how MS PowerPoint for the PC (PowerPoint 2010) functions, but there are some unique differences that we will highlight within this addendum.

What's the MS PowerPoint for Mac 2011 workspace look like?

Figure 5.27 is an example of MS PowerPoint workspace for Mac 2011.

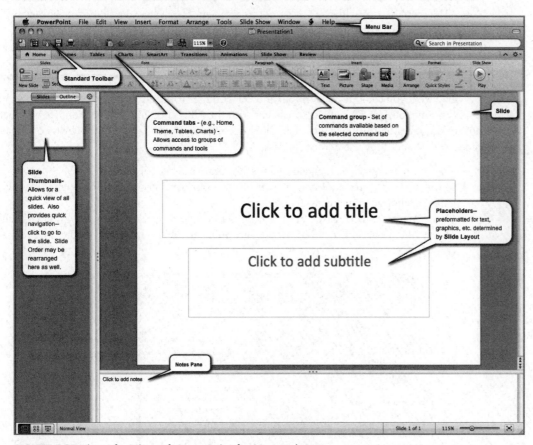

FIGURE 5.27 View of a Microsoft PowerPoint for Mac work area

What commands can be used?

Within the Mac version of MS Office, there are drop-down menu options, standard toolbar, command tabs, and command groups (see Figure 5.27). The tabs and groups are contextual, meaning that depending on what you have selected in the application, the content of these groups and tabs will change.

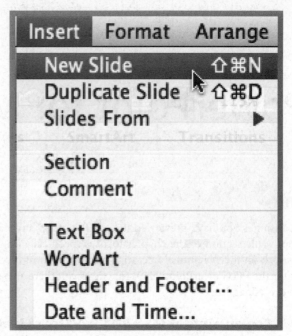

FIGURE 5.28 View of the Menu bar with drop-down Insert menu revealed

---

Note: The menu bar provides quick access to a variety of relevant dialog boxes. For example, when you choose to insert a slide via the menu bar, a number of options will be available to you. As shown in Figure 5.28 you can explore these menu bar options to see all of the different dialog boxes that can be accessed.

Likewise, you could use the ribbon and click on the **Home** tab >>> **Slides** command group >>> **New Slide** button. To remain consistent with the MS Office 2010 PC version, we will focus most of our comments on using the ribbon to accomplish the tasks within this text. Some basic things to note about the use of the ribbons:

- The command groups change based on the command tab selected.
- Many of the selected tool buttons within the command groups can be opened to reveal galleries of options related to that tool.
- Contextual tabs with associated contextual command groups appear when a specific object like a chart, formula, picture, graphic, or table is selected in the spreadsheet (see Figure 5.29).

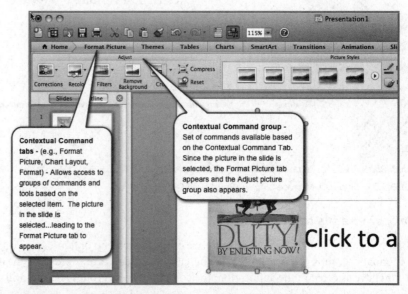

FIGURE 5.29 Selecting a specific item (e.g. chart, graphic) in the workspace reveals contextual tabs and associated contextual commands that can be accessed and used with the selected item

Orientation Workout

Return to the Orientation Workout on page 151 of this text and complete it as it is designed. The main purpose of this Workout is to get you familiar with how to enter data, work with formulas, and so on within the workspace as well as accessing and using the various tools on the menu bar and ribbons.

LEVEL 1: CREATING PRESENTATIONS TO TEACH

Scenario 1

To accomplish this Level 1 task, review Scenario 1 (page 158), specifically focusing on Figures 5.14, 5.15, and 5.16 and the formatting features highlighted by the callouts within those figures. Using Figure 5.14 to 5.16 as guides, re-create that document by following these steps.

No.	Feature	Steps to Get It Done
1.	Create a new slide	1. Click on the **Home** tab >>> **Slide** group >>> **New Slide** button. 2. A new slide will appear. 3. Use the Layout drop-down button to select the type of layout you wish to use on this slide.
2.	Add a title to the slide	1. Click on the area in the new slide designated for the title. Type in the title of this slide (e.g., *Individual Student Differences* . . .). 2. Click on the subtitle area of the slide and type in the subtitle (e.g., *Technology Integration* . . .). Note how the slide auto layout controls the location, font type, and size.
3.	Change the location of different elements of the slide	1. To move any element on a slide, click once on the item you want to move and handles (little boxes) with a line around the item will appear. 2. Move your cursor directly over the line and it will turn into a four-way arrow. 3. Click, hold, and drag the item to the new location on the slide and then release the button.
4.	Alter the text box size	1. Click once on the text box and the handles will appear. 2. Move the cursor over one of the handles and it will change into a two-way arrow. 3. Click, hold, and drag. The size of the box will change in the direction you are dragging. Play with the different handles and see their different effects on the size of the box.
5.	Change font size, color, and the like	1. Select (highlight) the words you would like to change. 2. On the main ribbon, select the Home tab and review all of the selections within the Font group. 3. Select the type, size, color, and special effects that you desire. 4. To see additional options, click the icon in the lower right portion of this group and the font dialog box will appear.

(continued)

6.	Add, size, and place a picture	1. Select the **Home** tab >>> **Insert** group >>> **Picture** drop-down button (see Figure 5.30).

FIGURE 5.30 Inserting photos and clip art

After inserting a picture you may need to size or place the picture to fit your needs.

1. *Size the graphic.* Once the graphic is selected, note that a box is drawn around the picture and handles are placed at each of the corners and in the middle of each of the sides. You can grab a handle by putting your mouse pointer on the handle (note that your pointer changes into a double-headed arrow) and click, hold, and drag to alter the picture. Try different handles and see what happens to the shape and size of the picture.
2. *Place the graphic.* Once your picture is inserted and sized appropriately, you can move it to a different location on the slide by putting the mouse on top of the graphic and clicking, holding, and then dragging it to the new location.
3. *Adapt or adjust the quality of the graphic.* Immediately on selecting the picture, a contextual tab, Format Picture, appears. The Format Picture tab houses several command groups that will assist you in modifying the picture. These groups include:

  - *Adjust:* Corrections, recolor, filters, remove background, crop, compress, and reset
  - *Picture styles:* Frames, borders, effects (including shadows, reflections, etc.), and transparency
  - *Arrange:* Arrange the picture in relation to other items (bring to the front, send to the back), reorder, rotate, and group
  - *Size the picture:* Crop, alter height and width

7.	Add a theme	1. On the main ribbon, click on the Theme tab and review all of the themes within the Theme group. Click on the theme you want applied to your presentation. If you need to change the theme, just make a different selection, click, and the new theme is applied.
		2. Once a theme has been applied, you can use other commands within the Theme group to alter the color, font, and the effect within your selected theme.

8.	Add a list of items that can be introduced (animated) one at a time: Custom Animation	1. Insert a new slide (**Home** tab >>> **Slide** group >>> **New Slide**).
		2. Select a layout for the new slide (see step 2) that will allow for a list of items to be entered.
		3. Click in one of the columns and add your content for each of the bullets (e.g., Developmental level, Intelligence).
		4. Select the content you would like to animate.
		5. Go to the main ribbon and select the Animations tab (see Figure 5.31).
		6. From the Animations tab, there are several groups that will be useful:
		• *Preview:* Test your animation and the selected features
		• *Entrance effects:* Modifies how text or objects enter a slide
		• *Emphasis effects:* Modifies how text or objects are emphasized while on the slide
		• *Exit effects:* Modifies how text or objects exit the slide
		• *Motion:* Modifies the motion path that a text or object uses
		• *Animation options:* Modifies the animation in terms of direction, start, timing, and so on.
		7. To remove an effect, simply select the element (e.g., the list) and click on the Remove button.

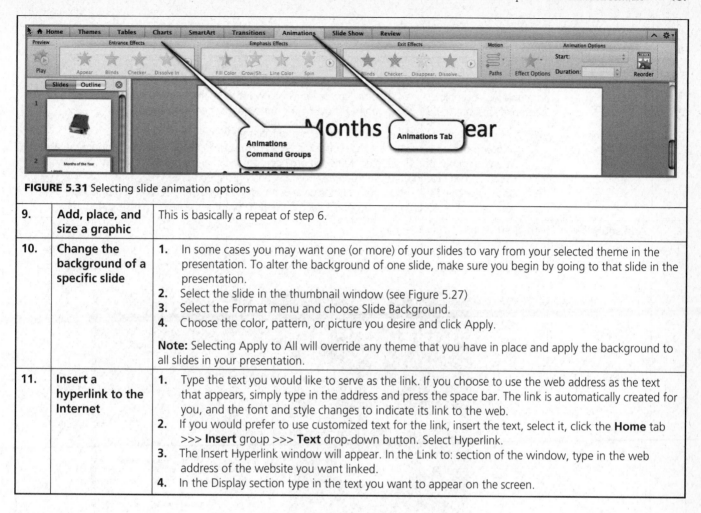

FIGURE 5.31 Selecting slide animation options

9.	Add, place, and size a graphic	This is basically a repeat of step 6.
10.	Change the background of a specific slide	1. In some cases you may want one (or more) of your slides to vary from your selected theme in the presentation. To alter the background of one slide, make sure you begin by going to that slide in the presentation. 2. Select the slide in the thumbnail window (see Figure 5.27) 3. Select the Format menu and choose Slide Background. 4. Choose the color, pattern, or picture you desire and click Apply. **Note:** Selecting Apply to All will override any theme that you have in place and apply the background to all slides in your presentation.
11.	Insert a hyperlink to the Internet	1. Type the text you would like to serve as the link. If you choose to use the web address as the text that appears, simply type in the address and press the space bar. The link is automatically created for you, and the font and style changes to indicate its link to the web. 2. If you would prefer to use customized text for the link, insert the text, select it, click the **Home** tab >>> **Insert** group >>> **Text** drop-down button. Select Hyperlink. 3. The Insert Hyperlink window will appear. In the Link to: section of the window, type in the web address of the website you want linked. 4. In the Display section type in the text you want to appear on the screen.

Scenario 2

To accomplish this Level 1 task, review Scenario 2 (page 164), specifically focusing on Figure 5.20 and the specific text formatting features highlighted by the callouts within that figure. Using Figure 5.20 as a guide, re-create that document by following these steps.

No.	Feature	Steps to Get It Done
1.	Select the theme for the presentation	1. Click on the Theme tab in the ribbon. 2. Select the theme you'd like to use by clicking. 3. Modifications to the theme can be made through the Theme Options group.
2.	Select a slide layout	1. Click on the **Home** tab >>> **Slide** group >>> **Layout.** 2. Select the desired layout from the presented gallery.
3.	Auto slide numbers	1. Click on the **Home** tab >>> **Insert** group >>> **Text** drop-down button. Choose Header and Footer. 2. The Header and Footer dialog window appears. Choose the options you'd like to include and select either Apply or Apply to All.
4.	Transitions between slides	Transitions allow for one slide to professionally evolve into the next slide during a presentation. For example, as the first slide fades, the next slide emerges from the center of the screen. 1. Click on the slide you would like to add a transition to. 2. Click on the Transitions tab. 3. Preview the transitions by clicking on the gallery selections. Click on the effect you desire. 4. In this same group of commands, you can also select the speed of the transition, whether to add a sound effect, and how to advance the slide (e.g., on the click of the mouse or by some predetermined amount of time).

(continued)

5.	**Custom Animation**	Refer to Feature 8 of Scenario 1 (page 186).
6.	**Clip art**	Refer to Feature 6 of Scenario 1 (page 186).
7.	**Animation of grouped objects**	At times, you may want to animate a group of objects simultaneously. Depending on how you set up the animation, it will be possible for you to begin a series of animations with simply a click of the mouse. A simple way is to first group the items you want to animate at the same time and then complete a simple custom animation as shown in Feature 8 of Scenario 1 (page 186). 1. Highlight all the objects you would like to group together within the animation. 2. To group these objects: Select the **Home** tab >>> **Format** group >>> **Arrange** drop-down button >>> **Group** button. All selected items will now be grouped together as a single item. You can also use this same procedure to ungroup a set of previously grouped items. 3. Once all of the different groups of items have been formed, open the Animations tab and make your selections. See Feature 8 from Scenario 1 (page 186) for more detail.
8.	**Add sounds**	To insert sounds from a file: 1. Click on the **Home** tab >>> **Insert** group >>> **Media** drop-down button >>> **Audio from File.** 2. The Media Browser will open. Select an audio file. Click and drag the file to the slide (see Figure 5.32). 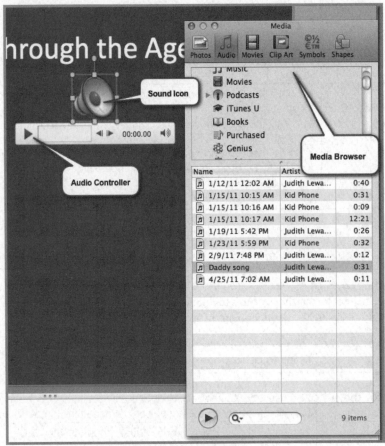 **FIGURE 5.32** Selecting an audio file to be included in the project 3. Immediately, a sound icon (a speaker) will appear along with an audio controller. Use the play button to preview the sound. 4. By clicking on the sound icon, the Format Audio tab will appear. Within this tab are several groups with features to enable you to customize the playback of the audio. 5. Under the Audio Options group, you can use the Start drop-down menu to determine when the audio begins and how long it lasts. Additionally in this same group, you use the Playback Options drop-down button to hide the sound icon during a slideshow, loop the music, or rewind. **Note:** From the Media drop-down button, it is also possible to record your own sounds. This could be very useful in student narration of work.

9.	Placement of objects	1. Select the object you would like to move by clicking on the outer edge. 2. Click and drag the object to the location you desire. **Movement Tips** (These work in all MS Office applications!): • *Nudging an object:* To move an item at very small intervals. Select the object. Press the Control key on your keyboard while pressing a directional arrow. • *Modify the order of objects* (e.g., bring to front, send to back, and so forth): Select the object and then select the order (**Home** tab >>> **Format** group >>> **Arrange** drop-down button). • *Rotate or flip an object:* Select the object and then select how you want it rotated or flipped (**Home** tab >>> **Format** group >>> **Arrange** drop-down button).
10.	Watermark backgrounds	Watermarks (also known as *washouts*) are images (e.g., pictures, clip art) that are semitransparent and often used in the background. 1. Add an image from Clip Art. (For more detail, see Feature 6 of Scenario 1, page 162). 2. Select the image. Use the **Format Picture** tab >>> **Adjust** group >>> **Recolor** to adjust the transparency of the image. 3. To send the image to the background, click the **Home** tab >>> **Format** group >>> **Arrange** button >>> **Order objects** menu >>> **Send to Back** button.
11.	Timed animation effects	After adding an animation to text or an object, select the animation. Click the **Animations** tab >>>**Animations Options** group >>> **Start** drop-down button. 1. Choose how you'd like the animation to start. 2. Also, in this same location, use the duration section to determine the length of time that the animation will function. **Note:** There are other methods to be used to auto run a slide show. Click on the Slide Show menu to view the options available.
12.	Printing	To print slides, handouts, or notes: 1. Select the **File** menu >>> **Print.** 2. In the Print window, several standard options appear, such as number of copies, printer location, and collating choices. 3. Unique to PowerPoint is the ability to print a variety of formats of your presentation. Use the **Print What** drop-down list to select the option that meets your needs. 4. If you choose to print handouts, you will have an additional series of choices within the Handout section (e.g., how many slides to print per page). 5. It is always good to Preview your choices before printing. The Preview button is located in the bottom left-hand corner of the Print window. **Note:** If you use the Print icon located in the standard toolbar, all slides in full color will be printed. This could lead to a lot of wasted paper, ink, and time.

Level 1a and 1b Workouts

Return to the Level 1 Workout found on page 169. Complete the Workouts using Figures 5.14 to 5.16 and 5.20 as guides for your work.

LEVEL 2: CREATING PRESENTATIONS TO LEARN

What should you be able to do?

The focus within Level 2 is to help you use Help and other resources to access and use various other features of the MS PowerPoint application.

Similar to Help in Windows, there is also Help in MS PowerPoint and most other sophisticated spreadsheet software. To use Help, click the Help button on tab bar of the standard toolbar (see Figure 5.27). As shown in Figure 5.33 you can also access the Help function through the Help drop-down menu on the menu bar.

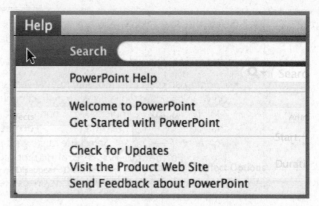

FIGURE 5.33 Accessing Help through the main menu bar in MS PowerPoint for Mac

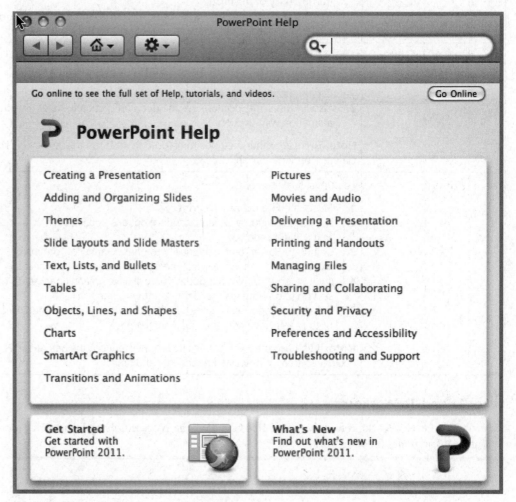

FIGURE 5.34 PowerPoint Help window for Mac

Clicking the PowerPoint Help button opens the Help window (see Figure 5.34). From here you can browse general Help topics, enter key words to search for a specific question that you might have, explore addition online Help topics, review tutorials to help you get started, and so on.

Note: In addition to the built-in Help in PowerPoint, expanded Help can be accessed online (www.microsoft.com/mac/how-to). Click on the PowerPoint Help link and a Help window similar to Figure 5.34 will appear. These topics have expanded topics that are not covered within the built-in PowerPoint Help.

Scenario 3

To expand your capabilities and begin to see how Help can be accessed and used to find additional features, review Scenario 3 on page 171, paying close attention to Figures 5.24, 5.25, and 5.26. Note the highlighted callouts of their various features. Using Figures 5.24 to 5.26 as guides, practice using the highlighted features by accessing and using each of the following word processing features.

Feature	Steps to Get It Done
Inserting customized action buttons	**Online help:** www.microsoft.com/mac/how-to Click on **Product Help** >>> **PowerPoint 2011** Select: *Transitions and animations* and then explore *Insert an action button to change slides* and *Create, edit, or remove a hyperlink* To add an action button: 1. Go to **Home** tab >>> **Insert** group >>> **Shape** drop-down menu and select **Action Buttons.** 2. Choose the button you want to use. Immediately, your mouse arrow becomes a + (or cross-hair). Click and drag to draw out a button. 3. When you release, the Action Settings window will appear. In this window, you can choose to link to a specific slide, run a program, play a sound, and so on. 4. Make your selection and click OK. **Note:** If you know that you want the button to go to a specific slide, choose Hyperlink to and select Slide . . . . This will allow you to link directly to a slide regardless of any changes or additions that are made to the presentation. **Additional note:** Action can be added to any item in a similar manner. Click the item, right click and select Action Settings. Follow the steps just given.
Using SmartArt graphics	**Procedure for creating and inserting:** **PPT Help** • Key words: SmartArt • Select: *Add* or *Add or edit a SmartArt graphic* and follow the given procedure. **Key features to note, explore, and try out:** • A quick way to get to the action buttons is to use the SmartArt tab. • Once a SmartArt design has been selected, you can add text, pictures, graphics, alter color scheme, and so on. (i.e., highlight the selected SmartArt graphic, then select the SmartArt tools above the Design tab).
Customizing sections of a graphic or object to serve as individual action buttons	To do this, you create an action button that is totally transparent, then you lay it over the top of the target graphic or object (e.g., a picture, graphic, word, SmartArt, and so forth.). Even though you can't see the button, it (and its associated action) will still be present. Clicking on the graphic or object with the transparent button overlay will produce the associated button action (that is, the button will work). • To create 100 percent transparency, select your action button, then click on the **Format** tab/**Shape Styles** group >>> **Transparency**. Set the Transparency to 100 percent. Repeat this procedure for the Shape Outline.
Placing action buttons on the Slide Master	Action buttons that you want to appear on all of your slides (e.g., buttons to link to the next slide) can be created once and put on the Slide Master. These buttons will then appear on all slides within the presentation. **General information on the Slide Master:** **PPT Help** • Key words: Slide Master • Select: Modify a Slide Master **Key features to note, explore, and try out:** • A quick way to get to the Slide Master: **View menu** >>> **Slide Master**. • Action buttons can be added anywhere on the Slide Master and they will appear in that position on all slides. Therefore, place them in a location that will be free of other items on all slides.

(continued)

Using movies or video clips	Procedure for incorporating movies or video clips: **PPT Help** • Key words: Add a movie • Select: *Add and play a movie in a presentation*. Review the Overview of movies and animated GIF files section. • Select: *Add a movie section* and follow the given procedure. **Key features to note, explore, and try out:** • A quick way to get to add a movie is **Home** tab >>> **Insert** group >>> **Media** drop-down button. • Movie tools can be accessed by selecting the inserted movie within your slide, then click the Format Movies tab (contextual tab will appear when you click the movie). Movie tools allow you to select when to show the movie and to select the volume, size, and arrangement of the movie on the slide.
Designing review questions with required interaction and feedback	With the use of action buttons, it is possible to present the learner with a question and several possible alternative responses on a slide. Having each of the possible responses as an action button allows you to have specific feedback slides linked to each alternative. In addition, the feedback may include information about why the response being made was correct or incorrect and additional information to help the student understand why his or her response was correct or not.

Level 2 Workout

Return to the Level 2 Workout found on page 174. Complete the Workout using Figures 5.24, 5.25, and 5.26 as guides.

6 DESKTOP PUBLISHING
MS Publisher: The Basics of Creating a Publication
(written in cooperation with Cindy York)

INTRODUCTION

What should you know about desktop publishers?

Desktop publishing (e.g., **Microsoft Publisher**) is designed to help you and your students create professional-looking publications. You need to know a few of its basics so that you can use it effectively. In this opening section, we want you to know the following:

- What a desktop publisher program is, what it can do, and how it can help in teaching and learning
- How to justify the use of the desktop publisher program as an effective tool—by knowing when and why it should or shouldn't be used

Terms to know		
border	computer applications	layout guides
boundary guides	fill color	Microsoft's Publisher

What is a desktop publisher and what does it do?

Desktop publishers are **computer applications** that allow you to design and produce professional-looking publications at home or school. Using desktop publishing is very similar to using a word processing program and allows you to create print publications, e-mail publications, or web publications. Desktop publishing allows for manipulation of the size and shape of print publications, allowing for things such as a one-page flyer, wall banner, index card, or greeting card, just to name a few.

Microsoft's Publisher provides many templates and ideas as well as blank publications that allow you to efficiently and professionally create newsletters, brochures, signs, banners, and even websites. This program allows for much flexibility and creativity on your part.

Types of publications

There are many different types of publications. The most common you'll find is print publications. These could be advertisements, signs, note cards, business cards, labels, and so forth. Within MS Publisher there are also e-mail publications and web publications. E-mail publications consist of e-mail newsletters, event or activity announcements, product announcements, and so on. Web publications can consist of the same things as e-mail publications as well as just about anything else someone would want to create on a website.

What are some commonly used desktop publishers?

- Microsoft Publisher
- Serif PagePlus
- Nova Development Print Artist Platinum 23

- Adobe PageMaker
- Adobe InDesign
- Broderbund Print Shop Professional 2.0
- Corel CorelDraw Graphics

Note: We focus on Microsoft's Publisher in this text. However, *all of what we show you can be done in any of the other desktop publishers listed*. So if you don't have access to Publisher, don't be alarmed—you can still complete the projects and learn the basic skills.

Why bother learning how to use desktop publishing?

- *Save money and time.* Professional publications can be expensive and time consuming. Publishing from your computer allows for quick and easy modifications to any document.
- *Quality publications.* Desktop publishing allows the use of clip art, graphics, and professional-looking fonts. Desktop publications look much more professional than those that are handwritten. A quality publication will grab someone's attention much better than one casually created.
- *Themes—templates, font schemes, color schemes.* Design sets allow you to keep a theme throughout different documents such as letterhead, envelope, and label. Publisher offers many templates, publication design ideas, color schemes, and font schemes.
- *Multiple uses.* It's easy to see how many different types of publications you can create using this software. From award certificates, to labels, to newsletters—you can create just about anything you might need.
- *Learning tool.* Desktop publishing can be integrated into various lessons, for example, the history of publishing. This lesson could begin prior to the printing press and lead into today's newspaper and magazine publishing. In another example, think of what can be learned by a student using Publisher to create a brochure about a specific concept, event, place, or person. By teaching others about a specific concept through the development of the brochure, the student effectively learns the needed material.

How can desktop publishing be used at school? A brief list of ideas

By the teacher:	By the student:
• Newsletters	• Classroom newspapers
• Flyers	• Book reports
• Signs or banners	• Club announcements
• Calendars	• School event flyers
• Nameplates	• Greeting cards
• Award certificates	• Brochures

ORIENTATION

What's the workspace look like?

Figure 6.1 is an example of the workspace of a common desktop publisher (MS Publisher). Note where you can enter your information and graphics. Similar to other MS Office applications, the ribbon is located along the top with common command tabs and command groups. The purpose of Publisher is to facilitate the process of creating and publishing documents; therefore, this application has many predesigned templates, page parts, themes, and so on that are included to help you create an effective design in a very professional and efficient manner. All of these helpful items can be accessed through the command tabs on the ribbon.

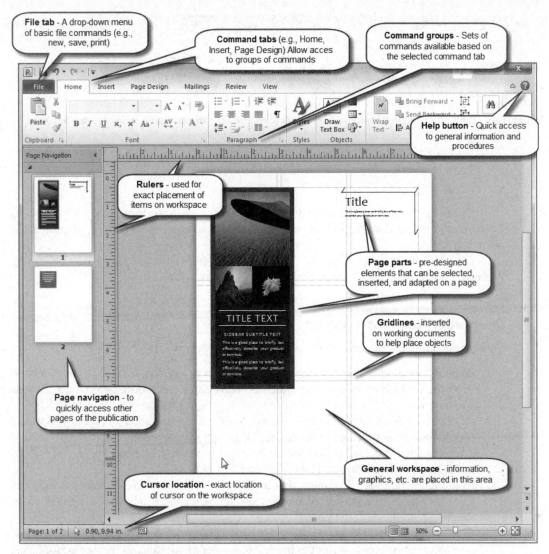

FIGURE 6.1 View of a Microsoft Publisher desktop publishing work area

What commands can be used?

As in all MS Office applications (e.g., MS PowerPoint, MS Word) there is a ribbon of tools that runs across the top of the work screen. Within each ribbon the actual tools that can be used to input, format, edit the information, and set up the page for publication are grouped together under the various command tabs (e.g., Home, Insert, Page Design, Mailings). Selecting a specific tab reveals an associated command set or group. Once a command tab has been selected this specific group remains visible and ready for use. Items within the set may appear as individual items or as a gallery of related items. For example, selecting the Insert tab (see Figure 6.2) in Publisher reveals a group of commands that deal specifically with the insertion of such things as tables, illustrations, page parts, text boxes, and hyperlinks.

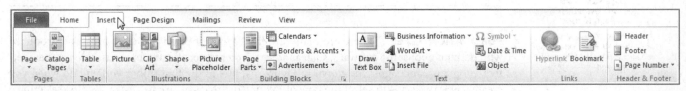

FIGURE 6.2 The ribbon holds the command tabs, command groups or sets, and individual commands.

FIGURE 6.3 Selecting a specific item (e.g. graphic, picture) in the workspace reveals contextual commands that can be accessed and used with the selected item

Occasionally, additional commands will be needed. As shown in Figure 6.3 (Drawing Tools) these contextual commands appear when a specific object like a picture, graphic, table, or chart is selected.

For more information about the Publisher ribbon and command tabs, please review the Publisher Orientation video on the website that accompanies this text.

Orientation Workout 1: Explore the territory

Turn on the computer and attempt the following:

1. Begin by selecting the type of publication you want to develop. Click **File** tab >>> **New**. From the available templates (e.g., Flyers, Greeting Cards, Letterhead) select a specific type you want to try.
2. Once your template type has been selected, MS Publisher gives you a number of optional specific templates from which to choose. These options are professionally developed and can be selected and used to help with the completion of your project. Try several options and view the different layouts that are generated by your selection.
3. Examine the template document that is now revealed within the Publisher workspace. Click on items in the workspace and see how different contextual tabs are highlighted on the ribbon as you select the various objects.
4. Click on an item within the template and alter it in some way. For example, if you click on a picture or graphic, attempt to move it to a different location on the workspace (click, hold, and drag), alter its style and shadow effect, or even adjust its color. For text, insert your own text and change the font in some way. As you make these changes note how the rulers monitor the exact position of the object on which you are working.
5. Play with it for a few minutes so you get a feel for what can be done and how easy it is to use.

Key features

Several key features have been incorporated within Publisher to assist you and your students as projects are identified, designed, and produced. Here are a few of the items that allow you to quickly and professionally develop projects such as brochures, programs, résumé, signs, cards, and so on.

Note: Each of these key features is demonstrated within a set of mentoring videos on the website that accompanies this text.

PUBLICATION TYPES. There are many different types of publications that can be produced with desktop publishing software, such as advertisements, certificates, brochures, flyers, newsletters, programs, and signs. As shown in Figure 6.4, one of the first things you will do when you create a new project is to select the type of publication that you are to design. By first selecting a type (e.g., calendars), you will then be given access to all kinds of examples and templates for that type of publication.

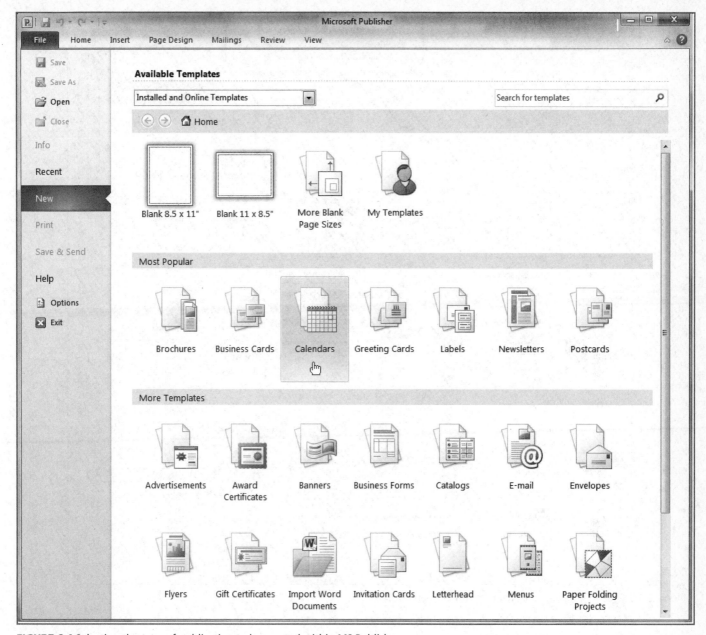

FIGURE 6.4 Selecting the type of publication to be created within MS Publisher

PREDESIGNED PUBLICATIONS AND TEMPLATES. Publisher has a number of different pre-made layouts created by professional designers available for your use. One or more of these may match what you need for your publication. Even if the given templates aren't a perfect match for your needs, they provide all types of ideas and possibilities of what can be created. As shown in Figure 6.5, once the type of publication has been selected (e.g., Calendars), then a new window exposing all of the different templates is brought up.

Selecting a template allows you to review the basic design and then add the written information and visual elements needed for your specific publication. Such templates can save you time and effort by giving you a quick, professional start to the project. It's always possible to start from scratch (a blank publication), but the templates allow you to start (and finish) in a much more timely fashion.

In addition, these templates are flexible—that is, you can customize them as needed. Note in Figure 6.6 that you can customize the type of color and font scheme used, paper size, and so on. Once you have created your own or customized one of the given templates, Publisher allows you to save the result as a new template. In this way, when you need it, the template will be available for your use and you won't have to generate it again.

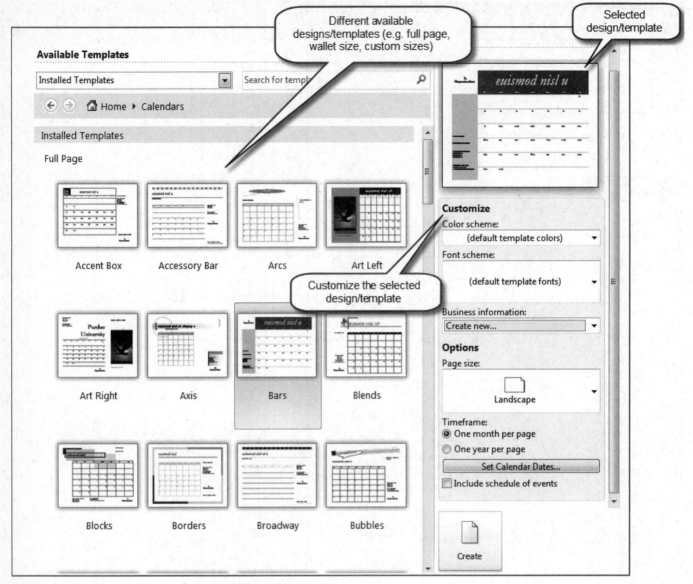

FIGURE 6.5 Selecting the design or template for the publication

---

Note: Within this template selection window, the templates have been grouped based on a specified design set (for the calendar templates, these sets include full-page calendars, wallet-size calendars, and some blank sizes that match specific paper sizes). You can access the various grouped sets by scrolling down with the vertical scroll bar.

COLOR AND FONT SCHEMES.   With the flexibility provided by this software, you can select all kinds of colors and fonts to be used within your publication. However, for some of us that can lead to potential problems—that is, we may select something that we think looks good but others find problematic. Designers have selected schemes or sets of colors and schemes of fonts that work well together within specific types of publications in addition to the templates offered in Publisher. This allows you to include a variety of color and fonts to add visual appeal, but at the same time you can confidently apply these schemes knowing that they work well together to help your publication be perceived as a professional creation. As shown in Figure 6.6, the Customize Color scheme task pane gives you access to drop-down menus of various types of color schemes (font schemes are accessible in the same manner). This will allow you to preview and select the color and font scheme that is most suitable for your work.

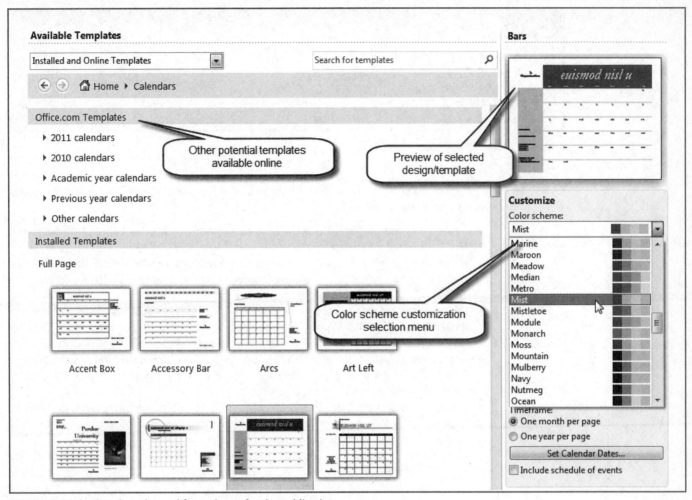

FIGURE 6.6 Selecting the color and font scheme for the publication

Note: As you work on your individual project, you can always change the font and color schemes by clicking **Page Design** tab >>> **Schemes group** and making your selection.

Another note: Additional templates for Publisher can always be accessed and downloaded from **www.office.com**. As shown in Figure 6.6 access to relevant templates requires an Internet connection and then simply clicking on the Office.com templates that you desire. The template should automatically download to your computer.

THE MASTER PAGE. Master pages contain the design and layout elements that you want to repeat on multiple pages in a publication. The design and layout elements may include headers and footers, page numbers, pictures, and page dimensions. The use of the master pages helps give your publication a more consistent look. For example, you may want your school logo and school colors to be consistent throughout your publication; therefore, you put the background colors and logo on the master page and they will show up consistently throughout your publication. The master allows you to create it once, and it automatically appears on all pages of the publication.

Within MS Publisher, each type of publication that you select to work with already has one master page associated with it (to provide the page layout). You can access that master and change the layout, add other design elements, and so on. You can also create additional master pages so you can adapt parts of your publication as it is developed (e.g., if you want the interior pages of a brochure to have elements on the master page that vary from those of the front and back page of the brochure).

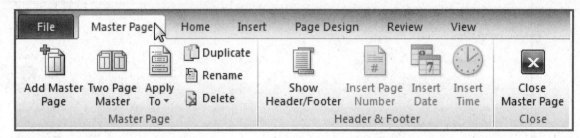

FIGURE 6.7 Master Page ribbon

Here's a list of what you can do with the master pages (note Figure 6.7 for reference on how to access most of these features):

- *Create a new master page:* **View** tab >>> **View** group >>>**Master Page**. With the Master Page tab selected you can select to Add Master Page.
- *Access and edit a master page:* **View** tab >>> **View** group >>> **Master Page**. With the master page now within the workspace, other tabs are available (e.g., Home, Insert, Page Design) with all of their groups of tools for editing.
- *Apply a master to a specific publication page:* **View** tab >>> **View** group >>> **Master Page** >>> **Master Page** group >>> **Apply To** >>> **Apply Master Page . . .** >>> the **Apply Master Page** window will occur and you can select which page(s) to apply the Master Page.
- *Place design or layout elements on to a master page:* Open the Master Page (**View** tab >>> **View** group >>> **Master Page**) and then select the Home, Insert, or Page Design tab to select and insert the needed page element.
- *Rename a master page:* Open the master page you wish to rename and click on the Rename button (**Master Page** tab >>> **Master Page** group >>> **Rename**). A Rename Master Page window will appear and you can rename it by filling in the description box.
- *Delete a master page:* Open the master page you wish to delete and click on the Delete button (**Master Page** tab >>> **Master Page** group >>> **Delete**).

BLANK PUBLICATIONS. MS Publisher offers a number of blank publications that you can use as a starting point for your own. These allow you to select a specific page size based on the type of publication that you want to create (e.g., booklets, postcards, name tags). The beauty of this selection is that Publisher has included selections that allow you to match your needed size with commercial products (e.g., Avery labels) so that when you create and print, your publication will match exactly the paper that you use from these commercial vendors (see Figure 6.5).

To access the various kinds of blank publications, simply create a new publication (**File** tab >>> **New**) and then click on the More Blank Page Size link. A set of alternatives from which to choose will appear (see Figure 6.8).

Orientation Workout 2: Explore the key features

While in Publisher:

1. Create a blank publication with more than one page.
2. Review the Orientation Workout 1 and add some content to your publication (e.g., text boxes with information, a picture).
3. Select and apply a color scheme and font scheme.
4. Create a new master page and add some elements such as a header or footer or page number.
5. Return to your pages and note the changes made on all of the pages using the master.

LEVEL 1: DESIGNING, CREATING, AND PRODUCING PUBLICATIONS

What should you be able to do?

Given specific guidelines and step-by-step procedures, you'll be able to use various tools and techniques of a desktop publisher program (specifically MS Publisher) to design, create, and produce a publication.

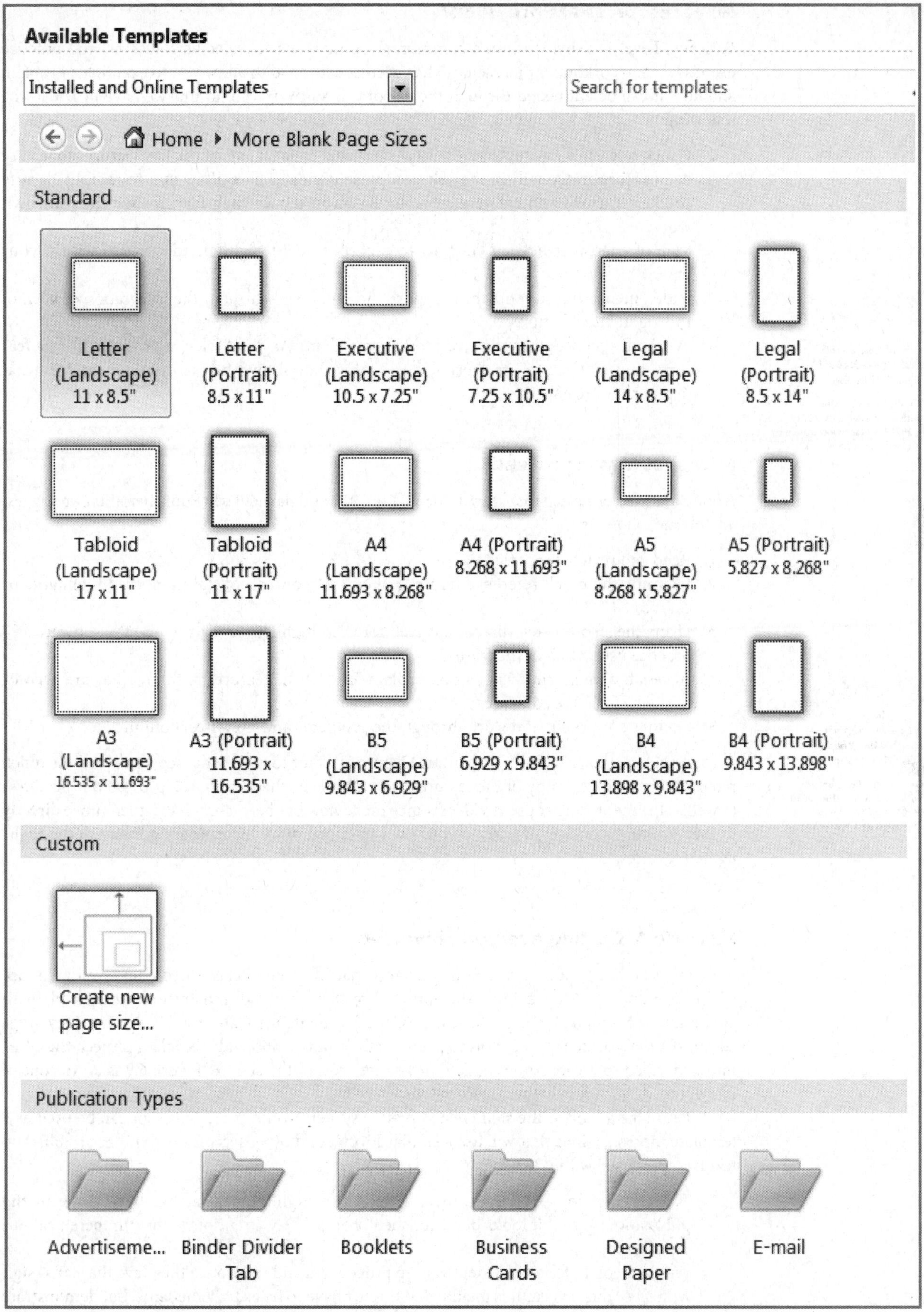

Available Templates

| Installed and Online Templates ▾ | | Search for templates |

⬅ ➡ 🏠 Home ▸ More Blank Page Sizes

Standard

Letter (Landscape) 11 x 8.5"	Letter (Portrait) 8.5 x 11"	Executive (Landscape) 10.5 x 7.25"	Executive (Portrait) 7.25 x 10.5"	Legal (Landscape) 14 x 8.5"	Legal (Portrait) 8.5 x 14"
Tabloid (Landscape) 17 x 11"	Tabloid (Portrait) 11 x 17"	A4 (Landscape) 11.693 x 8.268"	A4 (Portrait) 8.268 x 11.693"	A5 (Landscape) 8.268 x 5.827"	A5 (Portrait) 5.827 x 8.268"
A3 (Landscape) 16.535 x 11.693"	A3 (Portrait) 11.693 x 16.535"	B5 (Landscape) 9.843 x 6.929"	B5 (Portrait) 6.929 x 9.843"	B4 (Landscape) 13.898 x 9.843"	B4 (Portrait) 9.843 x 13.898"

Custom

Create new page size...

Publication Types

Advertiseme...	Binder Divider Tab	Booklets	Business Cards	Designed Paper	E-mail

FIGURE 6.8 Selecting a blank page size

What resources are provided?

Basically, Level 1 is divided into a common teaching scenario, selected solutions, and practice exercises (i.e., Workouts). The scenario has been constructed to allow you to examine a problem and how it can be addressed through the use of this software. To do this we have provided the following:

1. Quick reference figures that identify (via visual callouts) all of the key features that have been incorporated within the solution presentation. These allow you to rapidly identify the key features and reference exactly how to include such features within your own work.
2. Step-by-step instructions on how to incorporate all highlighted features within your work.
3. Video mentoring support that support and guide you through the integration of each of the highlighted features.
4. Workout exercises that allow you to practice identifying and selecting which software features to use, when to use those features, how they should be incorporated, and to what degree they are effective.

Go to PDToolkit for **Teaching and Learning with Microsoft® Office 2010 and Office 2011 for Mac** to locate the mentoring videos for Chapter Six.

How should you proceed?

If you have *little or no experience* with MS Office 2010 and particularly Publisher, then we suggest you do the following:

1. Read and review Scenario 1.
2. Examine the quick reference figure (Figure 6.10) and all of the numbered highlights or callouts.
3. Using the step-by-step directions given for each highlighted feature, use the software and practice using each of the features.
4. Access the mentoring videos that explain each of the features and how they are accomplished within the software.
5. Go to the Workout and work through the problems and exercises it outlines.

Go to PDToolkit for **Teaching and Learning with Microsoft® Office 2010 and Office 2011 for Mac** to locate the mentoring videos for Chapter Six.

If you have *experience* with Publisher 2010, you may want to review the scenarios and the quick reference figure first. If any of the features are unfamiliar, then use the step-by-step procedures as well as the mentoring support videos. Once the review has been completed, then move directly to the Workout exercise and create your own publication by incorporating many of the highlighted features.

Scenario 1: Getting everyone involved

Remember the aluminum can recycling project that Mr. Rena's classes were involved with (see Chapters 3 and 4)? After gaining the approval of the school administration for their plans to create a schoolwide recycling effort, the SCAR (Students for Can and Aluminum Recycling) committee was formed. In an effort to promote their new schoolwide recycling project, the committee decided to create some signs to distribute around the school. Figure 6.9 is a printout of one of the SCAR signs that was distributed.

Let's take a look at the sign created by this student committee. This sign can be used as a template for other signs that will use a similar format and other features. Several key publishing features were used within the sign.

- Take a close look at Figure 6.10. This figure highlights what has been done to the publication so that it looks like a finished product. Pay attention to the numbered callout bubbles.
- We want you to follow the step-by-step procedures and reproduce the "Save the Cans" sign with all of the key features included. It doesn't have to be exactly the same, but demonstrate that you can carry out the highlighted functions or features.

FIGURE 6.9 Sample sign created using MS Publisher

FIGURE 6.10 Highlighted sample sign

No.	Feature	Steps to Get It Done
1.	**Select a publication type and appropriate template**	1. Start Publisher and create a new publication (**File** tab >>> **New**).
		Note: From the Orientation section of this chapter, read the sections about Publication Types and Predesigned Publications and Templates .
		2. From the More Templates list, select the Signs type.
		3. A large variety of premade signs will appear. Select a design or template that you want to work with to develop your sign (e.g., For Sale #2 sign). Double left click on the selected design or template and the Publisher workspace will open with your selected sign ready to be adapted (see Figure 6.11).
		FIGURE 6.11 Selecting a template to start a new Publisher project
2.	**Insert and adapt a text box**	A text box is one of the best methods used to insert text onto a workspace and then control where it is placed and how it looks.
		To insert a text box:
		1. Select the Draw Text Box tool (**Insert** tab >>> **Text** group >>> **Draw Text Box**). This will make your cursor look like a large plus sign ╌╀╌ .
		2. Place the cursor in the approximate location of where you want the text box to be inserted, left click, and hold and drag your cursor to create the needed size of text box.
		3. Type text directly into the text box. Modify your text using font type, size, color, and style changes (**Home** tab >>> **Font** group).
		Note: As shown in Figure 6.12, with the text box selected, the contextual format tabs for both the Drawing Tools and the Text Box Tools appear on the ribbon. Using those tools you can make a variety of adaptations to the appearance of the text box as well as how the text within that box is formatted.
		FIGURE 6.12 Text Box Tools and Drawing Tools contextual tabs allow access to specific tools to adapt the selected text box and its contents

To adapt a text box within a template:

1. Click within the selected text box (a lined box with handles will appear around the edge of the selected text box) and select all words you wish to adapt.

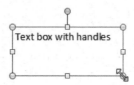

2. Enter the words that you desire.
3. Adapt the text (e.g., color, size, alignment) in the usual manner (**Home** tab >>> **Font** group or **Text Box Tools** contextual format tab >>> **Font** group).
4. Adapt the size of the text box by clicking once in the text box. Handles (i.e., small dots on the corners and sides of the text box) should appear. Click, hold, and move one handle to adjust the size of the box.
5. Adapt the looks of the box itself by clicking once in the text box and then selecting tool groups such as Shape Styles or Shadow Effects found on the Drawing Tools format contextual tab (see Figure 6.13).

FIGURE 6.13 Adapting text boxes with the Shape Styles and Shadow Effects groups can be accessed through the ribbon's Drawing Tools contextual tab

| 3. | Adapt the publication's color scheme | 1. You can adapt the overall color scheme for the entire publication when you originally select the template you with to use (see the Orientation section of this chapter: "Color and Font Schemes"), or as shown in Figure 6.14, you can adapt it at any time by simply selecting from the alternatives (**Page Design** tab >>> **Schemes** group). Move your cursor over the various schemes and you can preview the new look. Left click on your desired new color scheme.

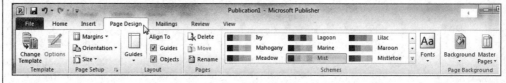

FIGURE 6.14 Publication color schemes can be adapted through the Page Design tab and the Scheme group of tools

2. If you want to adapt the color of any particular item within your publication, select the item (e.g., text box, picture) and then click on the contextual format tab that has appeared. Within the format tab, you can select various tools to adapt the color and other features. |
| 4. | Font type, size, style, and color change | 1. Select (highlight) the words you would like to change.
2. With the Home tab selected, adapt the formatting of the words using the Font group of tools. As shown in Figure 6.15 you can expand the Font group by clicking on the Font group expander button and the Font window will appear. Several additional and expanded tools become available. |

(continued)

FIGURE 6.15 Font window of tools used to adapt text in a publication

5.	**Change alignment**	1. Highlight the text (or object) to be aligned. 2. On Home tab within the Paragraph group, identify the set of alignment icons. 3. Click on the one that shows the text to be centered. 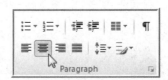 4. Try the other ones and see what happens. Then go back and center your text. **Note:** Alignment allows you to quickly line up text on the left, the right, equally between right and left, or in the center of your text box.

6.	**Insert, size, and place a graphic**

		1. *Get the graphic* (e.g., picture, clip art).
		  a. On the main ribbon, click **Insert** tab >>> **Illustrations** group >>> **Clip art . . .** The Clip Art task pane will appear.
		  b. In the Clip Art task pane, enter a key word that describes the type of clip art you are searching for (e.g., *sports*) and then click on the Go button. Various small versions of the clip art should appear in the task pane.
		  c. Scroll through the different alternatives that are presented in the task pane. Use the *Find more at Office.com* to expand your search if needed.
		  d. Click on your selected clip art and the picture will automatically be inserted within your publication.
		2. *Size the graphic.* If your inserted clip art is the perfect size for your publication, great—leave it as it is. However, in many cases, the size will not be perfect. So point your mouse at the picture and left click once. You will note that a box will be drawn around the picture and handles will be placed at each of the corners and in the middle of each of the sides. You can grab a handle by putting your mouse pointer on the handle (note that your pointer will change into a double-headed arrow), left click, and hold it. Dragging a handle will cause the picture to be altered. Try different handles and see what happens to the shape and size of the picture.
		3. *Place the graphic.* Once your picture is inserted and sized appropriately, you can move it to a different location on the publication by putting the mouse on top of the graphic and then clicking, holding, and dragging it to the new location.
		4. *Adapt or adjust the quality of the graphic.* You should also note that once you have selected your picture (the picture has the box around it with the handles) a special set of Picture Tools (see Figure 6.3) becomes available (look for the Picture Tools contextual tab immediately above the Format tab on the main ribbon).

		You can use these tools to: • Adjust the picture (brightness, contrast, color) • Change the picture style (**border**, shape, special effects) • Arrange the picture in relation to other items (bring to the front, send to the back) • Size the picture (crop, alter height and width) **Note:** Working with clip art and other graphic files may take a bit of practice. You'll find that some don't look very good when their size is changed to a drastic degree—others work great. You will also find that access to the Internet gives you an endless supply of various clip art, pictures, and so forth that you may want to use and insert within your documents. Just as a caution, copyright rules and regulations will apply for using any tangible item from texts, videos, pictures, as well as what is located on the Internet.
7.	**Insert and edit WordArt**	1. As shown in Figure 6.16, WordArt is a Microsoft object that provides you with various fancy text templates. You generally use WordArt to get attention and add interest to your publication. 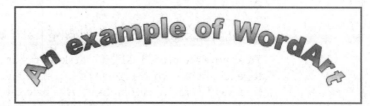 **FIGURE 6.16** An example of WordArt 2. To insert WordArt, simply click on the WordArt button (**Insert** tab >>> **Text** group >>> **WordArt**). From the drop-down menu select the style of your preference. An Edit WordArt Text window (see Figure 6.17) will appear and you enter your text at this point. In this window you select the type, size, and style of your font. Once that is completed, click OK and the text will be inserted into your publication. At this point, you can treat the WordArt as a text box and move it and size it in a similar fashion to usual text boxes. 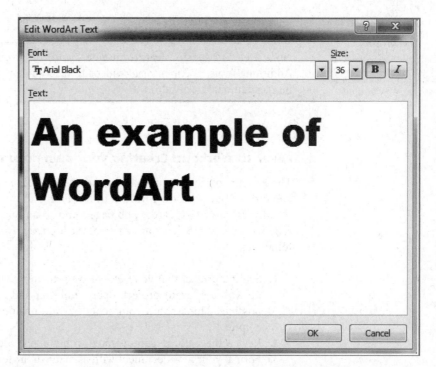 **FIGURE 6.17** The Edit WordArt Text window where text is entered and edited that will be shown as WordArt

(continued)

3. Once your WordArt has been inserted, a WordArt Format contextual tab will appear (see Figure 6.18). All kinds of tools allow you to alter and changes the WordArt and how it appears.

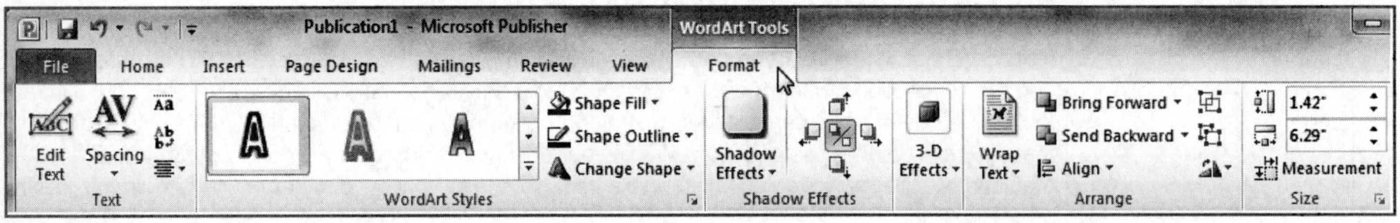

FIGURE 6.18 WordArt Tools contextual format tab and associated tools

Level 1a Workout: Practice using basic desktop publishing features

To acquire the needed skills for desktop publishing, you need to practice using **Publisher.** It generally isn't good enough to just read and watch how these features are developed. One way for you to accomplish this is by creating and formatting your own **publications.** As these documents are created, select and integrate the different features within your own work.

Here is a basic outline of what you need to do:

1. Review Figure 6.10 and all of the highlighted features that are in that figure.
2. Using Figure 6.10 as a guide, create your own publication for the SCAR committee.
3. Go through the list of features and practice adding them to your publication. **Don't worry** about matching the example figure exactly. You can adapt and change the features as you add them. Remember, this is a practice Workout—*practice integrating as many features as possible.*

PDToolkit

for
Teaching and Learning with Microsoft® Office 2010 and Office 2011 for Mac

Go to PDToolkit for **Teaching and Learning with Microsoft® Office 2010 and Office 2011 for Mac** to locate the mentoring videos for Chapter Six.

Note: Refer to specific feature numbers and the given step-by-step procedures as needed. Additionally, use the mentoring videos to help guide you through any specific procedure that needs additional clarification.

Level 1b Workout: Creating your own document

The benefits of desktop publishing software become very apparent when you begin to create and format your own publications. Think about all of the signs, brochures, newsletters, flyers, calendars, cards, web pages, and so on that you can create for your work, home, school—whatever. Select one or two of those currently in need of being completed and do the following:

1. Select a project that you need or want to complete. If you are having difficulty coming up with a relevant project, open Publisher and review the list of publications that are possible. Think about your school, work, or home and if any of those types would be helpful.
2. Review the features demonstrated within Figure 6.10.
3. Format your new document with as many of the features demonstrated in those figures as possible. Use Table 6.1 as a checklist to guide your efforts.

Table 6.1 Level 1 Workout and Practice Checklist: Creating and formatting a publication

Publication Content	___ Content is accurate and current.
	___ Content is relevant and cohesive throughout the document.
	___ Content achieves the proper level for the intended audience.
	___ Content is free from spelling and grammatical errors.
Publication Format	___ A new publication was created.
	___ Font size, style, and type were varied within the document to add emphasis to headings, and so forth.
	___ All text was placed and aligned in an appealing manner that allowed for clear understanding of the written material.
	___ Attractive, audience-relevant color and font schemes were employed within the publication.
	___ WordArt was employed effectively to gain attention to important text within the publication.
	___ Appropriate graphics (e.g., clip art, pictures, images) were properly selected, sized, and placed within the publication.

Note: Remember and implement the second rule to live by: *Save, save, save,* and then *save* your work again. This was a key principle mentioned at the beginning of this book. Make sure you do that or it will come back to haunt you sometime down the road.

Also think about concepts of Rules 3, 4, and 5: Keep things simple, watch how others accomplish what we have described in this chapter, and make sure you think about saving the publication as a template that can be adapted and used later as needed.

LEVEL 2: TABLES, TEMPLATES, AND OTHER GOOD STUFF

What should you be able to do?

You should come to recognize additional desktop publishing features and gain confidence using Help to create, edit, and format several original publications.

The key here is not to memorize all that the software is capable of—it's better to know some of the basics and when, where, and how to find assistance for all of the other stuff.

Getting some Help

Similar to Help in Windows and other MS Office applications, there is also Help in MS Publisher. To use Help, click the Help button on the tab bar of the main ribbon.

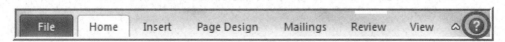

Clicking the Help button brings up the Help window (see Figure 6.19). From here you can browse general Help topics, bring up a general table of contents of all Help topics, review common commands, and complete a search for a specific question you might have.

By typing in key words or even a full question, Help will respond with a variety of potential answers for you to investigate. Help generally does not have all of the answers but it will have a lot of them. Make sure you become familiar with how it works and how often it can be of assistance.

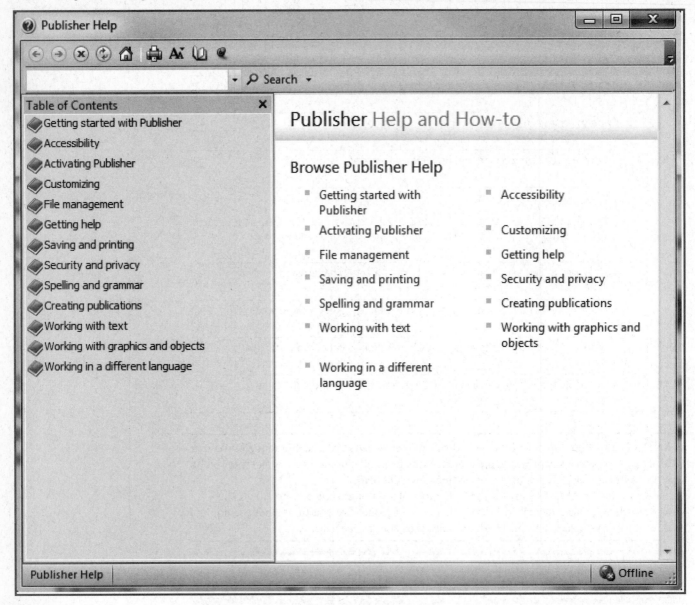

FIGURE 6.19 Publisher Help window

Scenario 2: The production

Mrs. Perez's fifth-grade class is putting on a play about the American Revolution at the end of the year. Although many have parts in the play, all of the students are involved with various parts of the production. An important part is the planning, designing, and production of the program for the event. Mrs. Perez's students chose the colors, pictures, and full layout of the program, as well as writing the information that the program will contain.

The final publication is shown in Figures 6.20 and 6.21. Remember that the program will be folded vertically down the center so the front cover and back page are side-by-side. Thus, it only takes one piece of paper for the four pages. Once this publication is completed, it will be used as a template for future play programs just by cutting and pasting new content as needed.

After reviewing the finished product (Figures 6.20 and 6.21), take a close look at Figure 6.22 and the highlighted sections of the interior two pages of the program. Following the figure there is a description of each of the features that have been added to those pages and how they were accomplished. More important, there is also a description of how to find much of this information within MS Publisher's Help. Take time to explore these features and also to examine the Help section and the explanations given on how to incorporate the features within productions such as this program.

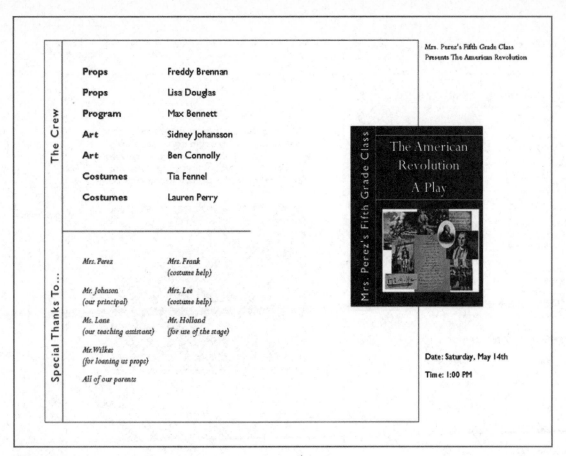

FIGURE 6.20 Program back and cover pages

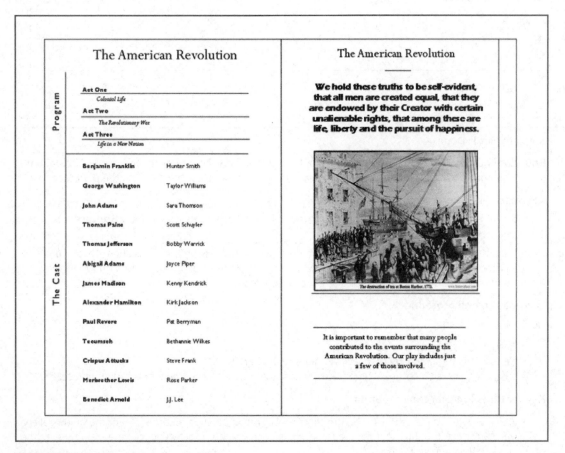

FIGURE 6.21 Program pages two and three

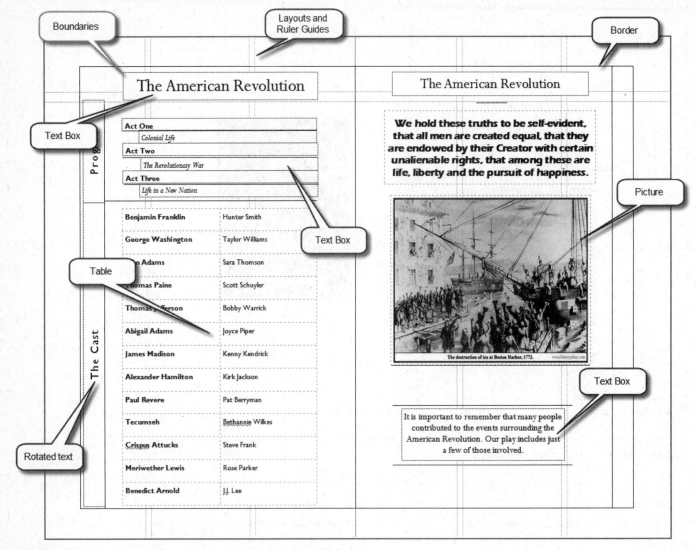

FIGURE 6.22 Program layout for pages two and three with highlights

Feature	Steps to Get It Done
Using object boundaries	**Boundary guides** allow you to see the edges of the items you are working with within your publication (e.g., a graphic, a text box). The boundaries allow for exact placement of the items on the publication. **Key features to note, explore, and try out:** • To view and use object boundaries, click **View** tab >>> **Show** group >>> check **Borders** and/or **Guides**.
Using layout and ruler guides	Layout and ruler guides are used to help position items with exactness on the publication. These guides are lines (that won't be seen when the publication is printed) that can be formed into a grid to ensure that exact placement of the elements on the page is completed. **Information and procedures:** Go to www.office.com • Search terms: **Layout guides** • Select: Structure the page with layout guides (Publisher 2010) • Also use the search terms: Align objects Publisher 2010 and review the article "Align objects." **Key features to note, explore, and try out:** • *Make the guides visible* (**Page Design** tab >>> **Layout** group >>> **Guides**): From the guide gallery, you can select from built-in ruler guides, no guides, or to input exactly your preference for where the guides should be included.

Baseline guides (horizontal lines running across the publication): To access and use a baseline guide click **Page Design** tab >>> **Layout** group >>> **Guides** >>> **Grid and Baseline Guides . . .** and a Layout Guides window will appear. From this window you can create exact margin, grid, and baseline guides.

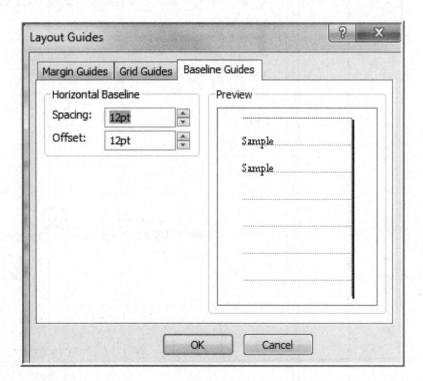

- *Ruler guides:* These are additional guides (lines) that can be added to the Publisher workspace. They can be used to help place elements on the publication. An important feature of these guides, however, is that you can move and place them as needed.

  To move a ruler guide: Once a ruler guide has been inserted, move your cursor over the top of the placed guide—the cursor will turn into a double-headed arrow. Click, hold, and drag the guide in the direction you desire it to move.

Inserting and adapting text boxes	**Information and procedures:**
	
	Publisher Help
	
	• Table of Contents task pane: Working with text
	• Select: Format Text Box Dialog
	
	Key features to note, explore, and try out:
	
	• Text boxes are used to position text on a page within a publication. The box allows you to control where the text is placed and how it looks and is emphasized.
	• To quickly insert or adapt a text box, review the explanation given within Scenario 1, Level 1, Feature 2 of this chapter (page 204).
	• There are a number of ways to emphasize the text box and catch the attention of those viewing it. Select your inserted text box and then open the Format Text Box window (once the inserted text box is selected (handles should appear around the border), click on the **Drawing Tools Format** tab >>> **Shape Styles** expander button). As shown in Figure 6.23, you should be able to do any or all of the following:
	
	  1. Put a border on the text box.
	  2. Change the color of the text box border.
	  3. **Fill** the text box with a **color**.
	  4. Alter the size, scale, and rotation of the text box.
	  5. Control how the text is wrapped within the text box.

(continued)

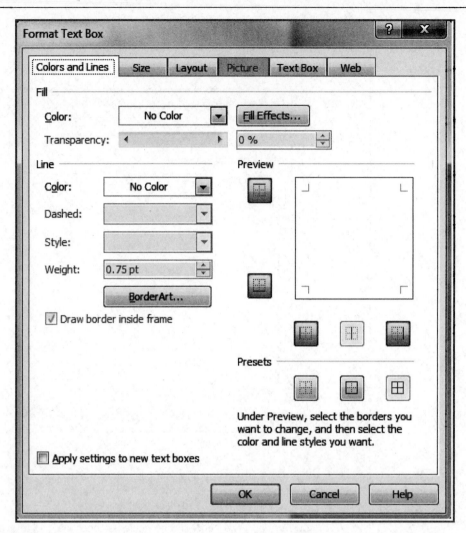

FIGURE 6.23 Use the Format Text Box window to alter the text box border, color, size, and so on within a document

- In addition, once text is inserted within the text box, all text formatting tools found on the **Home** tab >>> **Font, Paragraph, Styles, Objects**, or **Arrange** groups can be used to complete the following:
  1. Change the font size of text within the text box.
  2. Change the color of the text within the text box.
  3. Align the text.
  4. Change the style of the text.
  5. Wrap, align, and rotate the text.

Rotating text (and graphics)	**Information and procedures:** Go to www.office.com - On the Home tab, go to the Learning Resources section and within the Help by Product part, select Publisher. - In the Publisher 2010 section, select Working with text. - Select Text Box Tools Tab and read the section about Text Direction. **Key features to note, explore, and try out:** - To rotate the text box, select the rotate option (**Drawing Tools Format** contextual tab >>> **Arrange** group >>> **Rotate** button with drop-down menu). Options allow you to rotate exactly by 90 degrees or to free rotate.

- A quicker way to freely rotate the text box is to simply select the text box, then click, hold, and rotate the extended handle. The text will rotate as the mouse is moved in a circular fashion.

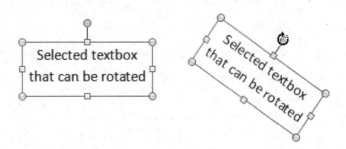

Use of the extended handle to rotate a selected text box.

Note: This technique also works for the free rotation of graphics

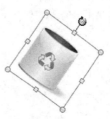

Creating, formatting, and moving tables	**Information and procedures:**
	
	Publisher Help
	
	    • Table of Contents task pane: **Working with text >>> Format Table Dialog**.
	
	Go to www.office.com
	
	    • Search term: Table Publisher 2010
	    • Select: Table Tools tabs
	
	Key features to note, explore, and try out:
	
	    • *To create a table:* **Insert** tab **>>> Table** and then select the number of rows and columns you desire. The table will then be inserted on the page. Click, hold, and move the table to the desired location.
	    • *To move a table to a new location:* Select the table and then click, hold, and drag one of the side borders of the table. The table will follow where you move the cursor. Also once the table is selected, the directional arrows on the keyboard will also move the table in the selected direction.
	    • *Once a table is inserted and selected:* You can format it by using the tools on the Design or Layout Table Tools contextual tabs. These tools can be used to format the table in ways such as:
	        • Using preformatted table designs
	        • Inserting cell borders with various line thicknesses and colors
	        • Rotating the full table or rotating the text within the table cells
	        • Inserting additional table rows and columns or deleting those that are not needed
	        • Formatting the position of the text within each individual table cell
	
	    • For additional ways to specifically format a table in Publisher, you can use the Format Table window (**Table Tools Design** contextual tab **>>> Table Formats** group expander button). As shown in Figure 6.24, tabs for Colors and Lines, Size, Layout, and so on will allow access to specific adaptations that can be made within the selected table.

(continued)

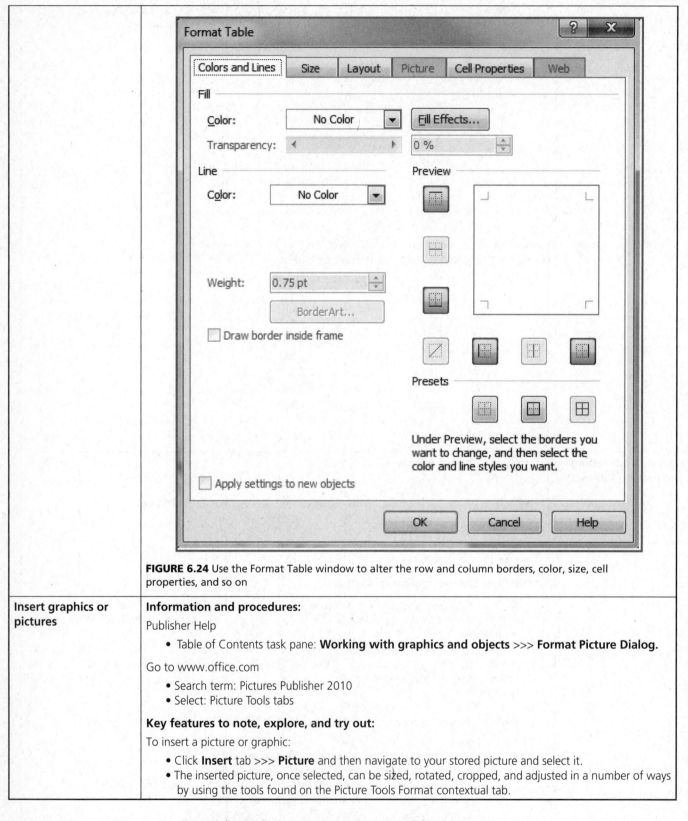

FIGURE 6.24 Use the Format Table window to alter the row and column borders, color, size, cell properties, and so on

Insert graphics or pictures	**Information and procedures:**
	Publisher Help
	• Table of Contents task pane: **Working with graphics and objects** >>> **Format Picture Dialog.**
	Go to www.office.com
	• Search term: Pictures Publisher 2010
	• Select: Picture Tools tabs
	Key features to note, explore, and try out:
	To insert a picture or graphic:
	• Click **Insert** tab >>> **Picture** and then navigate to your stored picture and select it.
	• The inserted picture, once selected, can be sized, rotated, cropped, and adjusted in a number of ways by using the tools found on the Picture Tools Format contextual tab.

Level 2 Workout: Creating your publication

Now you try it.

1. Think of a program for a play or perhaps a poster or sign you would usually create by hand to hang up in your room or use some other way.
2. Select a template for your publication. Try various styles of templates to ensure the most optimal selection.

3. Create text boxes in the workspace of the desktop publisher and enter the information.
4. Divide it into appropriate sections.
5. Put some of the information into tables.
6. Align, rotate, and format the title and all key headings.
7. Insert an appropriate picture, clip art, or graphic and place it within the workspace.
8. Adjust the picture or clip art in some way (e.g., change color, add a border, fill the picture background with a new color).
9. Redo these steps, except start from a blank publication (without the use of a template design). Note the differences in how the two publications were created.

Note: Each of these key features is demonstrated on the mentoring videos within the text's accompanying website.

for
Teaching and Learning with Microsoft® Office 2010 and Office 2011 for Mac

Go to PDToolkit for **Teaching and Learning with Microsoft® Office 2010 and Office 2011 for Mac** to locate the mentoring videos for Chapter Six.

LEVEL 3: INTEGRATION AND APPLICATION

What should you be able to do?

Here you need to think of how to use desktop publishing in terms of yourself and your students. You should be able to apply the examples given to generate ideas on how to integrate and apply desktop publishing to improve personal productivity as well as student learning.

Introduction

Within Levels 1 and 2 of this chapter, we focused on desktop publishing from the perspective of you learning to use it. However, to extend its use, you need to begin to think about desktop publishing as a means to enhance the learning experience of students. There are times when integrating desktop publishing within a learning situation may actually improve the learning opportunities and possibilities of the learners. However, there are other times when such integration would be more of a hassle than the potential benefits warrant. Learning to tell the difference can help you be successful in what you develop and use in your classroom.

Desktop publishing integration

Creating the enhanced learning experience: A partial lesson plan

TOPIC:

A study of the people, places, and culture of an African country.

OVERVIEW:

Mr. Carpenter, an eighth-grade social studies teacher at Lowell Middle School, is continuing to search for ways for his students to explore Zimbabwe, to find out about the country and its people. With the help of a former student, Jonathon Rogers (who is a university graduate student in Zimbabwe on an internship with an international health and education organization), Mr. Carpenter hopes to guide his students as they explore this fascinating country.

Through the use of e-mail, regular mail, digital photography, and audio recordings, Jonathon should be able to explore Zimbabwe and share his findings with the Lowell social studies classes of Mr. Carpenter.

SPECIFIC LEARNING TASK:

To explore present-day Zimbabwe, the students in Mr. Carpenter's classes are to investigate Zimbabwe and create travel brochures for the country. Each class is divided into smaller cooperative groups who are asked to address the following components in their travel brochure:

1. Country information—maps, climate, size, population, wildlife, currency used, major cities, languages spoken, religions, holidays celebrated
2. Tourist information—transportation, lodging, dining
3. Activities—historically significant sites, tours, safaris, entertainment

SAMPLE LEARNING OBJECTIVES:

Students will be able to do the following:

1. Identify and describe important elements about life in Zimbabwe.
2. Identify and describe areas of Zimbabwe that would be of interest to outside visitors.

PROCEDURE:

1. Break into the groups and brainstorm the key questions of inquiry to investigate about the selected topic.
2. Research answers for the questions from the view of Zimbabweans.
3. Create a table that lists the questions and potential answers determined through research. Reference the answers to the questions found within the research.
4. Plan a layout of the information to be provided in brochure style.
5. Design and create the brochure incorporating the information gathered.
6. Weigh the importance of information gathered and eliminate information that is not as important in order for it all to fit.
7. Present the final brochures to be distributed to all members of their class. This could be in the form of individual brochures or a display of some sort.

QUESTIONS ABOUT DESKTOP PUBLISHING INTEGRATION:

Obviously, this lesson can be completed with or without the use of desktop publishing software. Use these reflective questions to explore the value of potentially integrating desktop publishing within such a lesson as outlined by Mr. Carpenter.

- Within this lesson, in what way can desktop publishing be used by Mr. Carpenter, by Jonathon, and by the members of the social studies classes?
- How will the small groups cooperatively brainstorm and plan the publication? Can desktop publishing software be used to facilitate the planning process?
- Will the publication involve the use of visual graphics of some kind? Will the students have easy access to the collection of these graphics?
- In what ways can these brochures be presented to the class? Could other publications, such as bulletin boards, be used to help display the brochures?
- Are there potential problems or pitfalls if desktop publishing is integrated within this lesson and its respective assignments?

Level 3a Workout: Integrating desktop publishing

Now it's your turn. Complete the following steps to this Workout as you think about the future use of desktop publishing within an applied setting.

1. Read each of the following situations. Imagine being directly involved in the planning for each of these projects. Select one (or more if you wish) for further consideration.

Advertise a Service:

Students in Miller High School's math club want to help mentor elementary students who are having difficulty completing their math homework assignments. The high school students meet weekly with the elementary students but still there is a need to have more timely contact when questions arise. A suggestion is made to create some type of business card that would provide important contact information, online chat locations and times, and even important locations on the Internet that could give further help to the struggling elementary students. These cards should be simple, provide adequate information, easily updateable, attractive, and very inexpensive.

Service Learning Education:

In Jeffersonville, there is a real concern about the migration of various freshwater algae from one river to the next. A major cause of this migration is the lack of fisherman properly disinfecting their boots and waders as they fish in one river and then move to a different river. In order to help remind fishermen to go through the proper disinfectant process, there is a need to create posters and flyers to help educate the general public.

Classroom e-Newsletter:

Bramsonner Alternative School is a residential school for students who have had difficulties of one kind or another in the traditional school setting. To provide a constructive activity for the residents and to provide a means for them to work together, showcase their talents, practice their writing skills, and so on, they want to develop an electronic newsletter that could be distributed across the school's intranet. It could include items about school activities and programs, interesting teacher information, current news events, and even exemplary projects that have been developed. If it is completed in a successful manner, perhaps hard copies could be printed and sent to parents and grandparents.

2. Based on your selected project, consider the following questions found within the integration assessment questionnaire. Mark your response to each question.

Integration assessment questionnaire (IAQ)

Will using desktop publishing software as a part of the project:	
Broaden the learners' perspective on potential solution paths and answers?	__ Yes__ No__ Maybe
Increase the level of involvement and investment of personal effort by the learners?	__ Yes__ No__ Maybe
Increase the level of learner motivation (e.g., increase the relevance of the to-be-learned task, the confidence of dealing with the task, and the overall appeal of the task)?	__ Yes__ No__ Maybe
Decrease the time needed to generate potential solutions?	__ Yes__ No__ Maybe
Increase the quality and quantity of learner practice working on this and similar projects?	__ Yes__ No__ Maybe
Increase the quality and quantity of feedback given to the learner?	__ Yes__ No__ Maybe
Enhance the ability of the student to solve novel but similar projects, tasks, and problems in the future?	__ Yes__ No__ Maybe

3. If you have responded "yes" to one or more of the IAQ questions, you should consider the use of desktop publishing to enhance the student's potential learning experience.

4. Using the example lesson plan, develop a lesson plan based on your selected project. Within the plan, indicate how and when the learner will use desktop publishing. Additionally, list potential benefits and challenges that may occur when involving this software in the lesson.

Level 3b Workout: Exploring the NETS connection

PART A: Once you have an understanding of the features and applications of desktop publishing skills, it is important to provide a context for the professional purpose that these skills can have in the classroom. By using the National Educational Technology Standards (NETS) developed by the International Society for Technology in Education (ISTE), the next few tasks will provide a foundation for the importance of integrating this chapter's skill set into any teacher's professional practice. There are two sets of NETS: one designed for the skills needed by teachers (NETS-T), the other for the skills needed by K–12 students (NETS-S). A complete listing of these standards can be found in the Appendix of this book.

PART B: The following chart provides examples of how the use of a desktop publishing application can directly align with the NETS-T and the NETS-S. As you read these strategies, try to consider additional connections that could be made between these standards and this set of skills. Additionally, consider the answer to the focus questions presented for each unique standard.

NETS-T and NETS-S	Example Activities and Focus Questions
NETS-T 1. Facilitate and Inspire Student Learning and Creativity NETS-S 1. Creativity and Innovation	• A high school economics class that has been studying business and advertisements has been divided into small groups. Each group has been given a common household product. Their job is to take this product and create print advertising for it, including prices, as though the year is 2050. They must take into consideration what type of advertising to create, such as a catalog, flyer, coupon, and so on. 1. How can the use of desktop publishing software aid in the promotion of creativity in students? 2. What advantage is there in using a desktop publishing software over traditional art supplies to develop the advertisements described in this project?
NETS-T 2. Design and Develop Digital-Age Learning Experiences and Assessments NETS-S 4. Critical Thinking, Problem Solving, and Decision Making	• Elementary students at Lavenville School are finding out what service learning is all about. They have decided to work on a schoolwide project to raise funds for playground equipment for a local transitional housing group that is working on a housing project for homeless families. The students will create flyers, signs, and postcards to mail out to area residents that describe the housing project, the benefits it will be for the community, and the important impact the project will have on those in need and on the students helping with the project. Their ultimate goal is to raise awareness to the problem of homelessness and at the same time raise money to help with the playground. 3. In this scenario, how did the task promote critical thinking and problem solving skills? 4. Brainstorm other ways in which the use of desktop publishing can connect students with the community around them. What other types of community-related projects can you brainstorm?
NETS-T 3. Model Digital Age Work and Learning NETS-S 2. Communication and Collaboration NETS-S 3. Research and Information Fluency NETS-T 5. Engage in Professional Growth and Leadership	• A class that has been studying genealogy is creating individual family trees. They are to diagram the family tree using a software program to produce a professional-looking publication to laminate and keep for future generations. 5. Often times, research is done on concepts or facts. In this example, the research is based on one's own family history. What advantages and disadvantages does a project like this encompass? 6. Consider this statement: By creating a take-away project for the students that is important to them personally, the teacher has helped to underscore the practical relevance of using desktop publishing software. Do you agree or disagree? Explain.
NETS-T 4. Promote and Model Digital Citizenship and Responsibility NETS-S 5. Digital Citizenship	• Integrate a discussion of intellectual property when developing any desktop publishing project that incorporates images, text, or ideas from various sources. Incorporate appropriate citation skills throughout each task. 7. Under which subject area should citations, fair use, and copyright be taught? Explain.

NETS-T3. Model Digital-Age Work and Learning	Here are a few ideas that may help you model how the desktop publisher might be beneficial in a digital-age work and learning environment:
	1. Teach your high school students how to create a résumé.
	2. Have students create a flyer to announce the talent show.
	3. Design and create original bookplate or binder labels for classroom books.
	4. Create an e-mail newsletter to announce classroom events to parents.
	5. Compose and format different types of letters (e.g., business, personal, memo, cover letter, persuasive communication, letter to the editor) and then compare the different styles of writing.
	6. Have students develop a brochure about a specific historical topic (e.g., colonial America), their personal work history and skills (e.g., jobs they have worked and what they have done), or places they may someday travel (e.g., Australian Outback).
	7. Have learners create original poetry and combine it with an inspirational photo as a background to their written work.

Additional ideas on using the desktop publisher as an assistant

1. *Classroom rules.* A sign that highlights all of the rules of class conduct and consequences when the rule is not followed.
2. *Computer assignment chart.* A chart that allows you to monitor whose turn it is to use the computer.
3. *Certificates.*   Create certificates for extra effort and merit.
4. *Progress reports.*   Keep students (and parents) informed of what has been accomplished and what is still needed.
5. *Work sheets.*   Construct various types of work sheets and directions for projects.
6. *Calendars.*   Develop and use daily, weekly, and monthly assignment or work calendars.
7. *Weekly lesson planning.*   Develop a table template of all weekly planning for lessons and subjects.
8. *Badges and labels.*   Produce name badges for students, class helpers, parents, and others; labels for files, folders, and the like.
9. *Programs.*   Develop programs and handouts for school productions.
10. *Newsletters.*   Write weekly or monthly classroom newsletters containing relevant information for students and parents. Distribute in hard copies or via the web.
11. *Permission slips.*   Develop permission slips for events such as field trips, bus rides, and authorized school activities.
12. *Volunteer schedules and job responsibilities.*   Create a sign that explains job responsibilities and schedules for individuals who volunteer at the school.
13. *Reminders.*   Write memos to remind students about projects that they have been assigned or sign up to complete (e.g., bring snacks, give a report).
14. *Banners.*   Create banners to hang across the classroom for learning things such as the alphabet, numbers, or a new language.

GLOSSARY

accessibility settings Settings used to alter the computer's visual and auditory displays to facilitate its use.

action buttons In MS PowerPoint, a ready-made button that can be created, inserted, and hyperlinked within a presentation. By clicking on the button, the hyperlinked activity is carried out. See also *button.*

active window Describes the window that is currently selected or being used.

alignment How text is positioned on a screen, page, or specific portion of a page or screen. Left alignment lines all text flush on the left margin. Right alignment creates flush text on the right margin. Center alignment creates text that is centered in the middle of the page and full alignment creates flush margins on both right and left margins.

animations Special visual or sound effects added to an object or text. For example, in PowerPoint, having bulleted lists of items enter and leave a presentation at specific times or based on specific actions.

applications software Programs used by the computer to assist in specific tasks (e.g., word processing, desktop publishing, presentation development). See also *computer applications.*

audio clips Sound and music files that can be hyperlinked, accessed, and played within web pages and other electronic files.

background Pictures or text that are placed on a screen, slide, or within a text document to appear behind other elements. Backgrounds are generally used to add color and interest to the screen, slide, and so forth.

Boolean searches A specific type of search using the words *and, or,* or *not.* Boolean searches help to refine the information that is retrieved (e.g., search for information on Lincoln, *not* Nebraska).

border Lines around cells, tables, or pages that add emphasis, interest, and organizational clarity.

border art Selected graphics that can be inserted continually around the edges of a page, picture, or paragraph border within a document.

boundary guides see *layout guides*

browser Computer applications, such as Internet Explorer, Mozilla Foxfire, Apple Safari, or Google Chrome used for accessing the World Wide Web.

bullet list Dots or other symbols placed immediately before each item within a list. This design feature adds emphasis and facilitates organization of materials. See *number list.*

buttons A specific location on a computer screen that triggers an action when clicked.

cell A single block in a spreadsheet grid formed by the intersection of a row and a column.

cell reference Identifies a cell or a range of cells in a spreadsheet program (e.g., cell reference D5 identifies the cell where column D and row 5 intersect).

charts A graphic representation of a data set of numbers. Charts can add visual appeal and facilitate comparisons of patterns and trends in data. Charts are also referred to as *graphs.*

click To press and release a button on a computer mouse.

click and hold To depress the computer mouse button and keep it depressed until a specific action has occurred or been completed.

click, hold, and drag Used to move an item (e.g., icon) from one location to another on the computer screen. Completed by pointing the mouse pointer at the item to be moved, depressing the mouse button, holding the mouse button down, and then moving the mouse to the new location and releasing the button.

clip art Previously prepared graphics that can be accessed, selected, and inserted within files such as word-processed documents, presentation programs, or web pages.

clipboard Temporary storage in the computer's memory.

columns A vertical arrangement of cells in a table or spreadsheet. In most common spreadsheets the columns are initially designated by letters (e.g., column D, column F).

command groups Logical collection of tools or commands organized together under a specific tab on the ribbon (e.g., in MS Word on the Home tab there is a Font command group that includes commands to control font type, size, highlighting, color, and so on).

command tabs Various sections (e.g., File, Home, Insert) of the ribbon on the applications software that contain the various tools and commands. Tools with similar functions are grouped under the various command tabs on the application ribbon.

commands Tools used within application programs (e.g., the font color command within MS Word is the tool that allows for the selection of the font color to be used within the document).

computer applications Computer programs designed to perform tasks such as word processing, desktop publishing, mathematical or statistical calculations, and so forth. See also *applications software.*

contextual commands Tools or commands that only appear on the ribbon when a specific object is selected (e.g., if an image is selected, the contextual command tab for the Picture Tools appears on the ribbon within MS Office).

contextual tabs Tabs of associated contextual commands that appear only under specific situations (e.g., when a graphic is selected) on the software application ribbon.

control panel A location within the Start menu that stores programs that control how the computer functions (e.g., programs to install and uninstall programs, set the time and date, set the appearance and resolution of the screen).

custom animation A sound or visual effect that has been added to an object or text within a PowerPoint presentation. See also *animation.*

dashboard Within the Mac OS, a place where gadgets can be located. Accessing the dashboard then allows one to quickly access and view all gadgets placed therein.

database An organized collection of information, often stored on a computer.

design templates A prepared layout designed to ease the process of creating a product in certain computer applications, for example, a slide design and color scheme for presentation software or a standard web page layout.

desktop A description of the screen that appears after the computer has been turned on. The computer screen is commonly compared to the top of a desk that contains folders, files, and various tools for working.

dialog box expander A small button generally located next to the command group name on the ribbon. Clicking on this button opens a dialog box that is related to the associated command group. For example, clicking on the Font command group dialog box expander opens the font command dialog box, where additional selections can be made.

dock A location on the Mac OS desktop that displays icons for quick access to specific programs and files.

drag To move a selected item, icon, and text on a computer screen, point the mouse pointer at the target item, click and hold the mouse button, and move the mouse. The selected item will follow the mouse movement until the mouse button is released.

field Each individual category of information recorded in a database (e.g., a student's first name).

files Any data saved onto a hard disk or other storage device (e.g., a word document file, a spreadsheet file). Also, within a database, these refer to groups of related database records.

fill A spreadsheet feature that allows one to automatically continue a series of numbers, number and text combinations, dates, or time periods based on an established pattern. Commonly used in a spreadsheet program to automatically allow a specific equation or function to be applied to additional rows or columns of data.

fill color A feature that allows for a color, shading, or pattern to be added to an enclosed figure, text box, and so on.

fill handle A small box in the lower right corner of an active spreadsheet cell. It can be used to complete a fill. See *fill.*

filter A means to select a subset of records or data in a table or worksheet based on certain selected criteria.

finder A program in the Mac OS used to locate and organize the computer's application software and files.

folders An organizational device that represents where applications, documents, and other folders are located and serves a similar purpose as a file folder found inside an office filing cabinet.

font The appearance (typeface and size) of text on the computer screen and in printed form. Typefaces include Times New Roman, Arial, Courier, and so on.

footers Information that appears in an area at the bottom of a document page (e.g., page number, title of document, date, logo). Footers can be set to appear at the bottom of all or selected pages of multiple-page documents. See also *headers.*

format A process to design how a document will look (e.g., type of font, selection of borders, use of color). Also used to describe the preparation or initialization of a disk or other electronic storage device to receive digital information.

formula A mathematical expression (equation) that directs an electronic spreadsheet to perform various kinds of calculations on the numbers entered in it.

functions Predefined formulas used in spreadsheets or databases that perform calculations. See *formula.*

gadgets Miniprograms that are displayed within the sidebar of the Windows 7 screen or within the dashboard of the Mac OS. These miniprograms might include a display of the time, weather, stock updates, news headings, and the like.

gallery A collection (a group) of related, displayed items from which a selection can be made. For example, when WordArt or SmartArt is selected, a collection of alternatives (i.e., a gallery) is displayed within a pop-up window from which an alternative can be selected.

grammar check Ancillary feature of word processors that identifies a range of grammatical and format errors such as improper capitalization, lack of subject-verb agreement, split infinitives, and so on. Suggestions on corrections to the errors may also be provided by the check.

graphic Any pictorial representation of information such as charts, graphs, animated figures, or photographic reproductions. Frequently referred to (especially within web page development) as *images*.

gridlines Lines on a table or a spreadsheet that depict the location of rows and columns.

handles Small squares that appear around a selected object that can be dragged to alter the size and shape of the object.

Handout page A version of a PowerPoint presentation that can be printed. The handout page can be constructed to include various numbers of slides per page and space for notes to be written.

headers Information that appears in an area at the top of a document page (e.g., page number, title of document, date, logo). Headers can be set to appear at the top of all or selected pages of multiple-page documents. See also *footers*.

Help Built-in resource within most applications programs that supplies practical advice, tutorials, and demonstrations on the use of the software and its various features.

hold Depressing a mouse button and not releasing it until some task is completed (e.g., depressing until a specific menu appears on the screen or until the dragging of an icon has been completed). See also *click and hold; click, hold, and drag*.

HTML See *hypertext markup language*.

hyperlinks Connections between items or elements (e.g., text, objects) within a hyper environment. For example, an action such as the playing of a sound clip is executed when a connected (i.e., hyperlinked) icon is clicked. Hyperlink is frequently referred to simply as *link*.

hypertext markup language The authoring language used to define web pages. Commonly referred to as HTML.

icon A small pictorial or graphical representation of a computer hardware function or component.

images See *graphics*.

integration Within a classroom setting, the use of the computer in ways that facilitate the learning of subject matter or content (e.g., accessing additional information, incorporation of graphics, calculation and charting of data).

International Society for Technology in Education (ISTE) The international organization that has developed and promoted the National Educational Technology Standards for teachers, students, and administrators.

Internet A network of computer networks that links computers worldwide.

ISTE See *International Society for Technology in Education*.

jump list A feature in Windows 7 that allows you to right click on an icon of a program listed in the taskbar and a list of files that are currently or recently accessed within that program will be revealed.

keyboard The most common computer peripheral device used for inputting information. Keyboards can vary in size, shape, type, and arrangement of keys to input data.

layout guides Margin, column, row, and baseline lines used to create a grid of boundaries so that text, graphics, and objects can be properly aligned within a document or publication.

links See *hyperlinks*.

Mac (or Macintosh) A type of computer developed and distributed by Apple, Inc.

mail merge Inserting data from applications programs such as databases or spreadsheets into a form letter or document.

margin Blank space outside the boundaries of the text and images on a document page. A margin can also pertain to specific blank areas within table or spreadsheet cells.

master slide A template that stores information concerning font styles, placeholder sizes and positions, background design, and color schemes for a presentation program such as PowerPoint.

menus On-screen lists of available options (e.g., File menu consists of options to open a new document, save the current document, close the current document, and so forth).

menu bar Within the Mac OS, a bar of options that offers quick access to various commands (e.g., File, Edit, View, Window, and Help commands). The menu bar set of options is altered based on the current active program.

Microsoft Excel Spreadsheet software created by Microsoft Corporation to organize, analyze, calculate, and present data such as budgets and grades.

Microsoft Office A set of application software developed by Microsoft Corporation that typically includes programs such as MS Word (word processing), MS PowerPoint (presentation software), MS Access (database management), MS Excel (spreadsheet), and MS Outlook (planning and calendaring).

Microsoft PowerPoint Presentation software created by Microsoft Corporation to plan, organize, design, and deliver professional presentations.

Microsoft Publisher Desktop publishing software created by Microsoft Corporation to create professional-looking handouts, awards, brochures, calendars, newsletters, and websites.

Microsoft Word Word processing software created by Microsoft Corporation to plan, organize, and produce professional-looking text documents (e.g., letters, papers, reports).

mouse A pointing device used to select and move information on the computer display screen. As the mouse is physically moved, a pointer on the computer screen moves in a similar fashion. The mouse typically has one to three buttons that may be used for selecting or entering information.

normal view In MS PowerPoint, normal view is the main editing view used to write and design presentations.

Notes page In MS PowerPoint, each notes page shows a small version of the slide and the notes that go with the slide. This can be used as an easy way to create speaker's notes to accompany the presentation.

number list Sequential numbers or letters placed immediately before each item within a list. This design feature adds emphasis and facilitates organization of materials. See *bullet list*.

Office 2010 A suite of software applications developed by Microsoft that includes word processing (MS Word), spreadsheet (MS Excel), presentations (MS PowerPoint), publication (MS Publisher), and communications (MS Outlook).

Office 2011 for Mac A suite of software applications developed by Microsoft that is similar to Office 2010 but specifically designed for the Mac operating system.

page border Various types of line styles, graphics, and colors that can be added to the edge of a document page to increase interest and emphasis.

page orientation The direction (e.g., vertical or portrait, horizontal or landscape) of a page layout.

page setup Option that allows for the selection of page margins, orientation, layout, and paper size.

peek A feature in Windows 7 that allows you to move your mouse over the Show Desktop button and all open windows will become temporarily transparent allowing you to readily see the computer's desktop.

peripherals Devices (e.g., printers, external hard drives, keyboards) that connect to the computer.

point Manipulation of a mouse (or trackball, touchpad, and so on) to select a specific word, graphic, or location on a computer screen.

presentation software Computer software designed for the production and display of computer text and images, intended to replace the functions typically associated with the slide and overhead projectors.

quick access toolbar Generally located in the upper-left corner, this toolbar contains commands that are frequently used and that are independent of the tab currently being displayed. This toolbar is customizable and often includes such things as undo, redo, and save.

quick styles Allow one to select different colors, fonts, and effects that can be combined within a specific theme. Quick styles always match the theme and have been created by professional visual designers.

record A collection of related fields within a database of information. See also *field* and *database*.

recycle bin The location where deleted files are stored. Deleted files can be recovered from this storage location or can be permanently deleted by emptying the recycle bin.

ribbon The area within MS Office 2010 or Office 2011 for Mac applications that contains the command tabs, command groups, and individual commands. The ribbon is designed to hold logically grouped commands to facilitate the completion of specific activities.

rows A horizontal arrangement of cells in a table or spreadsheet. In most common spreadsheets the rows are initially designated by numbers (e.g., row 2, row 232).

ruler A bar displayed across the top of the document window that is marked in units of measurement (e.g., inches). Margins, tabs, and column widths, for example, can be set through the use of the ruler.

schemes Coordinated colors and fonts that complement each other. A predesigned color scheme allows you to select a set of complementary colors that work well together to present visual appeal.

screen saver A program that can be set to periodically alter the computer screen when it is on but inactive. A screen saver can save overall power as well as help to reduce damage caused by inactive computer screens.

scrollbar A feature that allows you to view information in documents that goes beyond the size of the screen. By using the scroll bar you are able to scroll or move the information so that what was previously off the screen can now brought to the screen to be viewed. The scrollbars are typically located on the right side and the bottom of the screen window.

search A common feature within application programs to find words, numbers, and characters within a file. Additionally, operating systems can use searches to locate specific files, folders, programs, and so forth.

section break A mark used to show the end of a section.

sections The layout of a document can be altered by dividing it into sections. Each section can be formatted in a different manner (e.g., one section with two-column format and another section with single-column format) and divided by the section break.

select To indicate that a text or object will be used or worked with by the program. To select, point the mouse pointer and click or drag across the text or object. Once selected, the text or object will be highlighted in some fashion (e.g., color change). To remove the selection, a mouse click on anything other than the selected item will remove the selected status.

shading A darkening or coloring of the background behind text or graphics. It is used to add emphasis and interest to a table, paragraph, cell, page, and the like.

shortcuts Icons of programs, documents, and so on that can be used to quickly locate and launch a program or document.

show desktop button A button on the taskbar that allows you to either minimize all current open windows or make them transparent so that the desktop of the computer can be viewed.

shut down Following a given procedure to properly turn off a computer.

sidebar A long, vertical area that is displayed on the side of the Windows 7 desktop. It contains gadgets that provide information (e.g., the weather, stock prices, time). Within the Mac OS the sidebar is used as an organizational structure that reveals the devices, places that can be accessed to get information and stored files, and places to be searched.

slide The fundamental unit within a presentation (e.g., PowerPoint). It can contain graphics, text, sounds, movies, and action buttons.

slide layout The manner in which elements (headings, text, lists, graphics) on a slide are arranged. In MS PowerPoint, for example, templates can be selected from the slide layout menu and used to automatically arrange slide elements.

slide reading view In MS PowerPoint, slide reading view facilitates reviewing an entire slide presentation by a single individual (not a group).

slide show view In MS PowerPoint, slide show view shows how the presentation will look when given to an audience. The full screen is used and all animations, graphics, links are activated.

slide sorter view In MS PowerPoint, this view is of the full set of presentation slides in thumbnail form. Slide sorter view allows for easy reorganization, addition, and deletion of slides, as well as the review of transition and animation effects and so on.

slide transition Within a slide presentation, a slide transition is how one slide evolves into the next slide in the presentation sequence. Examples include one slide fading as another begins to appear or one slide moving off screen to the right as another enters from the left.

SmartArt A gallery of predesigned visual layouts that can be adapted to communicate information, ideas, and messages.

sort Arranging data in a spreadsheet or database in ascending or descending order.

spell check A feature in applications programs that searches through a file and reports any instances of text that do not match a built-in dictionary. In most cases, it offers suggestions of possible alternative spellings.

split pane A feature that allows you to cut a document into parts and display those different parts concurrently on the same screen (e.g., in a large spreadsheet you can split the pane of the document so the headers of the columns can be seen at the top of the screen and then bottom of the screen reveals items in those columns that are in rows way beyond the normal viewing area of the screen when the headers are shown).

Spotlight A search feature in the Mac OS that allows you to search for anything located on the computer.

spreadsheets General purpose computer calculating tools. They are generally arranged in rows and columns. They can also hold various types of data (e.g., images, texts, numbers) which can be sorted and filtered similar to a database.

Start menu Options displayed when the Start button on the taskbar is clicked. Options generally include access to programs, help, search, and shut-down procedures.

start up Turning on a computer and having it prepare to perform the needed functions.

style Text style refers to the appearance of a character without changing size or typeface (e.g., using bold or italics).

system software The basic operating software that tells the computer how to perform its fundamental functions.

tables Data set up in a row-column format. Cells within the table can contain text and graphics. Tables are often used to organize and present information.

taskbar A bar usually displayed at the bottom of the screen that contains the Start button, open document icons, and buttons to activate programs.

taskbar preview A feature in Windows 7 that allows you to mouse over application buttons on the taskbar and a small preview window of what is currently running in the program will pop up to view.

task panes Small windows within an application program that provide easy access to commonly used commands.

templates Stored documents that contain previously generated formats or content (e.g., text, page layouts, columns). Use of templates as a starting point allows for the efficient creation of new but similar documents. For example, a template office memo allows for the previously created header, footer, school logo, and the like of the template to be included so that only new information needs to be added.

text box An object that can be added to a document, worksheet, web page, and so on that sets off or emphasizes a section of text. It can be readily positioned, colored, and borders can be added for extra emphasis within a document.

text wrapping The automatic arrangement of text from the end of one line to the beginning of the next line. Text may be wrapped within cells of a table or spreadsheet, within paragraphs on pages, and in reference to inserted graphics and objects. See *word wrap*.

themes Previously completed design settings (e.g., coordinated colors, fonts, styles that have been created by professional visual designers) can be applied within a document, file, or presentation.

toolbar Bars generally displayed at the top or bottom of a screen of application software that contain shortcuts to useful features and tools (e.g., shortcut to save a file, shortcut to open a document or create a new document). Use of the toolbars eliminates the need to go to the menu options.

touchpad Input device generally found on a laptop computer that serves a similar function as a mouse. The pad allows for a finger or stylus to be used to control the position of the pointer or cursor on the screen.

trackball Input device that serves a similar function as the mouse input device. The device is similar to an inverted mouse where the user rotates the ball with a thumb or forefinger to guide the pointer or cursor on the screen.

transitions See *slide transition*.

trash can A Mac OS feature similar to the Windows 7 recycle bin. It is a storage area for unwanted or deleted items. By "emptying the trash" the stored items can be permanently deleted.

URL Uniform Resource Locator. The unique address for every Internet or World Wide Web page containing the protocol type, the domain, the directory, and the name of the site or page.

video clips Digital video files that can be hyperlinked, accessed, and viewed within web pages and other electronic files.

view buttons Buttons within the applications program (e.g., MS Word) that allow the document or file to be displayed in different formats (e.g., as a web page, two pages side by side).

view menu A specific area where a selection can be made about how the workspace of an application should be set up (e.g., for editing, notes, outlining).

view tab A tab option on the main ribbon of most applications programs that allows one to select various ways to view a document or file of data as well as how the document should be displayed.

watermark Text or pictures that appear behind text in a document. For example, a picture of a mountain that is printed behind text about a trip to the mountains. Often a watermark is washed out, or lightened, so that it doesn't hinder how the main text is viewed. Watermarks are generally intended to add interest or information to printed documents.

web See WWW.

web browser See *browser*.

WebQuest An inquiry-oriented activity in which most of the information used by learners is drawn from the World Wide Web.

website A set of interrelated web pages usually operated by a single entity (e.g., company, school, organization, or individual).

what if? When using a spreadsheet program, statements beginning with this phrase are used to signify how the spreadsheet may be used to make predictions and estimations.

windows Portions of the computer screen that display information or a program. Multiple windows can be revealed at the same time (e.g., a window revealing an office memo in a word processing document, another revealing a spreadsheet chart, and another accessing information on the Internet). Size, number, and location of windows revealed on the computer screen can be altered by the user.

Windows Explorer A software program within the Windows operating system that allows one to navigate to and access various folders and files.

Windows operating system A specific type of computer operating system produced and marketed by Microsoft Corporation. Versions include Windows XP, Vista, and 7.

WordArt A gallery of predesigned text styles such as shadowed or mirrored text that can be included within a document.

word processing The act of creating a document through the use of word processor software.

word processors Computer programs for writing that support the entry, editing, revising, formatting, storage, retrieval, and printing of text.

word wrap A feature of a word processor that automatically shifts the next whole word to the next line of the document when a line of text in a computer document is filled. See *text wrapping*.

workbook A set or collection of worksheets from a spreadsheet program saved under a single file name.

worksheet An area of rows and columns in a spreadsheet program in which text, numeric values, and formulas are entered.

workspace The main screen space within an application program (e.g., word processor) where the main amount of work is completed (i.e., text, data, and graphics are inserted and edited).

WWW World Wide Web (or the **web**). An information retrieval system on the Internet that relies on a point-and-click hypertext navigation system.

INDEX